Revealing the Hidden Social Code

of related interest

My Social Stories Book
Edited by Carol Gray and Abbie Leigh White
Illustrated by Sean McAndrew
ISBN 978 1 85302 950 9

**Playing, Laughing and Learning with Children
on the Autism Spectrum**
A Practical Resource of Play Ideas for Parents and Carers
Julia Moor
ISBN 978 1 84310 060 7

Relationship Development Intervention with Young Children
**Social and Emotional Development Activities for Asperger Syndrome,
Autism, PDD and NLD**
Steven E. Gutstein and Rachelle K. Sheely
ISBN 978 1 84310 714 9

Enabling Communication in Children with Autism
Carol Potter and Chris Whittaker
ISBN 978 1 85302 956 1

Freaks, Geeks and Asperger Syndrome
A User Guide to Adolescence
Luke Jackson
Foreword by Tony Attwood
ISBN 978 1 84310 098 0

The Little Class with the Big Personality
Experiences of Teaching a Class of Young Children with Autism
Fran Hunnisett
ISBN 978 1 84310 308 0

Asperger's Syndrome
A Guide for Parents and Professionals
Tony Attwood
ISBN 978 1 85302 577 8

Caring for Myself
Christy Gast and Jane Krug
ISBN 978 1 84310 872 6

Revealing the Hidden Social Code

Social Stories™ for People with Autistic Spectrum Disorders

Marie Howley and Eileen Arnold

Foreword by Carol Gray

Jessica Kingsley Publishers
London and Philadelphia

First published in 2005
by Jessica Kingsley Publishers
116 Pentonville Road
London N1 9JB, UK
and
400 Market Street, Suite 400
Philadelphia, PA 19106, USA

www.jkp.com

Library of Congress Cataloging in Publication Data

Howley, Marie.
   Revealing the hidden social code : social stories for people with autistic spectrum disorders / Marie
Howley and Eileen Arnold ; foreword by Carol Gray.
      p. cm.
   Includes bibliographical references and index.
   ISBN-13: 978-1-84310-222-9 (pbk. : alk. paper)
   ISBN-10: 1-84310-222-6 (pbk. : alk. paper) 1. Autistic children--Education. 2. Autistic children--Reha-
bilitation. 3. Autistic children--Behavior modification. 4. Social skills in children--Study and teaching. 5.
Narration (Rhetoric)--Psychological aspects. 6. Narrative therapy. I. Arnold, Eileen, 1944- II. Title.
   RJ506.A9H675 2005
   618.92'85882--dc22
                                                              2005006231

British Library Cataloguing in Publication Data
A CIP catalogue record for this book is available from the British Library

ISBN 978 1 84310 222 9

Printed and Bound in the United States by Thomson-Shore, Inc.

Contents

Boxes

Figures and tables

Figures

Tables

Acknowledgements

Alderwood Living and Learning with Autism Residential Special School, Northampton, UK.

Meena Chivers.

Amy Fry, Kingsley Special School, Kettering, Northamptonshire, UK.

Carol Gray, The Gray Center for Social Learning and Understanding.

Laurel Hoekman, Executive Director, The Gray Center for Social Learning and Understanding.

Oliver Howley.

Rosie Howley.

Northamptonshire Society for Autism.

Deborah Verdino, Prince William School, Northamptonshire, UK.

Symbols used throughout book

The Picture Communication Symbols ©1981–2004 by Mayer-Johnson LLC. All Rights Reserved Worldwide. Used with permission.

Mayer-Johnson LLC
P.O. Box 1579
Solana Beach, CA 92075
USA
Phone: 858-550-0084
Fax: 858-550-0449
Email: mayerj@mayer-johnson.com
Website: www.mayer-johnson.com

Foreword

Social Stories™ are collectively a wonderful educational tool that enables those working on behalf of a child, adolescent, or adult with autism spectrum disorders (ASDs) to share information meaningfully and accurately about a variety of concepts, interactions, and situations. To accomplish this, each Social Story™ is written in a carefully personalized format and style, resulting in a friendly, unassuming document that possesses ten defining characteristics. First developed in 1991, Social Stories™ have aptly demonstrated their own sort of 'social talent' as evidenced by their ever increasing popularity and positive regard. Collectively, they have made it possible for moms, dads, aunts, uncles, teachers, social workers, therapists and many others to share a wide variety of important social information with those in their care. In the years since their introduction, experience and newly emerging research have taught us much about the writing, implementation, and effectiveness of Social Stories™. In turn, Social Stories™ have held informal, important and unexpected discoveries for those who write them – new insights into the often unique perspectives and untapped social abilities of individuals with ASDs. *Revealing the Hidden Social Code* is an interesting, enlightening, and reader-friendly summary of all this and more, as shared by two well-qualified professionals, Marie Howley and Eileen Arnold.

Every page of this book is evidence that Marie and Eileen genuinely understand and appreciate the significance of Social Stories™, and subsequently the information they share with you as a current or potentially future author of Social Stories™. Quite simply, they take writing *and* the education and welfare of individuals with autism spectrum disorders very seriously.

To write is to 'paint' with words in the mind of another person. One book may be invited into many varied hands, regarded by many minds and interpreted through the knowledge and experience of each. In turn, a reader may pass what they have learned and their own related ideas on to others – via conversation, e-mail, or by writing subsequent articles and books. In fact, whenever an author cites the work of another it creates a valuable link to the origin of an idea or concept. It is an incredible chain of concepts, images, and ideas – pictures that, when handled with care, are enhanced and ultimately rendered more valuable than they were before. The best authors are continually aware of and humbled by the invitations they may ultimately receive. For this reason, authors will write and revise and rewrite, continually working with words to create the very best images that they can on a canvas that is the mind of another person.

If an author 'paints pictures' in another person's mind, what is a Social Story™? Authors of traditional stories for children casually assume that the words they place on each page will be easily understood by – and create similar images in – the young minds that read them. As we write Social Stories™, the successful exchange of meaning is not assumed – it is a goal that we work very, very hard to achieve. We must carefully choose words and format most likely to be the effective messengers of our information. In addition, our Stories™ enter minds that are unique, in some ways unfamiliar to us, and often very young. What a staggering responsibility we assume when our pens hit the paper! We have been given a unique opportunity to meaningfully share and describe ideas, concepts, interactions, and situations – another perspective on life – with a child, adolescent, or adult with an autism spectrum disorder (ASDs). To write a Social Story is to create a bridge for information to cross between two minds that – while similar in many ways – may regard and perceive social situations from strikingly different vantage points. Every Social Story™ should be worthy of this purpose as well as this often unstated trust.

Fortunately, Social Stories™ are rapidly becoming a popular social communication tool in homes, schools, and workplaces around the world. Unfortunately, because they are so commonplace, to some the importance of a Social Story™ and the responsibility to write and implement it carefully may be overlooked in deference to factors of time, convenience, or sadly, profit. To others, though, that same importance and responsibility is an ever-present factor that, while initially very humbling and even a little intimidating, ensures the care and consideration that writing a Social Story™ requires. Thus, over the years, I have been disappointed by those who approach learning to write Social Stories™ with a teach-me-quick drive-thru mentality or haste, but am reassured by those who, in sharp contrast, understand that Social Stories™ must be developed and implemented with care.

I am absolutely comfortable that as you read these pages you are in the hands of two authors who are worthy of valuable attention and investment of time. Marie Howley is a Senior Lecturer at University College Northampton, England. Marie's professional background includes several years' experience as a specialist teacher with children with ASDs. In addition, Marie is a prolific author, and is the co-author of many articles and resources, including Accessing the Curriculum for Pupils with Autistic Spectrum Disorders. Eileen Arnold is a former speech and language pathologist with extensive training, knowledge, and experience supporting her continuing work on behalf of individuals with ASDs. The combined knowledge and personal experiences of Marie and Eileen collectively form a rare, conscientious, detailed, comprehensive, and multifaceted expertise on the development and implementation of Social Stories™.

In this book, Marie and Eileen translate this combined expertise into useful information. Their stated purpose to create a resource '...to reflect upon key principles of the approach and to provide writers of Social Stories™ with examples based upon extensive use of the approach in a diverse range of settings, including schools, home and work place, with many individuals with ASDs' is amply met. The reader-friendly text and clear case examples are a wonderful introduction for readers new to Social Stories™. At the same time the new ideas and insights throughout the book will re-ignite the excitement in those – like myself – who have written more Stories™ than they can count! For example, upon reading, 'Directives are often most effective when linked to the perspectives of others as this helps to explain how people may feel as a consequence of others' actions,' I reflected with interest on several Stories™ from my past and decided, 'That's an interesting point!' In fact, the margins of my original manuscript are filled with arrows that point to this and similar highlighted passages. And for those who don't know what a 'directive' in a Social Story™ is, that, too, is beautifully described along with the processes and defining criteria that distinguish these Stories™ from other documents. As a result, I am confident that this book will be a 'must read and must have' for all parents and professionals working on behalf of people with ASDs, with a wide breadth of information to meet their specific needs.

There is no doubt that Marie and Eileen have recently 'been there'. They have experienced the frustrations and triumphs of teaching individuals with ASDs in collaboration with their parents, teachers, and caregivers. Theirs is a compassion that is seasoned with the intangible social wisdom that is gradually acquired by those who work alongside children, adolescents, and adults with ASDs with open and observant eyes, minds, and hearts. In describing this book to a colleague, I commented that it is quite clear from chapter to chapter that not only have the authors 'been there' but they also 'get it,' referring to their time-vested understanding and appreciation of what the 'social impairment in autism' is all about. This is a book that creatively reflects the 'attitude' that professionals – and especially parents – claim is essential to creating those contexts where individuals with ASDs learn and thrive.

It is a personal, genuine honor for me to introduce you to the expertise and insights within this book; as it has reinforced and strengthened a very important bridge for the meaningful exchange of concepts, ideas, and information between varied human perspectives. I believe Eileen and Marie have written a book that is destined to be a classic contribution to the education and welfare of individuals with autism spectrum disorders.

Carol Gray
The Gray Center for Social Learning and Understanding

Chapter One

Introduction and Rationale for Social Stories™

Social interaction is a fundamental aspect of all of our lives. Most everyday situations and events require us to interact with others. Often success within our social encounters depends upon our skills in, and understanding of, social interaction. The need to develop effective interaction should be reflected in any curriculum, as for example indicated in the English National Curriculum (Department for Education and Employment/Qualifications and Curriculum Authority 1999a, 1999b), which identifies 'working with others' as a key skill for all pupils, embedded across the curriculum, stating that: 'if pupils are to work with others they must develop social skills and a growing awareness and understanding of others' needs' (p.21). The development of social interaction is crucial for children and adults, yet for many people with autistic spectrum disorders (ASD) social interaction remains an enigma and they are frequently socially excluded from a wide range of activities in the social world. Sainsbury (2000) recalls that it is as if 'everybody is playing some complicated game and I am the only one who hasn't been told the rules' (p.8). Such social exclusion may result in increased levels of stress and anxiety, low self-esteem and inappropriate social behaviours (Barnhill 2001; Volkmar and Klin 2000). Given that social interaction is essential in order to participate and enjoy our very social world, it is equally essential that we consider ways of developing skills and understanding in this area for those who are at great risk of social exclusion.

One approach that is increasingly used to develop social skills and social understanding with individuals with ASD is that of Social Stories™, originated by Carol Gray. The purpose of this book is to reflect upon key principles of the approach and to provide writers of Social Stories™ with examples based upon extensive use of the approach in a diverse range of settings, including schools, home and workplace, with many individuals with ASD.

Gray's Social Stories™ approach (1994a, 1998a) focuses upon the individual needs of people with ASD who face challenges in the area of social interaction every day of their lives. This chapter provides an explanation of the nature of social challenges that people with ASD may experience and explores the rationale for Gray's approach. An understanding of the theoretical framework for the approach is crucial to developing and writing Social Stories™. This is crucial to understanding how the approach can be used and how Social Stories™ enable some people with ASD to participate in social interaction more successfully.

The nature of the social impairment

ASDs are viewed as developmental disabilities, the difficulties associated with the disorder affecting all aspects of the individual's life (Mesibov, Adams and Klinger 1997). Since the original descriptions of an autism syndrome by Kanner (1943), cited in Frith (1991), the nature of ASD has been widely debated and is well documented (e.g. Frith 1989; Howlin 1986; Schopler and Mesibov 1986; Wing 1996). Wing and Gould (1979) defined a 'triad of impairments' associated with autism, suggesting that despite individual variation, individuals characteristically show impairments in reciprocal social interaction, verbal and non-verbal communication, and display a restricted range of activities and interests, stemming from an impairment in imagination. Diagnostic criteria (American Psychiatric Association 1994; World Health Organization 1993) identify these aspects as critical to diagnosis. Individuals with ASD will therefore face challenges, to a greater or lesser degree, in all three of these areas.

In particular, the social challenges facing individuals with ASD are well documented and accepted (e.g. Attwood 2000; Happé 1994; Howlin 1986; Schopler and Mesibov 1986; Wing 1996; Wing and Gould 1979). Wing and Gould (1979) identified a triad of social impairments, including impaired social interaction; impaired reciprocal communication; impaired socially oriented, imaginative, pretend play. They also defined three groups of individuals whose social interaction can be described as 'aloof', 'passive' and 'active but odd'. In 1996 Wing added a fourth group, described as 'stilted and over-formal' in their interactions. Individuals with ASD will of course vary in their abilities to interact with others: for example, an individual who may appear socially aloof in many contexts may, in a familiar situation where the topic is of interest to them, become more actively socially engaged. However, while there is much evidence reporting and describing the social behaviours characteristic of ASD, the nature of the social challenges facing people with ASD continues to be debated. As Baron-Cohen and Bolton (1993) point out, there is no single definition of the social impairment, rather there is a range of difficulties that varies from one individual to another. Moreover the difficulties characteristic of the social impairment are not restricted to the development of skills alone, rather the difficulties are all-encompassing, and include social skills and social understanding.

Social competence: social skills and social understanding

The need to develop social interaction skills is crucial as access to so much of life's events depends on an ability to interact with others. In addition, in order for an individual to be successfully included in social activities it is crucial that he or she develops a degree of 'social competence' (Harris and Handelman 1997). Howlin (1986) suggests that 'the essence of social behaviour consists of the ability to relate to others in a mutually reinforcing and reciprocal fashion and to adapt social skills to the varying demands of interpersonal contexts' (p.103). However, social reciprocity is frequently a challenge for people with ASD and the ability to generalize and adapt skills is often limited due to lack of social understanding. In addition, whilst the social impairment is acknowledged in ASD, Gray (1998a) also places an emphasis on the two-way nature of challenges to social interaction. By definition, social interaction requires at least two people to engage in a reciprocal exchange. Therefore, any 'problems' in interacting lie with all participants, not just the individual with an ASD. This is a key issue when considering the Social Stories™ approach. Any approach that addresses the social impairment in ASD must include the development of social skills and social understanding and take into account all social partners, rather than focus entirely upon the individual with ASD.

SOCIAL SKILLS

Social skills may be relatively easy to teach to individuals with ASD, although these may remain 'splinter' skills that are not necessarily used appropriately. A number of crucial aspects of social development are frequently not addressed by teaching specific skills in isolation. For individuals with ASD to develop 'social competence', it is crucial that social skills are taught within a broader, more meaningful social context. The development of social skills may be of minimal intrinsic value unless accompanied by the development of social understanding. In fact, developing skills without offering contextual information and guidance may be detrimental in the long term.

For example, Billy, aged 5, had difficulties accepting and initiating hugs with his parents who identified this as a priority area for development. Billy learnt relatively easily to hug his parents, first in response to their hugs, and eventually spontaneously. His parents were initially extremely pleased with this newly acquired skill and encouraged him to practise and demonstrate this behaviour with other family members and friends. However, it became clear over time that a number of more significant issues remained problematic. Although his parents were delighted that he now hugged them and his brother spontaneously, it became increasingly clear that he was unaware of how frequently he should hug them and for how long. Thus it became a problem when, for example, he continually approached his parents for a hug when it was inconvenient for them such as while preparing a meal. More importantly, Billy was not always able to distinguish between those he was allowed to hug and those who he should not. Consequently he began hugging strangers in a range of contexts such as at church, in shopping centres or on public transport. While this was perceived by some as mildly amusing and somewhat endearing at 5 years old, it became an increasing problem as he grew older. By the time he had reached his teens, it was a significant difficulty that became a priority area of concern. As a result, Billy now had to 'unlearn' a social skill he'd been taught previously, try to learn the appropriate times for giving hugs to his family and learn a new set of skills that were more appropriate (e.g. for greeting). This proved to be very difficult for him and caused great anxiety for his family. It is clear from this example that the social impairment was not restricted to the acquisition of skills alone. Billy was taught to hug, but knew nothing about who, when, how long for and where to hug. While he had indeed acquired a new social skill that was initially celebrated, it became clear that the difficulties he had in the broader areas of social development remained and continued to cause him significant difficulties in relation to social interaction. He was unable to make a social judgement about who and when to hug. He was limited in his ability to select appropriate behaviours for different contexts and he was unable to predict what was expected of him. Furthermore, he lacked social understanding to inform his decision making in different contexts. It is this area of social understanding that appears to be critical to the development of social competence.

It is generally accepted that individuals with ASD will need to continue to develop their social skills throughout adulthood (Howlin 1986, 1997; Mesibov 1986). A number of social skills programmes are available for developing social skills (Aarons and Gittens 1998; Schroeder 1996) and the role of social skills groups is also acknowledged (e.g. Attwood 2000). However, while it is agreed that the teaching of social skills is important, any social skills learnt by an individual will be of little functional use if taught in isolation. Volkmar and Cohen (1985) report that 'higher functioning' adults with autism who acquire a number of social skills still have major problems with relationships and social interaction. Howlin (1986) identifies areas of social functioning that continue to be problematic often into adulthood, including a failure to develop friendships and lack of empathy. Barnhill *et al.* (2001) suggest that when people with ASD initiate interaction with others, they are frequently rejected due to their lack of understanding about their inappropriate social behaviour.

It is the experience of the writers that it can be relatively easy to teach social skills in isolation, but that this results in little more than a series of unrelated tricks and splinter skills if not placed into useful and meaningful contexts and developed with a degree of social understanding of how and when to use those skills. Isolated social skills may not lead to increased social inclusion and individuals may therefore continue to experience high levels of stress, anxiety and low self-esteem (Volkmar and Klin 2000).

SOCIAL UNDERSTANDING AND SOCIAL COGNITION

Frequently individuals with ASD are described as behaving socially inappropriately, but invariably their social responses are based upon their unique experiences and understanding of the social world. This experience consequently impacts upon their social understanding of the world. Gray's approach, Social Stories™, is innovative in that the approach focuses not only upon developing appropriate social skills, but also upon developing social understanding. Rowe (1999) supports this view by suggesting that Social Stories™ are not about teaching isolated social skills, but rather more about providing information about the social world to the individual in order to develop his or her schema. Gray (1998a) suggests that social understanding should be taught as 'an integral and prerequisite component to teaching social skills' and the Social Stories™ approach is underpinned by this philosophy. Gray states:

> The goal of a social story is to share relevant information. This information includes (but is not limited to) *where* and *when* a situation takes place, *who* is involved, *what* is occurring, and *why*. (Gray 1998a, p.171)

Social understanding depends upon having some insight into how to use social skills in a variety of social situations. This is usually developed as individuals engage in social experiences and establish schemata for interacting with others. However, for individuals with ASD it is suggested that they may not experience the social world in the same way as those who do not have ASD (sometimes called neurotypicals), hence their reactions may seem unusual or inappropriate. The Social Stories™ approach has been developed in response to our growing understanding of the difficulties that people with ASD may face in relation to developing their understanding of social situations. The approach is underpinned by some of the key psychological theories that offer possible explanations for the social challenges in ASD, and which may account for their different experiences of the social world, in particular theory of mind and central coherence.

Theory of mind

Frith (1989) suggests there is a consensus that individuals with autism are 'socially inept', especially in relation to two-way interactions. She believes that it is crucial to look beyond the realm of social behaviour alone, as the overt behaviours are only symptoms of an underlying deficit; for example, a lack of a 'theory of mind'. Leslie (1987) proposes that individuals with ASD have difficulties attributing thoughts and feelings to others. It is suggested that they also have difficulties in taking the perspective of another person and are unable to 'mind read' (Baron-Cohen 1995; Baron-Cohen, Leslie and Frith 1985; Happé and Frith 1995). This research concludes that individuals with ASD have specific difficulties with understanding that other people may have different beliefs and intentions from their own. Baron-Cohen *et al.* (1985) suggest that individuals with ASD are unable to 'mentalize'; that is, they have difficulties understanding the thoughts, intentions and feelings of others. This would suggest an impairment of 'social cognition', leading to difficulties with reciprocal interaction.

Central coherence

Whilst lack of theory of mind may well account for many of the difficulties associated with social impairment, including a lack of ability to see another person's point of view, an egocentric view of the world and consequently an inability to understand social nuances of reciprocal social interaction, such a lack does not account for all the social challenges in ASD. Frith (1991) suggests that individuals with ASD lack what she calls 'central coherence'. This means that individuals are unable to extract meaning from information and ideas in order to integrate them into a meaningful whole. Frequently, individuals with ASD fail to see the 'whole picture', often focusing on irrelevant details and missing relevant and important cues which give meaning to the context. This is exemplified by the child who completes a jigsaw puzzle easily without seeing the picture. The individual pieces are not seen as an integrated whole picture; hence the picture clues most children would rely upon become meaningless. In relation to social contexts this means that they may not 'see' the whole 'social picture' and this may lead to inappropriate behaviour. For example, an office worker with ASD who is sent to another office with a message may not 'read' the facial expressions and gestures of the colleague who would like him or her to wait as they are on the telephone. The individual may deliver the message regardless of these signals. Such behaviour may be interpreted as impolite and inappropriate. As a consequence of weak central coherence, individuals with ASD are often unable to apply their knowledge to changing contexts and situations. They may fail to generalize their social skills and are unable to adapt skills to different social situations and contexts.

Lack of theory of mind and weak central coherence may mean that individuals with ASD are missing essential information in social situations. Often individuals may be trying to respond in social situations but their responses are based upon their different experiences of the social world. Gray (1998a) suggests that the ability to 'mind read' and to be aware of the perspectives of others, together with the drive for central coherence, means that 'most people are privy to a secret code' (Gray 1998a, p.169). She describes this code as 'a system of unspoken communication that carries essential information; a system that eludes and frustrates individuals with high functioning autism and Asperger syndrome'. This may account for some of the challenges they are faced with when interacting with others and with developing a shared social understanding.

Social understanding

Social understanding may be defined as an understanding of the underlying messages that underpin social interaction, described by Gray (1998a) as a 'hidden code'. Social understanding depends on an understanding of explicit and implicit social rules that govern everyday social encounters. It requires an ability to make decisions about the social skills we have in terms of when and where to use them. Gray (1998a) makes a direct link between the psychological, theoretical approaches described above and the purpose of Social Stories™, suggesting that they can:

- provide missing information about the perspectives of others
- provide missing information about relevant social cues.

The provision of this missing information helps to clarify the whole social picture, integrating information into a more meaningful whole.

Social Stories™ are designed therefore to provide accurate social information, thus allowing access to the 'secrets surrounding social interaction into practical, tangible social information' (Gray 1998a). It is the focus on provision of the missing or 'hidden' information to people with ASD that makes the Social Stories™ approach different from other social skills approaches. Revealing the 'hidden social code' and developing strategies to develop social understanding are central to the approach, which goes beyond skill development in considering the enhancement of social cognition and understanding.

Other features of Social Stories™

Visual cognition, motivation and predictability

In addition to considering the different ways that individuals may think about social situations, the Social Stories™ approach is also informed by our understanding of learning styles. Many studies have looked at the learning styles of individuals with ASD and it is widely agreed that the uses of visual support and visual teaching are, for many, effective intervention strategies (e.g. Dettmer *et al.* 2000; Hodgdon 1995; Mesibov and Howley 2003; Quill 1995; Schopler, Mesibov and Hearsey 1995; Schopler, Mesibov and Kunce 1998). This is further supported by personal accounts by individuals with autism such as Temple Grandin (1995, p.19), who says:

> I think in pictures. Words are like a second language to me. I translate both spoken and written words into full-color movies, complete with sound, which runs like a VCR tape in my head. When somebody speaks to me, his words are instantly translated into pictures.

The Social Story™ approach embraces this particular way of thinking and consequent learning style, presenting information visually according to the individual's level of visual cognition (i.e. objects, photographs, pictures, symbols, written words). Gray (1998a) suggests that 'one premise of social stories and Comic Strip Conversations is that materials and instructional methods used to present social information should be consistent with visual learning strengths' (p.170). The presentation of visual information within Social Stories™ may be key to their success (Howley 2001). This may be because the use of visual information reduces interpersonal demands and appears 'neutral' to the individual. Visual presentation of Social Stories™ is therefore explored in detail in Chapter 5.

In addition, motivational factors are also considered to be critical when developing effective educational approaches. Teachers need to utilize interests in order to motivate learning and Social Stories™ are specifically designed to take into account individual motivation and interests. Examples in this book illustrate the importance of utilizing interests and taking into account motivational factors.

Finally, Gray (1998a) refers to studies that show that predictability can improve the social responsivity of individuals with autism (e.g. Dawson and Adams 1984; Ferrara and Hill 1980). She suggests that Social Stories™ may be written to prepare individuals for new social situations to enable them to predict what may happen and what is expected of them, for example, during a first trip to a train station. Social Stories™ therefore introduce predictability to confusing situations that individuals with ASD are unable to understand, thus reducing anxiety and developing under-standing. As a result, the Social Story™ approach offers a strategy that may enable individuals to develop social judgement, prediction and under-standing. Examples within subsequent chapters will illustrate how Social Stories™ utilize individual interests and bring predictability to a social situation.

Personal autobiographical memory

Smith (2003) reminds us of the importance of helping individuals with ASD to develop their 'personal autobiographical memories', which may be limited due to their experiences of 'self'. Individual memories may be dis-jointed and may not facilitate any understanding of self. Gray (1998a) suggests that one purpose of the Social Story™ which is frequently over-looked is that of providing information about situations that may contrib-ute to the development of personal memories. For example, Social Stories™ may be written to record specific life events such as attending a family wedding, to record successes and achievements, and to highlight when an individual has responded well in a social situation. Thus a library of Social Stories™ may be developed that helps the individual to develop an autobio-graphical account, rather than focusing upon addressing difficult behaviours. For example, the Personal, Social and Health Education

(PSHE) curriculum at Key Stage 1 (age 5–7 years) in the National Curriculum in England suggests that children should 'feel positive about themselves (for example, by having their achievements recognised and by being given positive feedback about themselves)' (DfEE/QCA 1999a, p.138). Social Stories™ may be one method of providing positive feedback in a way that is more meaningful to the individual. Examples in this book will illustrate how this proactive and positive approach may be developed to help individuals to develop connections in their personal memories and to begin to 'feel positive about themselves'.

Behaviour

Schopler (1994) proposes that in order to address the behavioural challenges frequently associated with ASD it is critical that any management strategies should focus upon the underlying deficits which may be causing the behaviour. In order to develop more appropriate behaviour, the underlying difficulties must be addressed. The Social Story™ approach is primarily focused upon underlying cognitive considerations rather than overt behaviours alone. Gray (1998a) places an emphasis on 'gathering information' prior to writing a Social Story™ in order directly to observe the situation which is to be the focus of the intervention. Howley (2001) also stresses the importance of this, suggesting that the process of gathering information may be as important as the final product. However, as Smith (2003) suggests, it may be difficult to allocate sufficient time to 'get to the bottom of the problem' and this may impede the development and eventual success of a Social Story™. This will be explored in detail in Chapter 2 in order to inform and develop more effective practice.

Research evidence

Whilst many anecdotal claims are made as to the efficacy of the Social Stories™ approach, there is increasing research evidence to support these claims (Agosta *et al.* 2004; Barry and Burlew 2004; Bledsoe, Smith and Simpson 2003; Chalk 2003; Del Valle, McEachern and Chambers 2001; Erangey 2001; Gray and Garand 1993; Hagiwara and Myles 1999; Howley 2001; Kuttler, Myles and Carlson 1998; Lorimer *et al.* 2002; Moffat 2001; Norris and Dattilo 1999; Rowe 1999; Scattone *et al.* 2002;

Smith 2001a, 2001b; Swaggart *et al.* 1995). Many of these studies are small scale and therefore limited in their generalization, and some include two or more approaches, thus making it unclear which approach had an impact. In addition, many studies focused upon the impact of Social Stories™ on behaviours, with few exploring the development of social understanding. Nevertheless, some interesting issues are raised that may be central to the success of the approach. For example, Howley (2001) suggests that the use of visual cues that act as a reminder for the content of the Social Story™ may lead to increased effectiveness. Hagiwara and Myles (1999) also place an emphasis on visual cues with the use of a multi-media approach. This study supports the view that visual presentation may be a critical factor in presenting Social Stories™ and that this, combined with the use of information and communication technology, may provide additional motivational factors for some individuals with ASD. Thiemann and Goldstein (2001) also explore visual cues, specifically written text and video feedback, and their impact upon the social communication of children with autism.

The process of gathering information to inform the construction of a Social Story™ is identified as a critical element with regard to the eventual outcome of the story (Howley 2001). In addition, Howley concludes that Social Stories™ which result in a shift in social understanding are more likely to have a positive impact upon behaviour. This is also reflected in Rowe's (1999) study in which a pupil indicates 'now I'll know what to do', suggesting that with access to information that was previously 'hidden' the pupil was able to begin to understand why he should behave in a particular way. This is central to Gray's approach as one key aim of using Social Stories™ is for individuals to develop their social understanding in order to begin to determine appropriate responses in social situations for themselves.

Others focus upon how Social Stories™ are implemented. For example, Bledsoe *et al.* (2003) identify the importance of motivational factors and suggest that Social Stories™ may be more effective when used over a longer time period. Scattone *et al.* (2002) suggest that the consistency with which Social Stories™ are read may be important. Smith (2001b) comments on the need for frequent reading of the Social Story™ for it to have an impact.

Although many of these studies are small scale and some do not adhere to Gray's (1998a) criteria, nevertheless, such studies are helpful in developing a growing body of knowledge in relation to the efficacy of the approach. A number of issues are raised in these studies that indicate areas for further research:

- the role of visual cues
- gathering of information prior to drafting a Social Story™
- the role of the development of social understanding
- the importance of motivational factors
- the need for consistency and frequency of reading.

This book explores some of these areas and considers how Social Stories™ may be more successful when writers pay attention to these aspects.

The role of social partners

The focus thus far has been on individuals who have an ASD. However, social interaction involves social partners and any difficulties or challenges in an interaction are shared by all partners engaged in it. While the use of Social Stories™ may well develop the social understanding of individuals with ASD, it remains essential that those of us who are neurotypical (Gray 1997, 1998a) also develop our own understanding and awareness of the experiences of people with ASD in order to enhance social inclusion. After all, social reciprocity and competence depend not only on the individual with an ASD but also on the neurotypical individuals within society. Subsequent chapters explore the use of Social Stories™ to enhance interaction by considering the roles of social partners, in particular when combining the approach with other complementary strategies.

Conclusion and introduction to rest of the book

The social challenges facing individuals with ASD and those they interact with cannot be underestimated. Lack of social understanding, arising due to cognitive factors, frequently leads to confusion, inappropriate behaviour and isolation. Many people with ASD are frequently 'socially excluded' from a variety of life's events due to the nature of the social impairment. Social inclusion is of paramount concern for many of those who live or work with people with ASD, yet there are few strategies that provide us with the tools to develop social understanding which may lead to more successful inclusion. Social Stories™ provide one approach that focuses upon the need to develop social understanding in order to improve social interaction for individuals with ASD. The approach is based upon underlying principles that enable the approach to be used in flexible ways in order to meet individual needs.

Social Stories™ are founded upon our general knowledge and understanding of ASD and our specific understanding of individual needs. The approach is underpinned by psychological theory and is relevant to other work in this area. For example, Howlin, Baron-Cohen and Hadwin (1999) have developed strategies that aim to develop the ability to 'mind read'. They suggest that in order to make sense of social behaviour, it is important to teach individuals with ASD to 'mind read', developing social understanding as well as skills. Others have considered strategies to develop 'theory of mind' skills (e.g. MacGregor, Whiten and Blackburn 1998; Swettenham *et al.* 1996). In addition, Cognitive Picture Rehearsal (Groden and LeVasseur 1995) combines the use of pictures and scripts to enable individuals to rehearse appropriate social behaviours. Social Stories™ provide another vehicle for teaching individuals with ASD about the minds and perspectives of others and can be useful for revealing the 'hidden social code' of social interaction to people with ASDs. Examples in this book will highlight the focus upon developing social understanding, both in relation to thinking about others' minds and in developing appropriate responses in social situations.

This book aims to explore the development of Social Stories™, as established by Gray, and offers insights into how individualized Social Stories™ can be utilized. The emphasis lies on the 'process' rather than the finished 'product', with the intention of helping others to write more effective Social Stories™. The book is not intended to provide detailed training in the use of the approach and keen readers are urged to undertake relevant training. However, the book will be useful as an aide-mémoire for those who have completed Social Stories™ training or who would like to explore the approach prior to training. Examples are used to illustrate key points and also to discuss why Social Stories™ sometimes do not work. The examples in this book are not intended to provide 'off the shelf' Social Stories™ for readers to use; rather they illustrate the principles of the approach in order to help potential writers to develop their own Social Stories™, designed to meet individual needs. Each chapter focuses upon key teaching points and provides illustrations and discussion of how the approach may be developed and used effectively. Examples are based upon the authors' experiences of using the approach with many people with ASD, including children and adults and in many diverse settings.

Chapter 2 focuses in detail upon the process of gathering information prior to writing Social Stories™, as all too frequently this process is overlooked. This may lead to unsuccessful attempts and eventual abandonment of the approach. Suggestions are made for the types of information that may need to be considered and how to gather them. This is followed by two chapters that review Gray's guidelines for writing Social Stories™, including discussion of the sentence types and formula (formerly known as the sentence ratio) that she recommends. It must be stressed that these chapters do not amount to 'training' in the approach but serve to review the guidelines and offer examples to illustrate Gray's key principles, based upon our experience of using Social Stories™ with children and adults in a variety of contexts. Different ways of using Social Stories™ are also discussed in these chapters, including their use to celebrate achievements, to prepare for events and activities, and to direct behaviour based upon developing social understanding. Readers should note that examples of Social Stories™ in these two chapters are provided as text only; this is to ensure that readers focus upon sentence type.

Chapter 5 then explores principles for implementing the approach with detailed examples to illustrate the use of visual cues, text design, layout and presentation. Examples consider the use of objects, photographs, illustrations by the individual with ASD, symbols and the use of information and communication technology (ICT) to enhance meaning and emphasize relevant and important information within each Social Story™. Gray's guidelines for reviewing and monitoring are also considered as these are an essential part of the process.

In Chapter 6, the use of Social Stories™ to complement and enhance other strategies used with ASD individuals is explored. It is suggested that Social Stories™ may enhance other strategies, including the use of 'structured teaching' as advocated by the TEACCH (Treatment and Education for Autistic and related Communication handicapped Children) approach and social skills programmes. The role of social partners is also considered, particularly when exploring 'circles of friends' and 'jigsawed' planning. Examples illustrate how a combination of approaches has been effective for some individuals and it is argued that Social Stories™ enhance other strategies by developing social understanding.

Chapter 7 is based upon our experiences of those, including ourselves, who have written stories that may not have been Social Stories™ as described by Gray, and to encourage writers not to give up if they do not seem to work. Reasons for possible lack of success are explored and examples are provided to illustrate how to overcome apparent 'failure'. The appendices to the book comprise a set of checklists for developing and monitoring the approach.

The use of Social Stories™ has grown in recent years and many users of the approach provide anecdotal evidence of their success. However, there is often a mistaken belief that Social Stories™ are easy to write, when in reality the process may be lengthy and require a reflective and evaluative approach. Training in use of the approach is essential. Readers may then find this book useful in developing their use of the approach with individuals with ASD and to reflect upon the processes involved. The development of inclusive practices in schools and in wider society is essential when considering people with ASD who are at great risk of social exclusion. Social Stories™ may provide a very useful strategy in furthering our ability to include people with ASD in all aspects of society and the social world. This book is intended to complement the work of the originator of the approach, Carol Gray (to whom readers should refer if they have not been trained in use of the approach). It is hoped that readers will find it useful in their quest to improve the quality of life for people with ASD.

Chapter Two

Preparing to Write

Gathering Information

At first glance Social Stories™ may appear fairly simple and give the impression of being easy to write. However, this is deceptive as frequently individuals report that it is often quite difficult to write a successful Social Story™ and subsequently this may lead to abandoning the approach as 'not working'. This perception of Social Stories™ as being easy to write often leads to individuals attempting their first Social Stories™ quickly and without always considering in depth the need to gather information prior to developing a first draft. This chapter focuses upon the analysis needed before writing Social Stories™, emphasizing the need to gather information in relation to key factors, including:

- information to determine the topic
- information about situations and events
- information about specific behaviours (both undesired and more appropriate responses)
- information about the perspectives of others involved
- individual factors that will influence the development of the Social Story™.

The *process* of gathering information is often more important than the Social Story™ *product*. If you have gathered detailed information about a specific situation and your first Social Story™ is unsuccessful, the information you have already gathered can then be considered further in order to redraft. This process sometimes results in the drafting of a series of Social Stories™ in order for the individual to make progress (see Chapter 7).

Gray (1998a) suggests that 'a social story may not contain all of the information that is gathered. Still, a complete understanding of the situation is needed to determine information that is important to include in a story, as well as that which may be excluded' (p.174). This process is critical to the success of the approach. Thus the emphasis in this chapter is on process rather than product. Examples illustrate the types of information that should be sought relating to identifying a topic and ways of gathering information including observations, interviewing the people involved and assessing the perspective of the individual with ASD. Note that this chapter does not contain examples of Social Stories™. This is because the focus here is upon gathering information prior to writing Social Stories™. However, examples relevant to the scenarios depicted are provided in Chapter 3.

Identifying the topic

The need to develop a Social Story™ may be determined by a specific situation in which an individual is behaving inappropriately and showing signs of confusion in relation to what is expected in terms of an appropriate response. However, inappropriate behaviour may not necessarily trigger a Social Story™. Gray and White (2002) suggest that Social Stories™ can 'inform, reassure, instruct, console, support, praise and correct'. Social Stories™ may be developed to record an individual's successful behaviour in a specific social situation or to prepare and plan for a forthcoming event. Often writers begin by considering specific challenging behaviours as the focus of a Social Story™, but it may well be that the best first stories are those that describe successful behaviour and those that prepare for new events. Topics for Social Stories™ will arise then in different ways:

1.   *Recognizing achievements and celebrating success*: a Social Story™ may be written to celebrate success or an achievement for a behaviour which is already in place. These Social Stories™ can help to reinforce the appropriate behaviour and clarify the relevant cues that indicate success.

2. *Explaining, reassuring and preparing for events*: a Social Story™ may be developed to prepare an individual for a forthcoming event such as starting a new school or attending a party, or to explain and reassure when individuals are feeling confused. These Social Stories™ may help the individual to predict what will happen, explain how people may behave and respond and give suggestions for how the individual could respond, thus pre-empting potentially inappropriate behaviour.

3. *Changing behaviour*: a Social Story™ may be written to tackle a 'problem' behaviour such as answering all questions asked by the teacher, regardless of who they are intended for. These Social Stories™ indicate more appropriate responses and explain why this is important from other people's perspectives.

Social Stories™ that recognize achievements and celebrate success or prepare an individual for an event can be extremely useful as preparatory strategies to use before an individual is ready perhaps for more detailed social information; for example, the perspectives of others in relation to his or her behaviour. Chapter 6 explores the use of preparatory strategies in more detail.

Gathering information about the situation or event

Once a topic has been decided, it is essential that the process of gathering information to inform the development of a Social Story™ is undertaken. This requires direct observations of the event or situation that is the focus of the chosen topic and interviewing the people involved. Collecting information about a situation may differ according to the type of Social Story™ being written and those involved. However, the aims are the same:

- To identify what is actually happening.

- To ascertain consistency of factors surrounding the situation. Is the situation the same each time; for example, are different people involved on some occasions? Does the room layout differ and, if so, does it affect the behaviour? Are there different sensory components that affect the behaviour on different days?

- To consider the perspectives of those involved.

- To identify which cues the individual with ASD may be missing.
- To observe how (s)he is responding.

Direct observations
RECOGNIZING ACHIEVEMENTS AND CELEBRATING SUCCESS

If the topic relates to individual success in a specific context, gathering information may be fairly straightforward. If a Social Story™ is to be written to celebrate an individual's appropriate behaviour, then a period of observing that behaviour and people's responses to it may be sufficient to enable the story to be written. For example, Tom is 6 years old and attends a mainstream primary school. His teacher noticed that he had begun to put his belongings into his drawer independently. She wrote him a Social Story™ to praise this behaviour (see Chapter 3, Box 3.1).

EXPLAINING, REASSURING AND PREPARING FOR AN EVENT

If the purpose of the Social Story™ you are to write is to explain an event or to reassure an individual, observations of that event will be important in order to establish what is happening and to reassure the individual. For example, Cathy is 15 years old, has Asperger's syndrome and attends a mainstream secondary school. Cathy was preparing to undertake work experience in a local newspaper office. Information was gathered prior to the work experience. Box 2.1 illustrates the information gathered in order to write Cathy's Social Story™.

Box 2.1 Information gathered to prepare a student for work experience

Context, including information gathered through observations and interviews

Teaching assistant visited the office and interviewed the work experience supervisor, Mr Blackwell, to ask about office routines: start and finish times, break times, where to go at break time and what people do, who to ask for help, what to do at the end of the day.

The goal of the Social Story™

To provide information to Cathy about her forthcoming work experience, in particular to familiarize her with office routines. This is the first in a series of Social Stories™ about her work experience.

Social information being provided

- Office routines
- What people do at break times
- Who to ask for help
- Checking with Mr Blackwell at the end of the day.

Cathy's support assistant then wrote her a Social Story™ to explain about the office routines (see Chapter 3, Box 3.2). This was the first in a series of Social Stories™ to prepare her for general events whilst on work experience.

If the topic selected is to prepare an individual for a forthcoming event, it will be important to find out as much as possible about the event in advance in order to enable the individual to predict and prepare for it. In these cases, it is not always possible directly to observe the situation in advance and information gathering may rely more on interviews with key people who will be involved.

CHANGING BEHAVIOUR

If the topic addresses inappropriate behaviour or a 'problem', more detailed information will be needed. Direct observations will be necessary in order first to record information about a specific context in which the behaviour is occurring. This will include information about the context (where the behaviour is happening), the people involved, their responses and the individual's behaviour. This information should also be collected in order to establish a baseline assessment of the specific behaviour. The observation and description of behaviours in relation to the antecedents, behaviour and consequences (ABC) may be a useful starting point. However, as Schopler (1994) indicates, the underlying cognitive impairments in ASD must also be considered in order to determine how to intervene. This is critical when considering where the focus of a Social Story™

should be. For example, many pupils and students with ASD may answer all the questions a teacher or lecturer poses, but the reasons for this may differ. This means that for a Social Story™ to be successful it becomes essential to individualize the information presented. This can only be done if we consider the possible reasons for the behaviour of each individual.

Schopler's cognitive-behavioural approach and the iceberg metaphor (1994) are particularly useful in relation to Social Stories™. The iceberg metaphor places a specific behaviour at the tip of the iceberg and then suggests that it is crucial to identify key factors which may be causing the behaviour, including cognitive factors such as lack of theory of mind and weak central coherence (Figure 2.1).

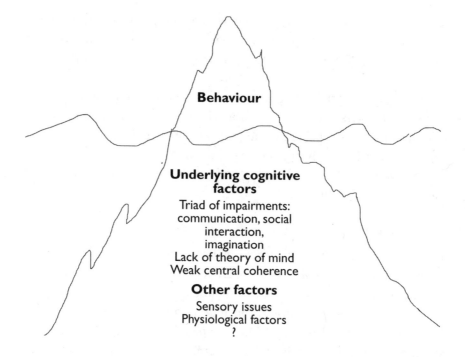

Figure 2.1 Iceberg metaphor

As discussed in Chapter 1, cognitive factors underpin the Social Story™ approach. Hence considering these must form an essential part of the information-gathering process. If Social Stories™ are to effect change by increasing understanding, it is crucial to consider the cognitive aspects as well as the overt behaviour. The iceberg metaphor gives us a useful model for considering the factors that may be influencing behaviour. The development of an individualized Social Story™ will therefore be informed by information gathered using, for example, the ABC method and identification of the potential underlying reasons for the behaviour using the iceberg metaphor. The following examples illustrate this problem-solving approach.

Jake is 10 years old and attends a mainstream primary school. He has Asperger's syndrome and has difficulties in the triad areas, especially in the area of social interaction. He has teaching assistant support for some of the school day. Jake is frequently corrected for answering all the questions posed by a teacher during lessons. This is problematic because he distracts his peers and consequently the lesson, and also because he irritates the adults and children. Information gleaned from the ABC chart reveals useful information about his behaviour, indicating that Jake is most likely to call out answers during whole-class teaching times. Analysis of antecedents shows that this increases when his teaching assistant is not in class and also when he is in less familiar classrooms. The behaviour described is consistent in that whenever the teacher asks the class a question, Jake calls out the answer. Frequently this results in a range of consequences, including Jake's peers laughing at him and Jake being corrected. On occasions he has been removed from the classroom, causing him to become tearful and distressed. By using the iceberg metaphor it is possible to consider the possible underlying reasons for Jake's behaviour, which may include:

- anxiety when not supported and in less familiar classroom contexts
- problems comprehending that the teacher does not always mean for Jake to answer (lack of theory of mind)
- literal interpretation of language – the teacher has asked a question, therefore I must reply
- lack of 'reading' of non-verbal cues such as body language, facial expressions and gestures from the teacher (weak central coherence, failure to respond to appropriate cues)
- misunderstanding peers' responses (lack of theory of mind)

- lack of ability to link 'cause and effect'; that is, he is sent out of the classroom because he has answered questions when he should not.

Analysis of information collected using the ABC method, together with consideration of the possible reasons for Jake's behaviour using the iceberg metaphor, allows us to identify the priority areas which may need addressing in order for Jake:

- to understand the impact of his behaviour on others (e.g. other children like to have a turn to reply – if Jake calls out all answers, nobody else gets a turn; the teacher needs to find out what different children know)

- to understand how he should behave (e.g. to raise his hand and wait for the teacher to choose a pupil to reply)

- to understand the impact this could then have and why (e.g. the teacher will be pleased as different children will get turns to reply to questions. Other children will not be so cross with him and/or will stop laughing at him. Jake can stay in class if he behaves as the teacher would like).

Information gathered about the behaviour, together with information gathered from others involved, should then be used to inform the drafting of an initial Social Story™ (see Chapter 3, Box 3.5). It is extremely likely that Jake would then require a series of Social Stories™ to address the different issues identified whilst gathering information. It is important to note that the information-gathering process may reveal a range of issues that cannot all be tackled in one Social Story™. Chapter 7 considers the need in some instances to develop a series of Social Stories™ that break down the content into one or two small steps per story.

Involving others and developing a collaborative team approach

Prior to beginning a first draft of a Social Story™, it is often important to consider other sources of information, including finding out about the perspectives of others involved. Once a topic has been determined, it is essential to interview those who are involved in order to clarify their perspectives. This will be important when drafting a Social Story™ as one of the aims of the approach is to help the individual with ASD to understand the perspectives of others. In order to ensure that this is accurate, interviewing those involved will be an important part of the information-gathering process. Observations will identify relevant people within the specific context for which you are writing a Social Story™. Discussions with key people will then inform the development of an individualized Social Story™. Such discussions may involve teachers, teaching assistants and other school staff such as lunchtime supervisors, workplace colleagues, residential care staff, peers, family members, and so on. The aim is to get as clear and accurate a picture of what is happening from everybody's perspective before attempting to accurately reproduce this information in a Social Story™ for the individual with ASD. Consulting others also establishes a collaborative and problem-solving approach to developing and using Social Stories™, with the aim of achieving consistency of approach amongst those involved.

RECOGNIZING ACHIEVEMENTS AND CELEBRATING SUCCESS

Sometimes direct observations provide enough information to write a Social Story™ that describes an event in which an individual was successful in some way; for example, Tom putting away his belongings. However, it may at times be essential or helpful to check with others involved to gain their insight. For example, when writing a Social Story™ to praise a child for greeting his grandparents when they come to visit, it would be useful to interview the child's parents and grandparents in order to share their perspectives and to identify relevant cues which provide feedback about the individual's behaviour.

EXPLAINING, REASSURING AND PREPARING FOR EVENTS

If you are intending to write a Social Story™ to explain an event, to reassure or to prepare for a new event, it will be crucial to interview those involved in order to collate relevant information that will inform the Social Story™. For example, preparing a child for starting a new school will require interviews with relevant staff at the school. For Cathy, who was being prepared for work experience, it was necessary to visit the workplace and to interview key staff to ascertain what information Cathy will need in her Social Story™; for example, information about office routines, break times, who to ask for help, and so on (see Box 2.1).

CHANGING BEHAVIOUR

Social Stories™ that aim to change an individual's behaviour will rely heavily upon the perspectives of those involved. Careful interviewing will be essential in order to establish how people feel about the behaviour of the individual with ASD and what they would like the individual to do as a more appropriate alternative behaviour.

In Jake's case it was important to establish the perspectives of the class teacher, other teachers who taught Jake's class including supply/substitute teachers, the teaching assistant and Jake's peers. Box 2.2 indicates the information gathered before writing Jake's Social Story™. It was important to establish what the teacher would like Jake to do as an alternative to calling out all answers and to agree how this could then be rewarded. This information is then used to inform the writing of a Social Story™ that clearly explains the perspectives of those involved to Jake and to clarify expectations of his behaviour.

Box 2.2 Information gathered to write a Social Story™ about answering all questions in class

---

Context, including information gathered through observations and interviews

- Support assistant and teacher recorded the number of incidences of answering all questions in the classroom to get a baseline measure of the behaviour.
- Pupils asked by support assistant how they felt about Jake calling out all answers. Observations showed that other children were getting irritated by Jake's behaviour; some were laughing at him.
- The Special Educational Needs Co-ordinator (SENCo) discussed Jake's behaviour with the teacher and support assistant and agreed upon an appropriate behaviour target for Jake.

The goal of the Social Story™

- To raise hand and wait for the teacher to ask him for his answer.
- If not asked for the answer, to write it in a notebook and show the teacher or support assistant later.

Social information being provided

- How the teacher, support assistant and children feel about the behaviour.
- How people will feel if Jake changes his behaviour.
- Consequence for Jake.

Gray (1998a) states that 'the goal of a social story is to share relevant information' (p.171). Interviewing those involved is essential for identifying *what is relevant* in terms of people's feelings, beliefs and so on in order to decide how to share this with the individual with ASD. Chapter 3 provides examples of the Social Stories™ written for Tom, Cathy and Jake.

Individual's perspective

In addition to clarifying the perspectives of those involved, it is also important here to consider the perspective of the individual with ASD. However, whilst we must attempt to understand the perspective of the individual, Gray (1998a) suggests that the perspective of the individual should not be reflected in the Social Story™ as it may not be accurate (see Chapter 3). The main purpose of gaining insight into the individual's perspective is to consider how she or he may perceive a situation in order to provide information to clarify the 'reality' of what is happening from his or her point of view. We have already established the importance of developing social understanding as 'an integral and prerequisite component' (Gray 1998a) to developing social competence (Chapter 1). However, how do we assess an individual's social understanding of specific situations and events? For example, what are the perspectives of Tom, Cathy and Jake? What is their understanding of the situations outlined above? This is somewhat problematic to determine as interviewing individuals with ASD is frequently fraught with problems due to difficulties with communication. Nevertheless, it is essential that we do try to identify the individual's perspective and understanding of a situation: first to inform the development of the Social Story™; second, and perhaps more importantly, to assess the impact of the Social Story™ upon the individual's social understanding. Direct observations and interviews will provide a useful baseline assessment of behaviour which can then be monitored and evaluated in order to establish the impact of Social Stories™ upon behaviour.

How then can we assess the individual's perspective to gain some insight into their understanding of a situation? This becomes essential to consider when evaluating the impact of the approach. Assessing an individual's social understanding in relation to a situation prior to introducing information through Social Stories™ will provide a baseline from which to measure any development in social understanding following its use. One possible approach for assessing the individual's perspective is that of Gray's Comic Strip Conversations (CSCs) (1994b, 1998a).

COMIC STRIP CONVERSATIONS

Comic Strip Conversations were devised by Gray (1994b, 1998a) to 'illustrate the art of conversation'. CSCs are defined by Gray (1998a, p.7) as:

> … an interaction between two or more people in which information is enhanced by the use of simple symbols, stick figure drawings and colour. These drawings serve to illustrate an ongoing communication, and provide additional support to students who struggle to comprehend the quick exchange of information, which occurs in a conversation. By slowing down and visually displaying an interaction, a student can 'see' and gain a sense of control and competence in a conversation.

The content of a conversation is illustrated, guided by a series of questions intended to support the individual with ASD to share information about a specific event or situation. Drawings, symbols and colour are used to illustrate abstract concepts in conversations, focusing upon selected topics (Gray 1994b). CSCs can be helpful in identifying what people do, say and think in a specific situation. Colour is used to visually identify the motivation that lies behind actions and statements (Gray 1998a). She advocates the use of simple drawings and symbols and describes the 'Conversation Symbols Dictionary' which contains eight conversational symbols to represent features of a conversation (Gray 1998a). CSCs can also be personalized to develop a 'personal symbols dictionary', shared by the individual with ASD and the parent or professional engaging in a conversation.

There are clear overlaps here with Social Stories™, underpinned by theoretical knowledge relating to lack of theory of mind in ASD. Both approaches are based upon the premise that people with ASD frequently think in visual ways (Quill 1995; Schopler *et al.* 1995) and that abstract concepts and the 'hidden' messages that elude people with ASD can be represented visually in order to develop their understanding of specific situations. Gray (1998a) argues that the visual imaging in CSCs allows some individuals with ASD to begin to visualize other people's feelings and perspectives and, importantly, helps them to visualize their own feelings about a situation. Gray goes on to suggest that the insights gained during a CSC can be important and may reveal something about the perspective of the individual with ASD. Therefore CSCs may offer us an opportunity to assess an individual's level of social understanding about specific situations and events. This information can then be incorporated into a Social Story™ and clarifications and explanations offered through the Social Story™ format to help the individual to develop their under- standing of the situation. Following the implementation of the Social Story™, it may then be useful to repeat the conversation to reassess the indi- vidual's perspective after being provided with information that had previously been 'hidden' from him or her. This may reveal any shift in social understanding that may have occurred. Chapter 7 provides an illus- tration of a Comic Strip Conversation and Social Story™ subsequently written for a pupil in a mainstream secondary school (Box 7.6). It should be noted here that not all individuals will respond to the CSC approach. Nevertheless it is important to try to ascertain the individual's perspective. Direct observations, individual discussions or multiple choice question- naires (written questions with pictures or symbols) may reveal their under- standing of a situation.

DEVELOPING SOCIAL UNDERSTANDING

The development of social understanding is a critical element of the Social Story™ approach; without this development Social Stories™, like many other strategies, would possibly remain in the domain of teaching isolated social skills. If individuals with ASD are to develop the ability to adapt and generalize their skills in different situations, it is imperative that their understanding of the situation develops. Successful Social Stories™ have illustrated the importance of developing this understanding. For example, the outcomes of a Social Story™ written for a child to help him to under- stand how to behave at lunchtimes hint at some development in understanding in the child's own comment: 'Now I'll know what to do' (Rowe 1999, p.4).

Howley (2001) suggests that the most effective Social Stories[TM] used with four pupils for various situations were those where a shift in social understanding took place. For example, a Social Story[TM] written for Sally to help her understand that she should listen when the teacher is talking to groups of children and the whole class, rather than only when the teacher talks to Sally individually, led to a shift in Sally's comprehension of the situation. Sally's understanding of when the teacher talks to the class changed from 'this is nothing to do with me' to 'it is to do with me and I should listen' (Howley 2001, p.100). Sally was able to generalize this new understanding when she transferred in to her new class the following term. Howley (2001) goes on to suggest that 'in order to develop effective Social Stories[TM] it is critical to identify an appropriate goal from the outset. This can only be achieved if an accurate assessment of the individual's level of social understanding is established' (p.104). Howley states that as a result of gathering information and accurately identifying the individual's current level of social understanding and skills, specific objectives can then be formulated against which the impact of the Social Story[TM] can subsequently be measured. Intended outcomes should be defined in measurable terms in order to ensure that progress can be monitored. The individual's perspective and social understanding should be considered carefully in order to identify an appropriate and relevant goal and to set specific targets, which can then be reassessed following the implementation of a Social Story[TM].

Conclusion

Social Stories[TM] often look simple and provide information in a straightforward manner. However, to achieve this apparent simplicity, the process of gathering information and assessing the understanding of the individual with ASD are critical factors. Overlooking this process may lead to Social Stories[TM] that are not effective and a potentially useful approach may be abandoned. Information gathered during this process may lead to a more effective Social Story[TM], with a real change in understanding, which may eventually lead to an individual being able to transfer and adapt social skills in different situations. In addition, if a Social Story[TM] is not effective, the information gathered during this process will be useful in order to reconsider and redraft. This *process* should underpin the development of the approach and must include direct observations, interviews with all involved and discussions with the individual with ASD, perhaps using the CSC technique, in order to establish his or her understanding and perspective.

Key teaching points

- Determine the topic. If you are new to this approach, it would be most useful to begin with a Social Story™ that recognizes achievements, celebrates success or prepares an individual for an event before using the approach to tackle inappropriate social behaviour.
- Gather information. Carry out direct observations and interview relevant people involved prior to writing a first draft (ABC and iceberg metaphor).
- Assess the individual's understanding of the situation prior to beginning a first draft (CSCs may help with this).

Chapter Three

Sentences and Structure

Descriptive, Perspective and Directive Sentences

Following the information-gathering process, this information is then used to begin to draft a Social Story™. Gray (1998a) identifies and specifies clear guidelines for writing Social Stories™. Whilst the content will be determined by the information gathered (Chapter 2), the structure should adhere to Gray's guidelines. This chapter focuses upon the core sentences that are used to write a Social Story™ and the basic sentence formula (formerly ratio) which Gray advises. Examples are provided to illustrate the principles devised by Gray.

Use of sentences

Gray (1994a, 1998a) describes three basic types of sentence that comprise any Social Story™. Other types of sentences are also used, which are explored in Chapter 4. Each type of sentence has a distinct purpose.

1. *Descriptive sentences* objectively describe a situation or event and introduce characters and roles. Gray (1998a) states that 'descriptive sentences objectively define *where* a situation occurs, *who* is involved, *what* they are doing and *why*' (p.177, authors' emphasis).

2. *Perspective sentences* describe the internal states of the characters involved in a situation. These sentences describe the physical and/or emotional perspective of the characters: wants, feelings, thoughts, beliefs and motivations of the characters involved. It

is important to note that the perspective of the individual with ASD is usually not described as we cannot be confident that our understanding of this is accurate. Perspective sentences are critical to this approach as they offer some explanation and provide information that may be 'hidden' for the individual with ASD. Perspective sentences may be most helpful in developing social understanding, rather than merely providing the individual with a list of 'to do' statements or directions. Social Stories™ should aim to explain why the individual should behave in certain ways and why other people behave the way they do.

3. *Directive sentences* 'define what is expected as a response to a given cue or behaviour' (Gray 1998a, p.178) and are used to direct the behaviour of the individual. Directive sentences need to be written very carefully to avoid a list of demands. Statements such as 'I will' or 'I must' should be avoided as they may be interpreted as demands for compliance and may also lead to a sense of failure. Gray advises that descriptive sentences should begin with phrases such as 'I will try to remember to', or 'I will try to work on'. Such statements may serve to reduce stress or anxiety that the individual may feel to 'get it right' first and every time. This is a more positive approach as the individual can then be praised or rewarded for efforts rather than outcome. Table 3.1 summarizes the three basic sentence types and provides examples to illustrate each type.

Basic sentence formula

In addition to identifying specific types of sentences to write a Social Story™, Gray also advocates the need to adhere to a 'Social Story formula' (1994a, 1998a). This formula 'defines the proportion of descriptive, perspective, directive…sentences in an entire Social Story' (Gray 1998a, p.179). A basic rule of the Social Story™ is that there should be more descriptive and perspective sentences than directive and that the Social Story™ sentence formula should be maintained regardless of the length of the Social Story™:

$$\frac{0-1 \text{ directive}}{2-5 \text{ descriptive and/or perspective sentences}} = \text{Sentence formula}$$

Table 3.1 Basic sentences

Type of sentence	Function of sentence	Examples
Descriptive sentences	Describe events and situations Introduce characters and roles	Work experience for pupils objectively in year 10 takes place during the summer term
Perspective sentences	Describe the internal states of the characters (not the perspective of the individual with ASD)	Some staff like to chat, others like to sit quietly
Directive sentences	Define expected responses and behaviour	I will try to remember to talk to other people at break time about the topics in my conversation topic book

Descriptive and perspective sentences

The sentence formula also means that Social Stories™ may comprise descriptive and perspective sentences and may contain no directives. This is an important point that is often missed as frequently Social Stories™ are introduced for individuals to tackle behaviour issues. Social Stories™ may be written to recognize and celebrate achievements, whilst some individuals with ASD may enjoy Social Stories™ written about familiar situations that describe events, characters and their perspectives, before introducing Social Stories™ that aim to direct behaviour. In Tom's case (Chapter 2) his teacher had noticed that he had begun to put his belongings into his drawer independently. She wrote him a Social Story™ to praise this behaviour using descriptive and perspective sentences (Box 3.1).

Box 3.1 Social Story™ using descriptive and perspective sentences to celebrate success

Putting my things in my drawer: A story for Tom

My name is Tom and I am six. I go to Redlands Primary School. I am in class 4. Usually my teacher is Mrs Brown. There are lots of other children in my class.

The children in my class have a drawer each with their name on. Mrs Brown likes children to put their things away in their drawers when she tells them to. She says, 'Pack away please.'

Mrs Brown is very pleased when children put their things away. It means our classroom is tidy.

Mrs Brown has noticed that I have been putting my things away by myself.

Mrs Brown is very pleased with me for putting my things in my drawer. She is going to tell my Mum that she is pleased with me. Mrs Holder, the head teacher, gave me a sticker that says 'Mrs Holder says well done'.

Cathy's support assistant wrote a series of Social Stories™ to prepare Cathy for her work experience in a newspaper office (Chapter 2). Cathy called her Social Stories™ 'social guides' and the first in the series used descriptive and perspective sentences to provide information about general office routines (Box 3.2).

Box 3.2 Social Story™ to prepare for an event

Work experience at *The Daily Journal* (Social guide 1)

Work experience for pupils in year 10 takes place during the summer term. My school have arranged for me to complete two weeks' work experience at *The Daily Journal* office on Jarrom Road.

Useful information

1. DATES. The work experience is on *Monday 1 June to Friday 5 June inclusive* and *Monday 8 June to Friday 12 June inclusive*.

2. TIMES. The office usually opens at 8.30 am. My working day begins at approximately 8.45 am and finishes at approximately 4.45 pm.

    Office break times are as follows:

    - Morning break 10.30 am – 10.45 am
    - Lunch break 12.15 pm – 1.15 pm
    - Afternoon break 2.30 pm – 2.45 pm

    Most staff take their break in the staff lounge. Some staff take a break outside. During breaks, staff can read magazines, make a drink and/or chat to their friends. Some staff like to chat, others like to sit quietly – this is OK.

3. GETTING HELP. Mr Blackwell is one of the office managers and he usually supervises students on work experience. Mr Blackwell tells students what jobs they are to complete and explains how things are to be done. *Mr Blackwell usually helps students* when they need it. Mr Blackwell likes students to ask him for help when they have a problem as he can explain what they should do.

4. END OF THE DAY. At the end of the working day (approximately 4.45 pm) Mr Blackwell likes students to check with him before they leave the office.

Directive sentences

Once individuals are familiar and comfortable with this approach, directive sentences can then be introduced to help them learn about expected behaviours. For example, Tom's teacher noticed that he forgets to put his things away in the afternoons when he is tired. A Social Story™ that builds upon the original one which celebrated Tom's success was written to encourage Tom to extend this new skill (Box 3.3).

Box 3.3 Story Story™ introducing a directive sentence

Putting my things in my drawer: A story for Tom

My name is Tom and I am six. I go to Redlands Primary School. I am in class 4. Usually my teacher is Mrs Brown. There are lots of other children in my class.

The children in my class have a drawer each with their name on. Mrs Brown likes children to put their things away in their drawers when she tells them to. She says, 'Pack away please.'

Mrs Brown is very pleased when children put their things away. It means our classroom is tidy.

Mrs Brown has noticed that I have been putting my things away by myself. Usually I do this in the mornings.

Mrs Brown is very pleased with me for putting my things in my drawer in the mornings. She would like me to put my things in my drawer in the afternoons as well.

I will try to remember to put my things in my drawer in the mornings *and* afternoons when Mrs Brown tells my class to 'pack away'. Mrs Brown will be very pleased. She will tell my mum and Mrs Holder. I might get a sticker from Mrs Brown, or Mum or Mrs Holder.

Similarly, Cathy's second 'social guide' (Box 3.4) contains directives, building upon the preparatory story already used to introduce the routines at the office where she undertook work experience. Monitoring of Cathy's progress during work experience revealed that she was unsure of what to do at break times and had begun to discuss her own topic of interest (motor racing) too intensively with work colleagues. Although not wishing to discourage Cathy from communicating with others, it was generally felt that her insistence on asking questions about motor racing would eventually lead to irritation on the part of colleagues and may eventually be problematic. Cathy's support assistant wrote a further Social Story™ to clarify what Cathy should do at break times and why this is important (Box 3.4).

Box 3.4 Social Story™ with directives

Work experience at *The Daily Journal*: break times (Social guide 2)

My school have arranged for me to complete two weeks' work experience at *The Daily Journal* office on Jarrom Road. Work experience began on Monday 1 June and ends on Friday 12 June.

Important information about break times

Office break times are as follows:

- Morning break 10.30 am – 10.45 am
- Lunch break 12.15 pm – 1.15 pm
- Afternoon break 2.30 pm – 2.45 pm

Most staff take their break in the staff lounge. Some staff take a break outside. During breaks, staff can read magazines, make a drink and/or chat to their friends. Some staff like to chat, others like to sit quietly – this is OK. People often talk about different topics during their break times. They might talk about:

- what they did last night
- what they are going to do at the weekend
- their family
- music
- shopping
- other topics.

During break times I could stay in the staff lounge or go outside. I could read a magazine, make a coffee or chat to other people.

Other people usually like me to talk to them at break times. People at the office usually like to talk about a variety of topics. Some people do not like motor racing; some people may become bored with conversations about motor racing.

I will try to remember to ask people at the office: 'Are you happy to talk about motor racing today, or would you like to talk about something else?'

I will try to remember to talk to other people at break times about the topics they choose *or* I can choose a topic from my conversation topic book. If I remember this, the other people in the office will be pleased with me. I can talk about motor racing to my Mum when I get home. I can also talk about motor racing to Mr James (work colleague) on Wednesday and Friday break time for five minutes – Mr James likes motor racing.

Cathy's social guide now tackles what may eventually be perceived as a 'problem' behaviour. Her social guide provides more information about break times and also refers to the 'conversation topic book' previously introduced by her support assistant. This contains phrases that Cathy could use to start conversations; her support assistant added some phrases that Cathy could use during office break times.

Directives are often most effective when linked to the perspectives of others as this helps to explain how people may feel as a consequence of others' actions. This is an important point as the perspective sentences in a Social Story™ are crucial to the development of social understanding. Perspective sentences are important as they provide 'hidden' information about others' perspectives. In Cathy's social guide a perspective sentence informs her that people do not like it when she talks about motor racing for the whole of break times and why they might not like it. The directive is then followed with another perspective that indicates the impact of her action upon the feelings of others.

It may be tempting to use too many directives in one Social Story™. This results in little more than what have been described as 'bossy books' (Smith 2003) and is likely to be unsuccessful. Stories that contain too many directives are not Social Stories™ and may be overwhelming for the individual and lead to increased anxiety. Numerous directives do little or nothing to increase the individual's understanding of the social situation and are therefore less likely to be successful in the longer term (see Chapter 7). Gray (1997) emphasizes that the more descriptive and perspective sentences and the fewer directive sentences, the more opportunity there is for the individual to determine their own new responses to a situation. For example, eventually Cathy may begin to figure out appropriate social responses for herself if she is able to access information about others' perspectives.

Social Stories™ should provide information to the individual about his or her behaviour and others' perspectives in relation to that behaviour. Expected behaviour is then described and the impact upon the perspectives of others to the new behaviour is made explicit in a perspective sentence – clearly linking cause and effect. Jake's behaviour in class was disruptive and irritated his peers who rarely had the opportunity to respond to the teacher's questions (see Chapter 2). After gathering relevant information about the situation, Jake's teacher and a specialist speech and language therapist wrote a Social Story™ for Jake using a combination of descriptive, perspective and directive sentences. Some perspective sentences follow the directive sentence in order to strengthen the directives and to facilitate Jake's understanding of 'why' (Box 3.5).

Box 3.5 Social Story™ using descriptive, perspective and directive sentences to guide behaviour and to increase social understanding

Answering the teacher's questions in class: Information for Jake and class 9

I am in class 9 at Bell Lane Primary School. My teacher is usually Miss Matthews and Mrs Taylor also helps me in class sometimes.

Miss Matthews often teaches the whole class together, especially when she is introducing the lesson and at the end of a lesson. When Miss Matthews teaches the whole class together, she often asks questions about the work. This is because she wants to know what children have learnt. Usually some children know the answers; some children may not know the answers. It is Miss Matthews's job to choose children to answer her questions.

Sometimes some children call out the answers to all of Miss Matthews's questions. Miss Matthews does not like it when this happens as she cannot choose which child she would like to answer. When children call out answers, Miss Matthews cannot find out what individual children know.

Lots of children like to try to answer Miss Matthews's questions. When some children call out the answers, other children do not get a turn to tell Miss Matthews what they know. This makes them feel upset, irritated or cross. Sometimes some children laugh at children who call out answers.

Miss Matthews has a new class rule:

> Answering questions: If you think you know the answer to a question, raise your hand and wait for Miss Matthews to choose a child to give an answer – thank you.

The rule is on the noticeboard to remind all children what to do when the teacher asks us questions.

> I will try to remember to raise my hand and wait for Miss Matthews to choose a child to give the answer. Sometimes I will be chosen, sometimes I will not be chosen – this is OK. Miss Matthews may choose me to answer a question later.
>
> If I remember to follow the rule, Miss Matthews and Mrs Taylor will be very pleased as they will be able to find out what different children know. The other children will probably not laugh. Children who follow the rule can stay in the classroom.

This Social Story™ clearly directs Jake's behaviour but in a calm and neutral way. Information is provided about *why* he needs to change his behaviour and how people are feeling through the use of perspective sentences. This is crucial as these sentences provide information that is 'hidden' from Jake and which is essential to develop social understanding. Further Social Stories™ will probably be useful for Jake: for example, to help him express his anxiety when the teaching assistant is not present or when he is in an unfamiliar classroom. Chapter 7 explores the need to consider writing a series of Social Stories™ in order to address complex issues that may be overwhelming if presented in a single story.

Other factors

Gray (1998a) provides further advice regarding the structure and drafting of Social Stories™. She suggests that there are a number of individual factors which need to be taken into account in order for Social Stories™ to be individualized. Gray recommends that the Social Stories™ should be written in a format that takes into account the characteristics of the individual:

1. *Developmental age*: this will be particularly important in relation to how the Social Story™ is presented (Chapter 5).

2. *Reading and comprehension ability*: the written style of an individualized Social Story™ is determined by the individual's reading and comprehension ability.

3. *Attention span*: the length of the Social Story™ will depend upon the individual's attention span. Some individuals will need a series of shorter Social Stories™ about a single issue, while

others may read longer and detailed versions. Consideration also needs to be given to the amount of information and visual images presented per page.

4. *Interests*: sometimes Social Stories™ are more motivating to individuals when they feature an element linked to their own interests.

5. *Preferred learning style*: the level of visual information that adds greatest meaning for the individual. Social Stories™ may utilize objects (Gray and White 2002), photographs, pictures and symbols to enhance meaning and to link to the individual's learning style. Some individuals may prefer audio, video, DVD versions or computer presentations that they can play back when they need to listen to their Social Story™.

Chapter 5 considers these guidelines in more detail in order to present Social Stories™ taking into account individual needs, strengths and interests. Additional guidelines for authors are also established by Gray (1998a) when developing individualized Social Stories™:

1. Describe events and cues objectively. Value judgements and opinions may lead to stress and anxiety for the individual.

2. Focus on relevant and important information. Highlight events, words and gestures that carry the greatest meaning.

3. Share information with literal accuracy. Social Stories™ need to be interpreted literally without losing meaning. Box 3.6 illustrates the use of 'sometimes' and 'usually'. Although these words may not seem significant, the tendency to literal interpretation for individuals with ASD means that the Social Story™ content should account for this. Words like 'always' and 'never' are therefore avoided. Chapter 7 considers this further in developing problem-solving strategies.

4. Write from the first person perspective, usually in present or future tense. Social Stories™ written from the third-person perspective may be relevant for adolescents and adults. (Chapter 5 provides an example to illustrate a Social Story™ written in the third person; see Box 5.6.) Gray (2004a) emphasizes that Social Stories™ should never use the first person to describe

negative behaviours. If it is essential to describe inappropriate behaviour, this should be described in the third person.

Box 3.6 Social Story™ with attention to language used to take into account literal interpretation

I go to Oak Tree House. Where are Mummy and Daddy? A story for Harvey

Sometimes I go to Oak Tree House. At Oak Tree House I do different things.

When I go to Northampton Road, Mummy and Daddy usually stay at home.

While they are at home they do different things. Sometimes they watch television. Sometimes they read books. Sometimes they hoover the house.

Sometimes they go out. Sometimes they go shopping. Sometimes they go to the cinema. Sometimes they go to a restaurant. Then they go back home.

When my stay at Oak Tree House is finished, usually I go home. Sometimes I go to Granny's.

Mummy and Daddy are happy to see me when I go home.

The title

The title of each Social Story™ is very important as the individual may decide immediately whether it is relevant to him or her or not. Gray (1998a) advocates that it helps to 'teach to the title' and that the title of the Social Story™ should indicate what it is about. Sometimes it may also be important to indicate who it is for, particularly for younger individuals.

Adolescents and adults will most likely prefer alternative terminology to 'story' and many will decide upon what they would like to call their library of Social Stories™; for example, 'social guides', 'social references'. The Gray Center for Social Learning and Understanding (2005) suggests the term 'Social Articles' as an alternative title to Social Stories™ for older individuals: 'Social Articles are more detailed, written in the third person, and geared toward the abilities, interests, and vocabulary of older or higher-functioning individuals.'

Conclusion

Social Stories™ are written using specific sentence types, the core ones being descriptive, perspective and directive. The basic sentence formula provided by Gray (1998a) determines the structure of each Social Story™. Additional guidelines, if followed, ensure that each Social Story™ is individualized according to needs and strengths. This chapter has introduced the core sentences and basic sentence formula. Readers are urged to try basic Social Stories™ before progressing to more advanced strategies. Appendix A provides a checklist to facilitate the development of individualized Social Stories™. Chapter 4 explores in detail how to further develop the approach and considers more advanced Social Stories™.

Key teaching points

- Write a Social Story™ with no directives to familiarize the individual with the approach.
- Introduce directives when the individual is ready. Ensure that you use words such as 'sometimes', 'often' and 'usually' to ensure literal accuracy.
- Follow directive sentences with a perspective sentence to emphasize the impact of behaviour upon other people's perspectives.
- Ensure that you follow the sentence formula (avoid 'bossy books' at all costs).
- Consider individual factors that may be crucial to success.
- Ensure the title is meaningful to the individual.
- Ensure Social Stories™ provide information about *where*, *who*, *what* and *why*.

Chapter Four

Advanced Social Stories™

Following on from basic Social Stories™, some individuals may be ready for more complex information that is not usually included in a basic Social Story™. Gray has devised Advanced Social Stories™ (Gray 1998b) and offers detailed guidance as to how to use the strategy to develop understanding of more abstract concepts, particularly related to thoughts and feelings, to offer the individual an opportunity to understand events taking place simultaneously, to explain choices which may be available or enable individuals to be prepared for varied responses from others (Gray 1998b). As individuals become familiar and comfortable with the use of Social Stories™ (and as writers gain experience and confidence in writing them), there are other forms of sentences within Gray's guidelines which can be used and incorporated into the sentence formula. These additional sentence types may highlight the role of the individual and other participants in a social situation and/or enable the individual to make contributions and incorporate some of their own ideas. It is more likely that these sentences will be used in Social Stories™ for older or higher functioning individuals.

This chapter focuses on additional Social Story™ sentences, the complete Social Story™ formula, Social Stories™ about abstract concepts, such as cognitive functions, and Split Section Social Stories™. It must be reiterated here that this chapter does not constitute training in Advanced Social Stories™ and readers are again urged to undertake relevant professional development training in order to implement Gray's approach. However, this information is crucial to this book as it is in this work that

Gray really moves on the approach from developing social skills to exploring social understanding.

Additional sentence types

Control, affirmative, cooperative and partial sentences

CONTROL SENTENCES

Control sentences are described by Gray (1998a) as 'statements written by a student to identify strategies the student may use to recall the information in a Social Story' (p.179). The intention is that individuals will read the story and add sentences of their own that help them to identify strategies in line with their own thinking style and interests which will clarify, reinforce and recall the information in the story. Gray (1998b) advocates that 'in assisting a student in writing a control sentence encourage the student to think of concrete, visual images (does this story make you think of any pictures?) that may help in developing a sentence that will retrieve important social information at the right time'.

For example, although able to hold a conversation on a number of different topics, Ashley would introduce his concerns about completing his work assignments at inappropriate times and with inappropriate people; once he opened this topic it was difficult for him to leave it. A Social Story™ was prepared to provide information about the effect this was having on other people and the appropriate people to discuss his work with. Ashley provided the following sentence: 'When I am out with my friends or family, I can park my worries about work in a lay-by and take them to my tutor later.' Box 4.1 illustrates the Social Story™ written for Ashley.

Box 4.1 Social Story™ with a control sentence

Discussing assignments with my tutor

Many university students occasionally become anxious about completing their assignments on time. Subject tutors are there to help students to plan their work and to give guidance as to how to complete it. This is part of their role.

Students have regular meetings with their tutors and can ask for help in organizing their work or for advice about any aspect of the work which is troubling them during those meetings. Most tutors also give their students information about how to contact them for help at other times as well. *The tutor* is usually the person who can give the most helpful advice about how to plan and complete work assignments on time. *This is important.*

Most people like to relax with friends or other members of their family occasionally. Sometimes friends or family members may invite me to join them. We might go to see a film, a football game or listen to a concert and sometimes we just meet for a drink and talk. When people meet together to relax they like to talk about the things they enjoy doing. They may look away, yawn, look at their watches or move away when someone talks about their work too much. This may be because it is not about a subject they are interested in or because they do not feel able to help very much.

When I am out with my friends or family, I can park my worries about work in a lay-by and take them to my tutor later.

Sometimes I have meetings with my academic mentor or my key worker or course coordinator. These are people who need to know when I am getting anxious about my work. They will tell me what I need to do or contact my tutor for me.

The Social Story™ in Box 4.1 helps Ashley to identify relevant and important information in relation to discussing assignments and also reminds him of who to discuss assignments with. The control sentence generated by Ashley is used as a reminder when he is with friends who do not want to discuss assignments.

AFFIRMATIVE SENTENCES

These sentences may be used to provide reassurance and may add to the calm and reassuring tone of the story. Examples of affirmative sentences include:

- 'This is OK' and/or 'This is important' to emphasize a point
- 'This is a helpful thing to do' to express a commonly held opinion within a given culture (Gray 1998b).

Box 4.1 also contains an affirmative sentence to highlight important information for Ashley.

COOPERATIVE SENTENCES

Gray (1998b) credits this type of sentence to Dr Demetrious Haracopos, Denmark. These sentences may describe the actions of others that may be helpful to the individual. Incorporating these in the story and identifying all those involved will serve to highlight to the individual with ASD and to all those involved the importance of their role and encourage a consistent response. Box 4.2 provides an example of a Social Story™ that uses a cooperative sentence: 'Mummy will show me a photograph of the hotel I am going to stay in when we go to Spain for our holidays.' This Social Story™ was written to prepare a child for a holiday, and in particular to let him know that the family would be staying in a different hotel from the one they had stayed in previously.

Box 4.2 Social Story™ with a cooperative sentence

Staying in different hotels

In the summer holidays Mummy, Daddy, Alison and I usually go to Calpe in Spain for two weeks. We went in July 2002 and July 2004. We stayed at the Hotel Mediteraneo, which was very near the beach and we could see the sea from the balcony of our room.

Next July we are going to go to Calpe for two weeks again. This year Mummy and Daddy have chosen another hotel for us to stay in. It is called Hotel Sol. This is because Hotel Mediteraneo is closed while builders paint it and build more rooms. Hotel Sol is not far away from Hotel Mediteraneo; it is also near the beach and has balconies with a view of the sea.

Mummy will show me a photograph of the hotel I am going to stay in when we go to Spain for our holidays. The hotel is called Hotel Sol.

The Social Story™ in Box 4.2 is a further example of how Social Stories™ can be used to prepare for events (Chapter 3). The cooperative sentence adds information for the child about how mummy will help and also clarifies for his mother what she can do to help.

PARTIAL SENTENCES

Gray (1998b) also suggests that for some individuals descriptive, perspective and directive sentences may on occasion be written as partial sentences for the individual to complete in his or her own words. Table 4.1 identifies the purposes of partial sentences and provides examples for each purpose.

Table 4.1 Examples of partial sentences

Purpose of partial sentences (completed by the individual)	Example sentences
Complete the information in a descriptive sentence relying on his/her own knowledge or experience	'Other children in my Maths group are _____.'
Identify the perspective of others	'When I remember to take my used clothes out of the bathroom other people in my family will feel _____.'
Identify what would it be helpful for others to do when completing a cooperative sentence	'When I make a mistake in my homework my Dad will _____.'
Suggest an appropriate behaviour in a directive sentence	'When other students are playing loud music in my bedroom I can try to remember to _____.'

Whoever prepares the Social Story™ for the individual may introduce the story and help them to complete the partial sentences. Sometimes the Social Story™ may be introduced with completed sentences initially and then reviewed with some sentences changed to partial sentences for the individual to complete. When completing partial sentences, the individual may reveal details or features of a situation that are important and significant to him or her, but which may not have been perceived as significant by the author and might not have been included by him. Sometimes individuals may suggest responses in completing a directive sentence that the author may not have thought of, but which are equally valid and appropriate and may have more strength and meaning as they came from the individuals themselves (Gray 1998b).

The complete Social Story™ sentence formula

The uses of control, cooperative and partial sentences are incorporated into Gray's basic Social Story™ sentence formula to form the complete Social Story™ sentence formula (Gray 1998b):

$$\frac{0\text{--}1 \text{ (partial or complete) directive or control sentences}}{2\text{--}5 \text{ (partial or complete) descriptive, perspective, affirmative and/or cooperative sentences}} = \text{Complete sentence formula}$$

The sentence formula is applied to each Social Story™ as a whole and may contain no directive or control sentences as in the basic Social Story™ formula (Gray 1998b).

Advanced Social Stories™

Further development of social understanding

Gray has developed her approach further to consider more advanced Social Stories™ for those individuals who are developing their awareness and understanding of others' minds. This is a real strength of the Social Stories™ approach as the emphasis focuses more intensely upon social understanding and how to provide missing social information that may enable individuals to develop their own appropriate social responses to social situations and social partners. This aspect of Gray's work is clearly underpinned by knowledge and understanding of cognitive functioning and has led to the development of a sophisticated approach to developing social understanding.

COGNITIVE FUNCTIONING AND THEORY OF MIND

While basic Social Stories™ often include references to other people's thoughts and feelings, Advanced Social Stories™ may include thoughts themselves as the topic of the story. Social Stories™ may be written about what other people think, feel or know. This approach is underpinned by theoretical perspectives such as the notion that individuals with ASD may lack theory of mind (Baron-Cohen 1995; Baron-Cohen *et al.* 1985). This type of information presented in a Social Story™ focuses upon other people's thoughts, knowledge or feelings and can be very helpful in guiding the individual with ASD towards a better understanding of others' behaviour and help him or her to determine more appropriate social responses.

Gray (1998b) states that 'the first step in writing about thoughts is to establish a basic vocabulary that will be used consistently'. Words connected to cognitive functioning can be introduced and their meanings explained to the individual, but they will need to be chosen and used with care. Gray utilizes the visual learning style of many individuals with ASD by using simple drawings and specific symbols to enhance the written descriptions of meanings of words such as: thoughts, think, know, guess, learn, forget, decide, idea, hope, believe, understand, opinion. These new terms are abstract and potentially difficult for the individual with ASD. Gray (1998b) feels that the meaning can often be made 'surprisingly simple, tangible and relatively easy to comprehend' when careful thought is given to providing visual representations, concrete examples and references to their use in common phrases. These words can then be built up into a Social Story™ dictionary specific to each individual.

Having introduced words such as 'think' and 'know', Gray (1998b) goes on to propose that the first Social Stories™ using these words may be 'Who Knows What?' stories. Initially the individual is asked to fill in a simple story about the things he or she likes to think about using partial sentences. Box 4.3 illustrates this approach as Danny indicates what he thinks about.

Box 4.3 Social Story™ about 'who knows what?'

My name is Danny. Sometimes I like to think about *Formula 1 racing cars, formula race meeting programmes or computer games.* I like to think about other things too.

Following this a parent or professional will then write a Social Story™ about what he or she likes to think about, following the same format. A catalogue or chart can be built up providing information for the individual about what other significant people in his or her life like to think about.

Advanced Social Stories™ may go on to provide information as to what knowledge other people may have. For example, Peter was 11 years old when his parents discovered that they were expecting a second child. Relatives had told Peter that he was lucky to be getting a new brother or sister who would be a lovely playmate for him. Peter's parents were concerned that Peter would have unrealistic expectations of the new baby and would not know how to relate to a baby. They also felt that he would have very little understanding of the impact a new baby would have on family life. A series of Social Stories™ was written in the remaining six months before the arrival of the baby to prepare Peter for this. These Social Stories™ focused upon the following topics and were designed to increase his knowledge about the impending event:

- What can babies do?
- Why do babies cry?
- What do mummies need to do to help babies?
- What do daddies need to do to help babies?
- How do brothers help to look after babies?
- What do babies like?
- What games do babies like to play?
- What do babies know about?
- How babies grow.

Peter enjoyed completing partial sentences where he could and adding photographs to his Social Stories™ about babies after his sister was born. This also provided a 'special times' activity for Peter and his parents.

Following on from the introduction of a 'thought vocabulary', Social Stories™ can be used that share information as to what other people may know or be thinking in social situations or interactions.

Split Section Social Stories™

Split Section Social Stories™ have been developed by Gray (1998b) to enable Social Stories™ to represent different actions or activities that could take place in the same period of time. These types of Social Stories™ are useful where choices of activities may be offered to the individual to suggest a choice of response that an individual might make or to describe the activities of several people or events, which may be taking place concurrently.

Split Section Social Stories™ are written according to the Social Story™ guidelines as any other Social Story™, illustrations are used and the Social Story™ is presented in a manner in line with the individual's abilities and interests, but will contain some split pages. In most cases the first one or more pages will be the 'scene setting' or opening part of the Social Story™, the middle will be the main part and the last part will be the conclusion. Any part of the Social Story™ may lend itself to split section pages, where the choices or information about what other people are doing at the same time or simultaneous events will be written and these pages will be split horizontally. These Social Stories™ will need to be presented in ring-binders or the pages split only part-way across, allowing for each part to be turned separately. Each section of the split page is numbered appropriately (e.g. 1a, 1b, 1c, and so on). The final pages will usually be the conclusion of the Social Story™ and will be presented as whole pages.

Split Section Stories™ *about choices*

Offering choices about activities in split-page format gives the person with ASD the opportunity to view information about those choices in visual form and to consider and compare the options. Gray (1998b) categorizes Social Stories™ about choice into three main groups: activities, playmates and partners, skills and responses.

ACTIVITY CHOICES

Split Section Social Stories™ about choice of activity can be useful when there is a choice about familiar activities or choice between familiar and unfamiliar activities or where plans are uncertain; for instance, when the weather conditions or other people's timetables may make it difficult to predict ahead of time which of a number of options may be possible. Box 4.4 provides an example of an activity choice Social Story™. This Social Story™ is presented with split pages in order to indicate that there are different options for a day out.

Box 4.4 Split Section Social Story™
with an activity choice

Page 1 (complete)

On Sunday Uncle Ben and Aunty Alice will come to my house.

Page 2 (complete)

When they come they are going to take me out in their new car.

Page 3 (split)

Page 3a

If it is raining we could go to the cinema to see *The Superheroes*.

Page 3b

If it is a sunny day we could go to the beach.

Page 4 (complete)

Uncle Ben and Aunty Alice will bring me home in time for tea.
They will stay and have tea with Mummy and Daddy and me.

Page 5 (complete)

If we do not go to the cinema on Sunday, Mummy and Daddy will take me to see *The Superheroes* on Tuesday.

PLAYMATES AND PARTNERS

These Social Stories™ focus on potential playmates, peers and social partners. The focal point in many cases will be to present information about the choices of activities and information about the likes, skills and interests of the peers who may have offered an invitation or who may be invited by the individual with ASD to join them in an outing or activity. This information will, for example, help the individual to decide which potential playmate or partner to invite on a trip. Box 4.5 provides an example.

Box 4.5 Split Section Social Story™: Playmates and partners

Page 1 (complete)

On Friday 16 August it will be my birthday. Mummy and Daddy are taking me to The Space Centre. I can choose a friend to come to The Space Centre with us.

Page 2 (split)

Page 2a

Mark is one of my friends. He watches Formula 1 Motor Racing. He has lots of magazines about Formula 1 Racing. He also likes to play computer games and other things. I can make a guess that Mark is interested in Formula 1 Racing.

Page 2b

Saeed often looks at the stars at night, he knows the names of all the planets. I can make a guess that Saeed is interested in Space.

Page 2c

Olivier has an aquarium with lots of different fish in it, he has lots of books about fish. I can make a guess that Olivier is interested in fish.

Page 3 (complete)

Many people who are interested in the stars would like to visit The Space Centre. I think the friend who would most like to visit The Space Centre is _____ .

Page 4 (complete)

Mummy will help me to fill in a card to invite _____ to come to The Space Centre with us. Mummy and I will give the card to _____ when we go to swimming club tomorrow.

The Social Story™ in Box 4.5 presents the individual with information about different children's interests to help him or her to decide who to invite on a trip. Gray's approach clearly provides the individual with ASD essential information that may be 'hidden' in order to encourage him or her to look for an appropriate response. This clearly moves the Social Stories™ approach beyond that of teaching social skills alone.

Stories about skills and responses

As we have seen earlier in this chapter, cooperative sentences can some-times be used to remind others of how they should respond to a new social behaviour that the individual is trying to implement. Cooperative sentences will help to ensure consistency of response. However, it is far more likely that there will be varied responses from others when a person is learning to use new social skills and behaviours. Box 4.6 develops the theme illustrated in the previous Social Story™ (Box 4.5) but lets the individual know that there may be different responses and outcomes after he or she has given his or her invitation.

Box 4.6 Split Section Social Story™: Social skills and responses of others

Page I (complete)

I have chosen to invite Saeed to come to The Space Centre with us next Friday. Mummy and I are going to give Saeed his invitation tomorrow.

Page 2 (complete)

Saeed will open the card and read it. He will need to show it to his Mummy too.

Page 3 (split)

Page 3a

Saeed and his Mummy will say that he can come to The Space Centre with us and he will be happy that he is going to come.

Page 3b

Saeed's Mummy may have to remind him that he has to go somewhere else on that day and that he will *not* be able to come.

Page 3c

Saeed's Mummy may say that she will have to check the calendar at home to make sure that Saeed does not have to go anywhere else on Friday and then she will telephone to let us know if he can come or not.

Page 4 (complete)

Saeed may be able to come to The Space Centre on Friday. If he is not able to come, I might invite a different friend on Friday. I can invite Saeed to come on another outing at another time.

Again, Box 4.6 clearly shows that the Social Stories™ approach is not focusing upon skills in isolation but rather upon providing 'hidden' social information, in this case about the different possible responses of Saeed and his mum, in order to help an individual to understand the social complexities of a situation.

In other instances, the split page technique may be used to offer varied ways in which social skills such as apologies, compliments, invitations, etc. can be made, with additional advice as to the occasions or situations when each would be the more appropriate choice. Social skills such as issuing invitations, making apologies and giving compliments are all useful to develop, but are all too frequently very difficult to comprehend and to master. Split Section Social Stories™ can be used to prepare the individual for some of the most likely ways in which such skills may be used.

In some cases where split books are used to offer choices, the first pages may 'set the scene' and the following split pages may give further information about the choices that are available. The initial split pages will state the choice (as at 2a, 2b, 2c) and the following split pages (3a, 3b, 3c, etc.) will give more information as to what is involved in that choice. For example, a Split Section Social Story™ was written for an individual attending a youth group. The Social Story™ is split into sections to provide information upon which to base a choice and to provide information about appropriate social responses and behaviour, depending upon the choice made (Box 4.7).

Box 4.7 Split Section Social Story™: Choices

Page I (complete)

On Thursday evenings I usually go to the Youth Group at my Church.

Sometimes when there is free time the Leader says we can choose what we would like to do for 30 minutes.

Page 2 (complete)

This story will tell me about some of the things I could choose from.

Page 3 (split)

Page 3a

I might choose to do puzzles.

Page 3b

I might choose to play skittles with some other people.

Page 4 (split)

Page 4a

There are puzzles in the cupboard by the window. It is OK to open the cupboard and choose a puzzle I would like to do.

Page 4b

I can take the puzzle to the table next to the cupboard and sit on one of the red chairs while I do the puzzle. Other people may be sitting at the table too. This is OK.

Page 4c

When I have finished the puzzle I can take it back to the cupboard and choose a different one.

Page 4d

The Leader will set up a game of skittles near the noticeboard. Three or four people usually play skittles together; they take turns to bowl balls at the skittles to knock them down.

Page 4e

Somebody will give the ball to me when it is my turn to bowl. While I am waiting for my turns I can watch to see how many skittles other people knock down.

Page 4f

Sometimes people do not knock any skittles down, sometimes they knock some of them down and occasionally all of them may fall down. Often people knock down more skittles after they have practised.

Page 5 (complete)

The Leader will usually say 'OK everyone, time for group time now.'

This means it is time to put the puzzle away and go to sit on a chair in the circle.

Page 6 (complete)

There are other activities to choose from at Youth Group. I can ask the Leader what other activities there are if I do not want to do puzzles or play skittles any more. This is OK. The Leader is there to help children and she knows about all the activities there are to choose from at Youth Group.

Social Stories™ *about simultaneous events or activities*

The split section format can also be used to share information about events and activities that are taking place in the same time slot, but which are not observable to the individual (Gray 1998b). For example, individuals with ASD often feel anxiety and confusion during the absence of a familiar person in their lives. This may be a family member who is away from home for a period of time, a teacher or learning support assistant, another child, or a supervisor or colleague at work. It may also be a problem for them knowing where other people are when they themselves are in a different environment; for example, at school, work, on holiday, in hospital, etc. Parallel schedules can be one way of providing visual representations of what others are doing in relation to the individual's own activities and when they will be returning. More comprehensive information may be given in a Split Section Social Story™. For example, a Split Section Social Story™ may help to identify for a child what his daddy is doing when he is away from home (Box 4.8).

Box 4.8 Split Section Social Story™: Simultaneous events and activities

Page 1 (complete)

My name is Marianne. I live at 104 Wordsworth Avenue with my Mum and Dad and my brother Robert. My Dad usually goes to work at about 7.45 am and comes home between 6 pm and 7 pm. He usually reads a story to me when I go to bed.

Page 2 (complete)

Sometimes my Dad needs to go to other towns to do work and he may need to sleep there. When Dad needs to sleep in other towns, he does not come home that night and Mum reads a story to me when I go to bed. Dad is going to London on Wednesday; he will sleep there on Wednesday night and come home on Thursday between 8 pm and 9 pm.

Page 3 (split)

Page 3a

On Wednesday my Dad will get up very early to go to London.

Page 3b

I will probably still be sleeping in my bed when Dad goes to London on Wednesday.

Page 4 (split)

Page 4a

I will get up and have my breakfast and go to school.

Page 4b

Dad will be travelling to London in his car.

Page 5 (split)

Page 5a

I follow my schedule at school and Mum will come to meet me when school finishes. Mum will bring me home.

Page 5b

Dad will work in an office in London. When his work is finished he will go to a hotel to have his supper and go to bed. Mum will show me a picture of the hotel Dad is staying in.

Page 6 (split)

Page 6a

Mummy will read a story to me when I am in bed.

Page 6b

Dad is in a bed in the hotel.

Page 7 (split)

Page 7a

I will get up and go to school and follow my schedule. Mum will come to meet me when school finishes and take me home.

Page 7b

Dad will have breakfast in the hotel and go to work in the office in London. When Dad finishes his work he will start to drive home.

Page 8 (split)

Page 8a

Mummy will read me a story in bed.

Page 8b

Dad will probably come home before the story is finished. He will finish reading the story to me.

Page 9 (complete)

On Thursday Dad and I will both get up at the usual time and I will go to school and he will go to work. Many Dads go away to work sometimes. This is OK.

Cooperative efforts

Finally, in the school and often the work setting working cooperatively or as part of a team has become more and more important. This presents further challenges for people with ASD who may not be aware of how their role 'fits' with others' roles. Gray (1998b) suggests that Social Stories™ may also provide useful information about 'cooperative efforts', showing the individual how his or her activities or piece of work fits in with that of others to produce an end result. They may also be used to give insight into different reactions and approaches to common experiences. This strategy could be utilized to give information about working in groups, preparations for social events such as birthday celebrations, festivals or outings, towards which many different people would be working cooperatively. Such Social Stories™ may well be particularly useful when combined with other approaches. This is explored in detail in Chapter 6 when considering the use of Social Stories™ with 'jigsawing' and 'structured teaching'.

Conclusion

This chapter has focused upon Gray's (1998b) recommendations for writing Advanced Social Stories™. The chapter has introduced advanced sentences, developed by Gray, namely control, affirmative, cooperative and partial sentences. The technique of Split Section Social Stories™ has been explored in relation to the key areas for which Gray promotes their use.

The focus of these strategies enhances the commitment to developing social understanding inherent in the Social Stories™ approach. Chapter 1 considered the theoretical perspectives that underpin this approach and it is in the realm of Advanced Social Stories™ that this really comes to the fore. Whilst social skills programmes have value, the focus upon developing social understanding, taking into account social cognitive factors, makes the Social Stories™ approach innovative and of particular importance. The rest of this book considers presentation of Social Stories™, preparatory strategies, complementary approaches, and the development of a proactive, problem-solving approach to their use. Whilst fully acknowledging Gray's approach and guidelines, examples are provided based upon the writers' experiences in order to illustrate key principles. Examples used illustrate how the Social Stories™ approach is placed within the current climate in relation to inclusive practices as the approach provides an inclusive strategy for promoting the social inclusion and participation of those with ASD.

Key teaching points

- Introduce additional Social Story™ sentences to develop understanding of more abstract concepts, to highlight the role of the individual and other participants and to encourage the individual to make contributions and incorporate their own ideas.
- Ensure that you follow the complete Social Story™ sentence formula.
- Introduce Social Stories™ about thoughts to further develop social understanding.

- Use Split Section Social Stories™ to develop flexibility and understanding of choices, to develop understanding that there may be varied responses from others or to provide information about simultaneous events and/or cooperative efforts.

Chapter Five

Presenting, Implementing and Monitoring

Presentation

The way in which a Social Story™ is presented may be a critical factor in relation to the eventual outcome. One possible advantage of the Social Story™ approach to providing individuals with 'hidden' information is that the information is presented in a neutral way, without added pressure of social interaction. An individual may feel more able to absorb the information presented in a Social Story™ than being told what to do by another person. Information presented in this neutral, asocial way may mean that the individual is more likely to be able to respond to the information being presented. It is important therefore to consider how to present each Social Story™ in order for the individual to be able to access the information being presented in a calm and neutral way, without the pressures of trying to comply with the social demands of others.

Social Stories™ need to provide information to the individual that is not readily available to them, 'revealing the hidden code' (Gray 1998a). For this to be effective, Social Stories™ need to be individualized. If individual factors are taken into account, as recommended by Gray (1998a), it quickly becomes apparent that Social Stories™ will take different forms for different individuals, depending upon their individual needs. Gray identifies a number of individual factors to consider when presenting Social Stories™, including developmental age, reading and comprehension ability, attention span, interests and preferred learning style (Chapter 3). Writers of Social Stories™ will need therefore to consider these factors when making decisions about how each Social Story™ will be presented. It is likely then that a Social Story™ for a young child with a short attention span who relies upon picture cues when reading is likely to be presented in a short form with pictures to enhance the meaning of the text. Conversely, a Social Story™ for an adolescent with a longer attention span and a wide vocabulary will be presented differently. Social Stories™ may therefore be presented in many different forms including picture/ text booklets, single-page text, detailed reports and through the use of information and communication technology (ICT).

This chapter considers different ways of presenting Social Stories™ taking into account individual needs, with an emphasis on the use of visual cues including illustrations, layout and text design in order to add interest, enhance meaning and highlight important information. Examples will illustrate different ways of presentation in order to provide ideas for those who wish to develop individualized Social Stories™. Finally this chapter also considers the implementation and review of Social Stories™, monitoring progress and fading the approach.

Visual cues

The use of visual cues to add meaning and highlight relevant information in Social Stories™ may be a key element of the approach and may influence the outcome. Visual cues may be provided through illustrations and/or text design. People with ASD are often described as visual learners who may respond well to visual teaching strategies. This preferred visual learning style is integral to other approaches. 'Structured teaching', as advocated by the TEACCH approach, lays great emphasis upon the use of visual structure and information (Schopler *et al.* 1995) and the Picture Exchange Communication System (PECS) provides a visual alternative communication system for individuals with ASDs (Bondy and Frost 1994). Howlin *et al.* (1999) use visual images in their approach to teaching children to 'mind read' and Cambridge University (2004) makes use of visual imagery through ICT to develop 'mind reading' and an understanding of emotions. Howley (2001) suggests that the use of visual cues can influence the outcome of a Social Story™ and reports greater effectiveness of Social Stories™ that make use of visual cues than those without. Visual cues may enhance the meaning of the text and can be used to highlight relevant and important information. It may also be the case that visual cues serve as visual reminders of Social Story™ content. For example, a Social Story™ written for a pupil to encourage him to use an appropriate volume of voice when reading to an adult in class incorporated a number scale on a bookmark (Howley 2001). The Social Story™ was read with the pupil prior to the activity and the bookmark then served as a visual reminder of key information in the Social Story™. This approach was perceived as very successful by the pupil's teacher and teaching assistant, with the bookmark reminding the pupil of the correct volume of voice and the Social Story™ content explaining why this is important in a classroom.

The important question to ask when developing an individualized Social Story™ is: what level of visual information adds greatest meaning for the individual? Social Stories™ may utilize objects (Gray and White 2002), photographs, pictures and symbols to enhance meaning and to link to the individual's learning style. In addition, consideration of presentation layout and text design may also be important in enhancing meaning and highlighting relevant information. The following examples illustrate different ways of presenting Social Stories™, taking into account the individual factors identified by Gray (1998a) and the use of visual cues. As Gray and White (2002, p.22) suggest: 'The ideas are endless; a little creativity and effort can go a long way to clarifying and expanding the meaning of a Social Stories set.'

USING OBJECTS

Some young children and individuals with additional learning difficulties may find it helpful to have their Social Story™ 'illustrated' with objects. Gray and White (2002) suggest that objects from a Social Story™ may be used for role play, giving an example of a 'set' of Social Stories™ about visiting a grocery store (p.22). Objects may be useful for enhancing meaning in a Social Story™ and may provide additional motivation. A Social Story™ illustrated with pictures may also have a collection of objects that can be used when reading the Social Story™ with the individual. The Social Story™ in Box 5.1 was written for a young child with ASD to prepare him for going on an overnight trip to his grandmother. The Social Story™ was accompanied by familiar objects that enhanced the meaning of the Social Story™ and which Andrew's mum knew he would find motivating. The objects used when reading the Social Story™ are indicated in italics at the end of each phrase.

Box 5.1 Social Story™ accompanied by objects

Going to Gran's for one night: A story for Andrew

My name is Andrew. I am 5. I live with my mum and dad at home. I have a blue train at home. (*train*)

I am going to Gran's house on Saturday. Gran has lots of balls and a yellow digger at her house. (*ball*)

I am going to stay at Gran's house on Saturday night. I can take my blue train to Gran's. I can play with the balls. (*ball*)

Gran and I can play with the blue train and the yellow digger. We can watch a video too. (*video case*)

I will go to bed at Gran's house on Saturday night. Gran will read me a story and kiss me and say, 'Goodnight Andrew.' (*teddy*)

Mum and Dad will come and get me on Sunday morning after breakfast. We will go home. (*Mum's keyring*)

This Social Story™ also incorporated pictures, but assessment of Andrew's needs led to the decision that concrete objects would enhance the Social Story™ content. The Social Story™ was read regularly to Andrew to prepare him for sleeping at his grandmother's. The Social Story™ was presented as a book and kept in a 'story sack' with the objects.

PHOTOGRAPHS

Some individuals prefer photographs and may find these more meaningful in Social Stories™, particularly if they have not yet reached the stage of recognizing more abstract symbols. Their use can help to personalize Social Stories™ with photographs of real objects, people and/or activities to enhance understanding. However, it is important to remember to edit photos to minimize any irrelevant, potentially distracting or misleading information. Photographs should be used carefully to highlight relevant information, enhance meaning and add interest or motivators. Box 5.2 illustrates a Social Story™ written for Tim who is being prepared for a train journey. Tim's mother decided to take Tim to visit the station and watch the trains before attempting to board one for a journey to see his grandparents. She wrote a Social Story™ to prepare Tim for his first visit to the station.

Box 5.2 Social Story™ illustrated with photographs

Waiting for a train: A story for Tim

My name is Tim and I am 6 years old. I live with my mum in Kettering. I have a Nanna and Pop who live in London.

Mum is taking me to the train station. When we are at the station we might see these things:

Station entrance

Station platform

Seats to wait on

The railway lines

A train

My mum would like me to:

- walk into the station
- walk to the platform
- sit on a seat
- wait for a train.

My mum will be there to help me.

The train will be loud when it arrives at the platform. My mum will take care of me.

Some people will get off the train, some people will get on. The train will leave when the people have got off or on. When the train has left the platform the noise will stop.

When the train has gone Mum and me can go home.

Another day we might go on a train to see Nanna and Pop. They will be very happy to see me.

Photographs provide realistic information for Tim about the context, including the station entrance, the platform, the bench to sit on and wait, the railway line (which his mother knew he liked looking at in books) and a train. Note that the photos do not include people. This is because Tim may think that any passengers appearing in a photograph would be the same when he actually goes to the station to board a train. Further Social Stories™ can then be introduced to prepare Tim for his visit to his grandparents.

DRAWINGS AND PICTURES

Social Stories™ may be illustrated with drawings and pictures, again with the purpose of enhancing meaning and highlighting relevant information. Some individuals may prefer to illustrate their Social Stories™ with their own drawings and this may add to their motivation. For example, Peter, aged 9, had problems with lining up in class. A Social Story™ was written to help him to understand the teachers' expectations. Peter illustrated his Social Story™ (Box 5.3).

Box 5.3 Social Story™ illustrated by the pupil

Line up quietly: A story for Peter

My name is Peter and I am in class 7 at Hawthorne School. My teacher is usually Mrs Hayes. Sometimes other teachers teach my class and me.

Class 7 often leave the classroom to go to other lessons. We might go to PE in the hall, music in the music room, assembly in the hall. Class 7 also go outside, if it is not raining heavily, at playtimes.

When class 7 needs to leave the classroom together, Mrs Hayes likes us to line up at the door. This is so that she can make sure that all the children are ready. Mrs Hayes usually says: '*Class 7, time to line up please.*'

Other teachers also like children to line up quietly. They may say 'Class 7, time to line up quietly please.' They may say something else. This is OK.

Most children get into line when asked. Sometimes some children are not in line. This means the class have to wait to leave the room. Usually Mrs Hayes and the other teachers let the children leave the classroom when we are all lined up.

When Mrs Hayes says 'Class 7, *time to line up please,* I will try to remember to line up. I will also try to remember to line up when other teachers ask class 7 to line up.

Mrs Hayes will be very pleased if I remember to do this. Usually she will give me a star for my star chart. Other teachers might also give me a star.

Some individuals take ownership of the Social Story™ if they are involved in its development. Adding illustrations can be an additional motivating factor for some.

SYMBOLS

Symbols can also be used effectively to highlight important information and to enhance meaning in a Social Story™. A Social Story™ presented as a booklet may be illustrated with symbols on each page. Box 5.4 illustrates a Social Story™ that uses symbols to clarify meaning for Leila, a 7-year-old girl who has been invited to a birthday party.

Box 5.4 Social Story™ with symbols: Birthday party

Going to a birthday party: A story for Leila

Lots of people have a birthday party on their birthday or on a day near to their birthday.

 Happy Birthday!

At birthday parties people like to do different things; sometimes they watch a magician, dance or do other things.

 magician   dance

Most children have a birthday cake at their party. Usually everyone sings 'Happy Birthday' when the candles are lit on the cake.

 birthday cake

When children have a birthday party, they usually invite other children. I have been invited to Jenny's birthday on 30 July.

Jenny's party is at Jenny's house and starts at about 3 o'clock. My mum or dad will take me to the party in the car.

 car

They will take me to the door and speak to Jenny. They will probably say 'Happy Birthday Jenny.' They might speak to Jenny's mum. Then they will go shopping. They would like me to stay at the party until it finishes.

When the party is finished, Mum or Dad will collect me and take me home in the car.

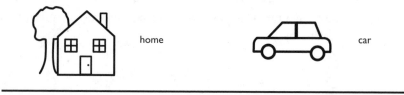

home   car

This Social Story™ contains no directives but is intended to prepare Leila for the event. Further Social Stories™ may then go on to explain related party topics; for example, giving the present, joining in games, and so on. Although Leila is a confident reader, it was felt that her anxiety about the party may interfere with her understanding and so symbols are used to enhance key aspects of the content.

Similarly, symbols were used for Joe, aged 6, who switches off his mother's washing machine. Information gathering indicated that this was usually when the spin cycle began and an interview with his mother revealed that she thought Joe disliked the noise of the machine. A Social Story™ was written to explain to Joe why his mother would like him to leave the washing machine switched on and what he could do to avoid the noise. Joe had a real interest in books, so his story was written as a small booklet and illustrated with coloured symbols (Box 5.5). Note that others may require photographs of the actual objects being described for the Social Story™ to be relevant and to have meaning for them.

Box 5.5 Social Story™ with symbols: Washing machine

Switching the washing machine off: A story for Joe

Page 1
My name is Joe. I live at 27 Slater Street. I live with my mum, dad, Emily and Paul.

Page 2
Usually, my mum puts washing in the washing machine every day.

Page 3

The washing machine is noisy when it spins the washing.

Page 4

If the washing machine is switched off before the washing is finished, Mum sometimes feels cross.

She is cross because the washing does not get finished. Then she has to start the washing again.

Page 5

When the washing machine is noisy Mum would like me to *play in my room or in the garden*. The noise will not be so loud in the garden or in my bedroom.

Page 6

Mummy would like me to leave the washing machine switched on.

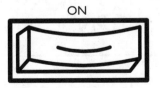

Page 7

I will try to remember to *play in my room or in the garden* when Mummy is doing the washing.

Page 8

I will try to remember to *leave the washing machine switched on* when Mummy is doing the washing.

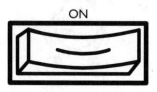

Page 9

Mummy will be very happy if I leave the washing machine switched on.

Page 10

She will usually switch the washing machine off when the washing is finished. Mummy will give me a dinosaur sticker for my chart.

Symbols may also be used effectively to highlight key information in a Social Story™ that is primarily text. A student at a high school would frequently call out in class. He was familiar with the Social Stories™ approach. He was also a keen member of the school newsletter publishing team. A Social Story™ was written for Mike in the form of a newsletter report with two symbols to clarify the important message. The Social Story™ in this case was written in the third person and was printed in the newsletter, with Mike's permission and delight (Box 5.6).

Box 5.6 Newsletter Social Story™ with one symbol to emphasize important information

Pupils call out in class at St John's Secondary School!

Teachers at St John's Secondary School often ask the students questions during lessons.

Some pupils know the answers to the questions. Some pupils call out the answers every time they know the answer.

When students call out answers, it does not give other students the opportunity to tell their answers. This makes some of the teachers and students unhappy.

The teachers and students at St John's Secondary School have agreed that students should **stay quiet** and **raise their hand** to get teachers' attention.

The students will try to remember to **stay quiet** and **raise their hand**, when teachers ask questions.

Teachers will ask different students for their answers. The teachers try to make sure that lots of students have the opportunity to answer questions.

The teachers and students at St John's Secondary School will be pleased if the students raise their hand to answer questions. St John's Secondary School has found a solution to calling out!

(Reporters: Mike S. and Mr Luker)

Note the different presentation of this Social Story™ compared to that of Jake (Chapter 3, Box 3.5). This example illustrates the flexibility of the Social Stories™ approach. Consideration of individual needs is the key and the presentation of any Social Story™ should incorporate these individual needs and interests.

In a classroom setting, a symbol used in a Social Story™ may also be used within the classroom at appropriate times to serve as a reminder of the Social Story™ content. Howley (2001) provides an example of how this idea was used in a mainstream classroom to remind a pupil, Sally, that when the teacher talks to a group or to the class she is also talking to Sally. Displaying the appropriate symbol on the teacher's desk during whole-class teaching provides a reminder to the pupil with ASD and to other pupils who may also need reminding to listen.

Older individuals with good reading and comprehension may prefer text only. Social Stories™ will need to reflect the language and vocabulary used by the individual. The Social Story™ in Box 5.7 was written for a student at university, Stuart, who needed to consider how to improve his ability to work on assignments with other students.

Box 5.7 Textual Social Story™ for university student

Working with other students on assignments: Tutors' expectations

University students attend a range of different modules during their degree course. Taught modules depend upon the subject of the degree. Taught modules are usually delivered through lectures, seminars and tutorials.

Students are expected to work independently during taught modules and for independent study time. Students are also required to work together during some modules. Different tutors have different expectations: sometimes they will ask students to work alone, sometimes they will ask students to work in groups. Sometimes the tutor will set a paired or group assignment. This means that two or more students work collaboratively on an assignment and submit a group response to the assignment title or question. The work is then marked for the group. Sometimes the assignment is marked for the work of the group or pair; sometimes there is an individual component and students receive a group mark and an individual mark.

Paired and group assignments require students to work together. This is very important and is a requirement of pass in some modules. Students who do not work together on an assignment when required may fail the assignment. If a student in a group does not work with the other students in their group, the other students may feel angry and resentful as they may fail the assignment.

Tutors intend students to work together and to **co-operate** and **collaborate** with each other. The group will need to **negotiate** with each other how they will organize the assignment.

Definitions (Oxford Dictionary)	**French translation (complete if you wish)**
Co-operate *work or act together (with person, in or on task, for purpose)*	**Cooperer**
Collaborate *work jointly with*	**Collaborer**
Negotiate *confer with a view to finding terms of agreement*	**Negocier**

Tutors may allocate some marks to students for evidencing their group cooperation, collaboration and negotiation; for example, minutes of planning minutes, work allocation and monitoring progress.

The tutor for each module will be particularly pleased when students work together when required. I will try to remember to work with other students when required for assignments. If I am experiencing any difficulties it is OK to seek assistance. The module tutor, my student buddy and/or my academic mentor can help me with aspects of cooperation, collaboration or negotiation if necessary.

This Social Story™ does not incorporate symbol or picture cues but is presented as text, using language familiar to the student. Stuart is provided with dictionary definitions of key words. As he enjoys 'playing with languages' and English/French translation he has space to translate these definitions if he wishes to do so. The Social Story™ is not presented as a 'story' but nevertheless conforms to Gray's guidelines and sentence ratio. The perspectives of other students are included to help Stuart to understand why they may be angry if he does not work with them. The relevance of working together is also linked firmly to pass/fail criteria. Cooperative sentences serve as a reminder for Stuart as to whom it is appropriate to seek help from if he needs it. This generic Social Story™ about working with other students can then be personalized for specific module assignments as appropriate.

ICT AND SOCIAL STORIES™

Social Stories™ may also be illustrated with the use of ICT. Individuals with ASD are often highly motivated when using computers and this may be useful in presenting Social Stories™. Hagiwara and Myles (1999) designed a 'multimedia social story intervention' in which Social Stories™ were presented on a computer. They claim that 'the multimedia social story intervention embodies the characteristics of social stories in a structured, consistent, and attractive presentation with ample visual stimuli and sound made possible by the computer system' (p.83).

The use of ICT to support the Social Story™ approach may have several benefits including high motivational factors and the use of visual information to enhance meaning. Hagiwara and Myles (1999) also suggest that individuals with ASD may become involved in creating their own Social Stories™ by illustrating them with computer graphics or by recording their own voices reading the Social Story™ to be incorporated into the software program.

The Social Story™ in Box 5.8 was written for Emmy, aged 9, who hugged people indiscriminately. Her family and teacher prioritized this behaviour and together gathered information to help them to draft a Social Story™ for Emmy. They decided that one Social Story™ should focus upon who Emmy is allowed to hug and introduce new skills for greeting other people. Emmy's mother was anxious that her daughter might also overuse these new skills so the Social Story™ needed to indicate how she could find out which skill to use. Emmy's family and two other people (her teacher and Mr Green in the local shop) were involved in this Social Story™ to provide Emmy with safe and regular opportunities to practise her new skills.

Box 5.8 Social Story™ using ICT

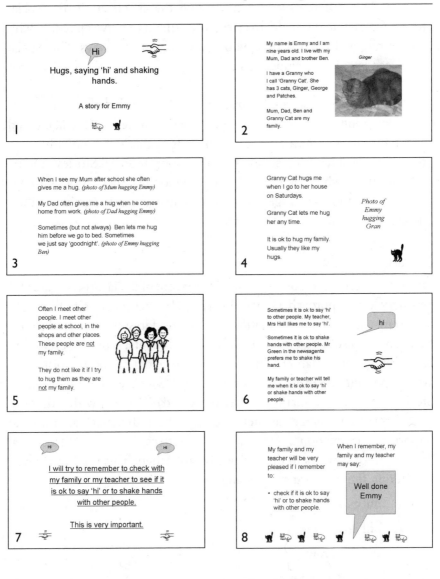

Emmy's interests (cats) were incorporated into the Social Story™ and the decision was made to present it using ICT software as she was highly motivated when using the computer. Emmy's family were presented in the story with colour digital photographs while 'other people' were illustrated with symbols. This different way of presenting the characters in the Social Story™ was intended visually to clarify the difference between family who you can hug and other people who you greet in other ways. This Social Story™ can later be developed to include more 'other people' and to introduce the concept of strangers.

Video feedback may also provide a useful media for some individuals to reflect upon the content of their Social Stories™ (Thiemann and Goldstein 2001). It must also be acknowledged that some individuals do not prefer visual teaching styles. Audio versions of Social Stories™ can be useful for those who prefer to read and listen to their Social Stories™ independently. Similarly, younger children may like an audio version of their Social Story™ to listen to as they read.

Text design and layout

The visual presentation of the text and the layout of Social Stories™ are also pertinent to the approach. Gray (1998a) emphasizes the need to highlight important and relevant information in order to address weak central coherence. The range of visual cues identified in this chapter is one aspect of this. However, the presentation of the text and the layout of Social Stories™ are also important. Readers will see in the previous examples of Social Stories™ that key information is often presented differently within the text. Text format and layout can help to draw the individual's attention to important information including the directives, sentences that reveal 'hidden' information and the perspectives of others. This can be achieved by altering the text format by changing:

- font type
- font size
- colour of font
- lower and upper case letters
- underlining, italicizing, emboldening.

Similarly, the layout of Social Stories™ should enhance meaning and the most relevant information for the individual. For example, a picturebook/ textbook may present one key piece of information on a page, the directive may feature as a single page, bullet points may be used within a longer text. These may appear to be small details, but given the tendency of individuals with ASDs to focus upon detail, they should not be overlooked and may be an extremely useful strategy for helping to reveal the 'hidden social code'.

Individualized Social Stories™ ought therefore to be presented in different ways in order to take into account individual needs. The length, style and presentation of each Social Story™ should be determined by the needs, strengths and interests of the individual for whom it is being written. Once a Social Story™ has been written and individualized, how then should you implement it with the individual?

Implementation

Writers of Social Stories™ often ask some key questions when they come to introduce the Social Story™ to an individual. Frequently asked questions include:

- How often do we need to read the Social Story™?
- Who reads it with the individual?
- How long do we read it and when do we stop?

Gray (1998a; Gray and White 2002) provides detailed guidance on how to implement Social Stories™, suggesting the following strategies:

1. Find a place with limited distractions to encourage the individual to focus upon the Social Story™ content.

2. Sit at the person's side and slightly back, so that the individual engages with the Social Story™ rather than with you.

3. Read through once or twice when you first introduce a Social Story™. Observe and record the individual's reactions and comments as these will inform any redrafting that might be needed.

4. Briefly explain how the Social Story™ will be used: for example, when you will read it, how often, who else will read it and so on. Explain or discuss where the Social Story™ will be kept.

After the first reading, it may be necessary to redraft the Social Story™ in the light of the individual's responses to it. Remember that sometimes individuals will be pleased to read the Social Story™ and it will instantly have meaning. Others may resist some of the ideas presented or may become distressed. When you are satisfied that the Social Story™ is appropriate, Gray then goes on to suggest that a review schedule needs to be considered:

- In some circumstances it is advisable that the Social Story™ is read approximately once a day, before the targeted situation.

- Develop a consistent approach to reviewing the Social Story™ with the individual.

- Share the Social Story™ with all others involved.

Regular reading of the Social Story™ will depend in part upon the developmental age, attention span and comprehension of the individual. Some will require numerous readings whilst others may respond quite quickly to the content. Be guided by the responses of the individual when deciding if a Social Story™ is no longer needed or if it is time to draft the next in a series.

It is important to encourage individuals to take ownership of their Social Stories™ and author and individual will decide together where they will be kept. Some children like to keep their Social Stories™ in their school drawer or in a safe place at home. Older individuals may wish to file them in a ring-binder or filing box or store them on a computer. Some individuals will enjoy 'collecting' their Social Stories™ in a series and may be motivated by having a logo for each set collected. Wherever they are kept, individuals should have easy access to them so that they may refer to the content when they feel it would be helpful. Some individuals will begin to read their Social Stories™ by themselves. This is an important step in beginning to determine responses in social situations for themselves.

Monitoring

Changes in behaviour and social understanding

Once a Social Story™ is in place and being read regularly with the individual, it is important to monitor progress and to assess any change in behaviour and social understanding. Again, Gray (1998a) gives clear guidelines for ongoing monitoring, suggesting that it is important to monitor the behaviour and any comments made by the individual. It may be relatively straightforward to monitor overt behaviours and any changes through direct observations. It is also important to assess whether there has been any development in relation to social understanding when a behaviour has changed. This should be assessed in a similar way to the original assessments to discover the individual's perspective and understanding: for example, using Gray's (1994b, 1998a) CSCs approach, individual discussion or multiple choice, written questionnaires. Whilst it may not be straightforward to assess any change in social understanding, it is a crucial part of monitoring the individual's progress as developments in social understanding may indicate progress that goes beyond behavioural compliance. If we are to encourage individuals with ASDs to begin to assess a situation and to determine the correct social responses in that situation, developments in social understanding will be crucial. Ongoing monitoring of behavioural responses and social understanding should therefore form an integral part of the process of using the Social Story™ approach. (Appendix 2 provides a pro forma for ongoing monitoring of both behaviour and social understanding.)

Fading

Monitoring individual responses to a Social Story™ will inform further development of the approach. When a Social Story™ is successful, it will be possible to fade its use. Fading of the Social Story™ must be determined by the individual's needs. Even when you feel it is no longer necessary to read the Social Story™ regularly, the individual should still have access to it should they wish to check the content at any time. Adolescents and adults sometimes like to keep their Social Stories™ within a filing system so that they can refer to them as they wish. Following the decision to fade a Social Story™, a further decision will need to be made with regard to the next step in the process. Sometimes a Social Story™ is withdrawn because it has not been helpful and needs rewriting (see Chapter 7). Gray also suggests that it may be useful to revise the review schedule; for example, to read the Social Story™ more or less frequently, depending upon needs. Further ways of fading include reducing the number of directive sentences and/or reducing the verbal cues provided while reading the Social Story™ with the individual, leading to the individual reading the Social Story™ independently.

Conclusion

The presentation of Social Stories™ is a crucial element of the approach and may influence the outcome. Taking into account individual needs, interests and preferred learning styles will increase the likelihood of success. Careful consideration of how to present a Social Story™ will include how the Social Story™ looks and what types of visual cues will be incorporated. The review schedule will indicate how, when and where the Social Story™ will be read and discussed and ongoing monitoring will inform the fading process. Observations and discussions with the individual will help you to identify how the individual is responding to the Social Story™ content and enable you to determine actions to take once a Social Story™ has been successful.

Key teaching points

- Identify the form of any visual cues that will add meaning and highlight important and relevant information for the individual.
- Consider the design and layout of text and visual cues to emphasize relevant information.
- Decide on the review schedule – when will you read it, where, how often?
- Monitor behavioural responses and changes in social understanding.
- Fade when appropriate.
- Decide upon the next action.

Chapter Six

Introductory Social Stories™
and Complementary Strategies

Social Stories™ aim to increase social understanding of social situations and events, as well as to encourage appropriate behaviour in those contexts. The aim of increasing social understanding underpins the approach and makes it different from other methods that may target social skills and behaviour. The Social Stories™ approach is flexible and responds to individual needs. Thus it is possible to consider other ways of using the approach. This may include the use of introductory Social Stories™ that may develop into Social Stories™ that focus upon more complex and abstract social information, and combining Social Stories™ with complementary strategies in order to enhance the overall approach to developing social skills, understanding and interaction. This chapter explores how you might use introductory Social Stories™ and how you might combine strategies to enhance outcomes in relation to behaviour and understanding.

Introductory Social Stories™

Some individuals, depending upon age and stage of cognitive development, will benefit from Social Stories™ that introduce basic information which prepares the individual for what to expect in a variety of situations. It may be more appropriate to begin to teach some individuals to understand sequences of events and perhaps to introduce the social skills that may be useful to them. In this case introductory Social Stories™ provide information without overloading individuals with information that they are unable to process meaningfully. Later, when the individual may be ready for further development of their social understanding, they will be familiar with the Social Stories™ approach and format. This familiarity with the approach means that their learning can focus upon the new content of the Social Story™, rather than on trying to learn a new strategy.

Gray and White (2002) provide a range of examples of Social Stories™ aimed at younger children. Social Stories™ are grouped according to topic and the individual is introduced to new information one step at a time. For example, 'What is a Watch?' is one of several Social Stories™ to increase understanding of time-related concepts:

> A watch is a very little clock that people wear on their wrist. A watch helps people know if it is time to eat, play, work, sleep, or do something else. (pp.82–83)

This Social Story™ is an important first step in introducing the idea and in preparing the child for more detailed Social Stories™ at a later date. This information prepares the child for further Social Stories™ that present information about more sophisticated time-related concepts, and how people may feel, such as being on time, hurrying up and being late. 'What Does It Mean to be Late?' (Gray and White 2002, pp.84–85) illustrates how the approach introduces perspectives with sentences like 'They may feel embarrassed when people watch them walk in late' and 'When they start to feel a little nervous about being late they hurry up.'

Social Stories™ that introduce situations may be useful for young children and for individuals who have additional learning difficulties. Whilst Social Stories™ are generally thought to be most successful for individuals with Asperger's syndrome or high-functioning autism, the approach should not be automatically ruled out for individuals with learning difficulties who may well benefit from introductory Social Stories™. The example in Box 6.1, which is one of a series of Social Stories™ about shopping, illustrates how introductory Social Stories™ can be useful. Pravin's mum found shopping trips stressful as Pravin (aged 6) disliked the shops, often tried to run out and wanted to go for a burger.

Box 6.1 Introductory Social Stories™

Going to the shops: A story for Pravin (1)

My name is Pravin. I live with my mum and sister.

On Saturdays, my mum usually takes me to the shops.
Sometimes we go to (*list shop names*).

When mum has finished shopping, usually we get a burger and milk-shake.

Going to the shops: A story for Pravin (2)

My name is Pravin. I live with my mum and sister.

On Saturdays, my mum usually takes me to the shops.
Sometimes we go to (*list shop names*).

When we go shopping, my mum will give me my pictures of the shops.

When mum has finished shopping, usually we get a burger and milk-shake.

Going to the shops: A story for Pravin (3)

My name is Pravin. I live with my mum and sister.

On Saturdays, my mum usually takes me to the shops.
Sometimes we go to (*list shop names*).

When we go shopping, my mum will give me my pictures of the shops we are going to. She would like me to look at the picture of the shop we are in. Mum will help me by showing me the picture.

When we have been in the shops and I have looked at every picture, shopping is finished.

When mum has finished shopping, usually we get a burger and milk-shake.

Going to the shops: A story for Pravin (4)

My name is Pravin. I live with my mum and sister.

On Saturdays, my mum usually takes me to the shops.
Sometimes we go to (*list shop names*).

When we go shopping, my mum will give me my pictures of the shops. She would like me to look at the picture of the shop we are in. Mum will help me by showing me the picture.

It is important to stay in the shop until mum tells me it is time to go.

The pictures show me when mum and me can go for a burger.

I will try to remember to stay in the shop and look at my pictures until mum tells me it is time to go. She will show me the next picture.

Mum will be pleased if I stay in the shop and look at my pictures.

When we have been in the shops and I have looked at every picture, shopping is finished.

When shopping is finished, usually we get a burger and milk-shake.

The Social Stories™ written for Pravin were illustrated with photographs to enhance meaning. A number of photos were taken and Pravin was encouraged to choose which photos to include in his Social Stories™. Photographs of the shops to be visited were included in the Social Story™ and put into a book for Pravin to take shopping. These examples illustrate how Social Stories™ can provide information incrementally, depending upon the needs of the individual for whom it is written. Some individuals may need to read introductory Social Stories™ for a long period of time before they are ready to be presented with more detailed social information. This makes the Social Stories™ approach accessible to individuals with a wide range of individual needs and includes younger children and those who have additional learning difficulties.

Visual directions and jigs

Another way of preparing individuals for Social Stories™ involves the use of visual directions and 'jigs' (a visual representation of how to complete a task) as described in the TEACCH 'structured teaching' approach (Mesibov and Howley 2003; Schopler *et al.* 1995). Step-by-step instructions are presented in a visual format in order to enable individuals to complete sequences of actions so as to achieve a goal or complete a task. Commonly these visual directions are utilized to enable individuals to complete academic tasks and self-care routines. However, it is also possible to use this approach to identify actions required in social situations. The use of visual directions 'allows a degree of flexibility that is uncommon in ASD, but essential for effective learning and vocational and community functioning' (Mesibov and Howley 2003, pp.13–14).

Flexibility is critical to adjusting social behaviour according to social context. Gray's Social Stories™ often focus upon helping individuals with ASD to 'see' and perhaps eventually to figure out for themselves the social behaviour and flexible responses appropriate to different social situations. For individuals who are not yet ready for this level of abstract information, visual directions may well be helpful in assisting the individual to begin to understand the sequence of actions necessary in a given situation. Gray and White (2002) incorporate sequenced visual directions in their Social Stories™ about brushing teeth (pp.33–35). In this example, other sentences are also used to begin to explain this event; for example, 'Adults teach children to brush their teeth.' The use of visual directions as a part of the structured teaching approach can therefore support Social Stories™. The example in Box 6.2 illustrates how visual directions can be used effectively to enable individuals to understand the sequence of activities within a situation or event and to develop appropriate responses. In this case visual directions provide essential information about what to do if there is a fire drill.

Box 6.2 Visual directions and jigs

What to do in a fire drill

When there is a fire drill at (*place name*), the bell will ring. These are the rules when the fire bell rings:

1. Stay calm.
2. Walk quickly to the nearest exit (front door or back door), with staff.
3. Walk to the bottom of the garden.
4. Wait at the sign.

Once an individual is able to follow visual directions, he or she may be able to develop flexible responses in different contexts. Later it may be possible to begin to add descriptive, perspective and directive sentences to the visual directions in order to begin to explain why those responses are appropriate. For example, Billy (aged 19) lives in a residential facility. He is disturbed by the fire drill and staff believe this is because of the noise level. The visual directions in Box 6.2 are explained for Billy in a Social Story™ (Box 6.3) with information about people's perspectives, why the fire drill is used and what he could do to respond.

Box 6.3 Developing Social Stories™ from visual directions and jigs

What to do in a fire drill: A social story for Billy

When there is a fire drill at Southfields House, the bell will ring loudly and usually everyone follows the fire drill rules. The fire drill rules are:

1. Stay calm.
2. Walk quickly to the nearest exit (front door or back door), with staff.
3. Walk to the bottom of the garden.
4. Wait at the 🔔 sign.

It is important to follow the fire drill rules; this is because if there is a real fire it is dangerous to stand still.

I will try to remember to follow the fire drill rules.

Jane and Steve and other members of staff will be pleased when I remember the rules and follow them. These rules are for my safety. If I follow these rules I should be safe.

When the fire drill is finished I can go back inside. Usually the bell will stop ringing.

Thus the visual directions guide the behaviours and responses required, telling the individual *what to do*. Social Stories™ can then add information about *how people feel* about the situation and *why* certain responses are more appropriate than others. Gray (1998a) strongly advocates the use of visual information to enhance meaning in Social Stories™. Visual information can be presented in the form of directions and jigs which may later be developed and incorporated in Social Stories™ that add social information. This may make the approach more accessible for individuals with ASD and learning difficulties. For example, this approach was used in a special school for a pupil who has ASD and learning difficulties. During whole-class work, David often moved his hands in patterns and would be distracted by this. His movements also distracted other pupils in the class. David's teacher wrote some directions and added visual symbols to remind David what to do with his hands during whole-class time (Box 6.4).

Box 6.4 Visual directions/rules symbols

Class-time rules

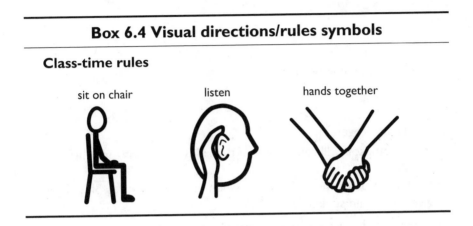

sit on chair   listen   hands together

David's teacher later wrote a Social Story™ for him incorporating photos, symbols and the class-time rules that also included a perspective sentence about how she would feel if he followed the rules (Box 6.5). Further Social Stories™ may later be written as appropriate to help David to understand how others might feel when he waves his hands around.

Box 6.5 Social Story™ to develop understanding of class-time rules

Hands on lap at class time: A story for David

My name is David. I go to Hazelwood School. I am in yellow class. (*with photo*)

    Usually Mrs Thompson is my teacher. (*photo*) Usually Mrs Thompson teaches us at class time.

    Mrs Thompson has some class rules. She has made a poster that looks like this:

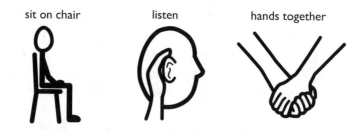

Class-time rules

I will try to remember to:

1. Sit on chair.
2. Listen.
3. Hands together.

Mrs Thompson will remind me of the rules by showing me the poster.

Mrs Thompson will be happy when I follow the rules. She might give me a train sticker.

Thus we can see that it is possible to write Social Stories™ that describe situations for an individual in preparation for further Social Stories™ that may add essential social information. In addition, complementary strategies such as the use of visual directions and jigs may also be used to prepare an individual for the Social Stories™ approach. Complementary strategies such as those of structured teaching outlined above may also be used to enhance the use of Social Stories™. This is the focus of our next discussion.

Complementary strategies

The use of visual directions and jigs as part of the structured teaching approach illustrate how visual directions can be applied in preparation for perhaps later introducing Social Stories™. Social Stories™ can then be written to add essential social information to develop understanding of a particular situation or event. This is important as whilst an individual may comply with rules and directions, ultimately the aim should also be to help the individual to understand *why* we would like him or her to follow these directions. Individuals who begin to develop this level of social understanding may eventually be able to determine for themselves appropriate social responses in other contexts. This must be an essential goal: that is, to help the individual to work out what to do, based upon reasons why, rather than rote compliance. Complementary approaches and strategies, including structured teaching, the use of social skills programmes, the 'circles of friends' approach and jigsawing, are explored in relation to the use of Social Stories™. It is argued here that combining strategies may lead to greater understanding for the individual and ultimately to improved, more meaningful and enjoyable social interaction.

Structured teaching

Individuals with ASD frequently have difficulties understanding 'meaning' (Powell 2000). This applies equally to understanding the meaning of social situations. Social Stories™ focus upon helping individuals to understand the meaning of social activities and events by clarifying relevant information, highlighting important information and introducing different perspectives. Other approaches also address issues relating to meaning. For example, visual information is advocated as part of the structured teaching approach to highlight important and relevant information and to clarify concepts (Mesibov and Howley 2003). Gray's use of visual information within Social Stories™ is complementary to structured teaching approaches and the two methods can be used in combination to enhance meaning. The use of visual directions and jigs illustrates how structured teaching strategies can be applied as a preparatory strategy to introducing Social Stories™ and to complement the Social Stories™ approach. In addition, other elements of structured teaching can be used to complement the use of Social Stories™; equally the use of Social Stories™ can enhance structured teaching strategies.

For example, structured teaching employs the use of visual schedules in order to provide information to individuals about sequences of activities. Schedules can also include other essential information such as who a pupil is to work with, what changes there are to the day, and so on. Schedules may sometimes incorporate reminders and rules for individuals about appropriate behaviour. It is suggested that such reminders may reduce the need for constant verbal prompting. Figure 6.1 illustrates how a written reminder is incorporated within the schedule to encourage a pupil to put away unfinished work at the end of a lesson.

Wednesday

AM	Literacy	Break	Numeracy	Lunch and break
PM	Music	PE	Messages	Home

Remember, put my unfinished work into the unfinished work box.

unfinished work

Figure 6.1 Schedule incorporating reminder from Social Story™

This strategy can be enhanced when used in combination with a Social Story™ as the Social Story™ adds information about *why* unfinished work needs to be put away at the end of lessons (Box 6.6).

Box 6.6 Social Story™ used in conjunction with reminder on a schedule

---

What to do with work that is unfinished at the end of the lesson: A social story for Gary

I attend South Brook Primary School. I am in Mr Bowers' class, class 6.

Mr Bowers usually tells us what he wants us to do in each lesson. Sometimes the work should be finished by the end of the lesson. Sometimes children do not get the work finished.

When work is not finished, I try to finish it. Mr Bowers tells class 6 to stop working and pack away. The class then move on to the next lesson.

Mr Bowers likes all the children to pack away when he tells them to. Work that is unfinished should be put into the box labelled 'unfinished work' on Mr Bowers desk. Mr Bowers likes children to pack away and put unfinished work into the unfinished tray so that he can begin to teach the next lesson. This is important.

I will try to remember to put my unfinished work into the unfinished work box.

unfinished work

Then I will be ready for the next lesson and Mr Bowers and class 6 will be very pleased. I can finish the work later – Mr Bowers will tell me when.

    If I remember to put my unfinished work in the unfinished box, Mr Bowers will usually give me a house point. He will tell my mum that he is pleased with me. My mum will be pleased too.

The reminder on the individual schedule can also act as a visual reminder of the Social Story™ content. It is particularly useful to use consistent phrasing, so the directive provided in the Social Story™ ('I will try to remember to put my unfinished work in the unfinished box') is also used on the schedule ('remember, put my unfinished work in the unfinished work box'). The use of this reminder on the schedule means that the individual is frequently reminded of the rule (every time he or she refers to his or her schedule) without 'nagging' and is also reminded of the Social Story™ content.

    In addition to schedules, the structured teaching approach uses 'work systems' to enable individuals to develop independent organizational skills (Schopler *et al.* 1995). Mesibov and Howley (2003) also suggest that the work system can be used to provide real opportunities for encouraging spontaneous communication; for example, by providing a visual cue card reminding an individual to ask for help whilst working (p.74). This could be enhanced by using a Social Story™ to explain why we should ask for help when needed and about the responses of others to this request. For example, Harry, aged 9, was often observed getting distressed when working independently yet he never asked for help. His teaching assistant would provide help when he became distressed. After a period of gathering information, it was agreed that an appropriate target for Harry would be for him 'to ask for help when needed during independent work'. A Social Story™ was introduced, together with a visual cue card which could be used within the independent work system that Harry already knew how to use (Box 6.7).

Box 6.7 Social Story™ used to support communication target within work system

Asking for help during independent work: A social story for Harry

I am in class 8 at school. My teacher is usually Mrs Jenkins. Class 8 has a teaching assistant too – Ms Wells is usually the teaching assistant.

Sometimes Mrs Jenkins helps children with their work; sometimes Ms Wells helps children with their work. If children get stuck with their work during independent work time, Mrs Jenkins and Ms Wells like them to raise their hand and wait for them to come. This tells them that a child needs help. When Mrs Jenkins or Ms Wells come, they like children to tell them what they need help with. Mrs Jenkins and Ms Wells usually like to help children with their work when they are stuck. Often they will come and help. Sometimes they might be too busy and they might tell children to try again by themselves. If they try again and then still need help, children can raise their hand again. Mrs Jenkins or Ms Wells will usually come and ask them what help they need.

I will try to remember to raise my hand when I need help with my work at independent work time.

I will try to remember to wait until Mrs Jenkins or Ms Wells come to me, then I will try to tell them what help I need.

Mrs Jenkins and Ms Wells will be very pleased if I remember to raise my hand when I need help with my work. Usually they will give me a credit in my book.

Harry was encouraged within his independent work system to ask for help when needed. The visual cue reminded him how to do this. In addition, a Social Story™ provided information for Harry to help him understand the process, including what to do, why, and the effects upon others. Thus the two approaches complement and possibly enhance each other.

Social skills programmes

A number of useful programmes are available to teach and develop social skills (Aarons and Gittens 1998; Schroeder 1996). Social skills programmes focus upon developing various social skills in a range of contexts: for example, greetings, apologies, compliments. Many programmes also focus on explaining emotions and feelings. Structured programmes, often used in structured social skills group contexts, may be extremely helpful in helping individuals to identify and develop appropriate social skills and to explore feelings. Combined with the use of Social Stories™, however, their effectiveness may be enhanced as crucial information is provided through the Social Stories™ about *why* specific social skills are appropriate in specific situations, about emotions and feelings, particularly about the perspectives of others. For example, Schroeder (1996) provides a structured programme with varying activities around the theme of 'Let's Be Friends' (pp.43–97). One topic within this unit focuses upon 'How to Make New Friends' (pp.83–85). A question and discussion session is suggested to help individuals to identify 'How Do You Make New Friends?'. Individuals are encouraged to consider how they could make friends with a new child at school. This is supported by role play and completion of 'making friends' worksheets. This session is one of several that focuses upon a range of friendship issues over a period of weeks.

Social Stories™ can be used to enhance this type of programme by reinforcing the messages within these activities and providing information that may be missing for the individual with ASD about others' perspectives. Schroeder suggests various responses that may be useful if you want to make a new friend such as:

- introduce yourself
- show the new pupil around
- smile at them
- ask them if they would like to play with you (p.83).

Individual pupils may also make their own suggestions. Role play is used to practise these skills in a less stressful situation before trying them out for real. A Social Story™, or probably a series of Social Stories™, may then be written to reinforce the social skills programme. For example, a Social Story™ was written for Steve, who attends an inclusive community college.

Steve attends a weekly social skills group and has been exploring 'friendship' for half a term. One Social Story™ in a series about 'friendship' focuses upon how to be friendly to new pupils (Box 6.8).

Box 6.8 Social Story™ used in conjunction with social skills programme

Being friendly towards a new pupil at Valley Community College: Social information – FRIENDS – NUMBER 6

I attend Valley Community College and am in year 8. There are many pupils at this community college. I know some of the pupils, especially the pupils in my tutor group. Sometimes new pupils start at the community college. I may not know them. Pupils who are new to the community college may feel shy or nervous. They might appreciate it when other pupils are friendly towards them. If I see a new pupil, I could try to be friendly (see social information – FRIENDS – NUMBER 3). I could say 'Hi, my name's Steve, what's your name?' I could smile at the new pupil. If I remember to try to be friendly, new pupils might feel welcome to the community college. Ms Jones will be really pleased if I remember to try to be friendly to new pupils. She will help me to think about what to do to continue new friendships in the social skills group on Monday lunchtimes.

This Social Story™ is one of a series and is used to support the work undertaken during weekly social skills groups. The social skills programme is used to help individuals to learn new social skills, while Social Stories™ reinforce the social skills, but also add to the development of social understanding. The social skills group is a useful forum to introduce new skills and to rehearse them, for example, through role play. Social Stories™ can then be used to consider missing social information such as about others' perspectives. In this case, Steve is provided with information about how new pupils may be feeling and an explanation about why being friendly is a good response to try. As Gray (1998a) suggests, it is essential to teach 'social understanding as an *integral* and *prerequisite* component to teaching social skills'. Combining social skills programmes with Gray's Social

Stories™ approach may provide us with a useful combined strategy for developing social skills and social understanding.

Circles of friends

Successful social interaction involves many different social partners in many different contexts. Problems that people with ASD may face with social interaction are not only their responsibility but also the responsibility of potential social partners. The role of social partners must be considered in addition to the responsibilities of the individual with ASD. All of us need to accept our responsibility within any interaction. Others have begun to recognize the importance of the role of social partners; for example, Gus (2000) emphasizes the importance of 'promoting peer understanding'. Social interaction is essentially reciprocal, relying upon the responses of all partners, not just the individual with ASD. Thus the potential social partners of individuals with ASDs need to be involved in developing more successful social interaction. However, for social partners to develop their ability to interact with individuals with ASD, a degree of understanding of the nature of ASD and the strengths and difficulties of the individual is vital.

One approach that focuses upon the role of social partners and peers is 'circles of friends' (Newton, Taylor and Wilson 1996; Whitaker *et al.* 1998). This approach considers the role of peers and aims to develop empathy with the individual with ASD. A circle of friends supports the individual and suggests strategies to help them to interact more successfully and behave more appropriately. If this is to be successful, it is logical that the peers involved in the circle of friends need to have some understanding of individual needs, strengths and interests and ideas about the kinds of strategies that may be helpful for the individual. It may be helpful to involve a circle of friends in drafting a Social Story™ as often peers can identify information that is relevant both to the context and to the individual with ASD. The following example illustrates how a circle of friends can contribute to the Social Story™ approach.

Danny is 8 years old and in a mainstream primary school. He has a diagnosis of ASD with particular difficulties in relation to social interaction and social behaviour. Danny has been causing distress to other pupils at playtimes as he chases others and squeezes their cheeks. His teacher believes that he is attempting to interact, which is positive, but that he is not aware of how he should initiate interaction. An individual behaviour plan identified targets focusing upon stopping this behaviour, with stickers as rewards and exclusion from playtimes as a sanction. Despite this, Danny's behaviour did not change.

It was decided to ask Danny's circle of friends for their suggestions as they had previously suggested strategies for Danny in relation to interaction in the classroom with some success. The circle consisted of Amy, a friend of Danny's, and five other children. A speech, language and communication therapist also worked with the circle of friends and introduced the Social Story™ approach. She suggested that the peers should be involved in 'gathering information'. As a result, the children in the circle made a number of useful observations: Danny did not particularly like stickers; Danny liked marbles; Danny did not know what to say if he wanted to be friendly. A Social Story™ was drafted by the speech, language and communication therapist, who then shared it with the circle of friends who made some suggestions: use marbles as a reward, tell Danny what he could say. The Social Story™ (Box 6.9) aimed to help Danny to understand why other children did not like him to squeeze their cheeks, what he could say to be friendly and how that would make people feel. The circle of friends decided upon the phrase that they could teach Danny to use to ask children to play at playtimes. Marble rewards were built into the Social Story™ for additional motivation. The Social Story™ was illustrated by Danny and his circle of friends and additional visual cue cards were used as reminders at playtimes.

Box 6.9 Social Story™ used with a circle of friends

Asking children to play at playtimes: A Social Story™ for Danny

1. My name is Danny and I go to Briars School. I am in class 5. There are other children in my class and Mrs Hewitt is usually our teacher. Amy is in my class too.

2. Usually we have playtime in the morning and after we have eaten our lunch. If it is dry, we usually play outside. At playtimes, children often play different games like tig and chase, skipping, hide and seek. Lots of children like to play these games.

3. Mrs Hewitt, the grown-ups and the children would like it if I asked to play with the other children. I could say 'Hi, can I play with you?' They also like children who keep their hands by their sides when they say this. Amy likes it when I keep my hands by my sides while I say 'Hi, can I play with you?'

4. I will try to remember to say **'Hi, can I play with you?'** to children at playtimes. I will try to remember to keep my hands by my sides.

Sometimes children will say
'Yes, you can play.'
Sometimes they will say 'No.'
This is OK. If they say 'No' I
could ask another child or I
could talk to a grown-up.

5

Sometimes, some children
squeeze other children's
cheeks in the playground.
Usually other children do
not like it when people
squeeze their cheeks – this
is because it might hurt
them. Teachers and other
adults may feel cross with
children who hurt others
and they may send children
who hurt others into
school.

6

Mrs Hewitt, the grown-ups
and the other children will
be pleased if I remember to
say **'Hi, can I play with
you?'** and if I remember to
keep my hands by my sides.
Amy will be pleased too.

7

When I remember to ask to
play and to keep my hands
by my sides, my teacher, or
another grown-up, or Amy
will usually give me a marble.
I can put the marble in the
jar on Mrs Hewitt's desk.
Usually on Fridays I can play
with the marbles in the jar
during golden time. Class 5
will usually get extra golden
time when I have
 marbles in the jar.
Class 5 will be
happy to have
extra golden time.

8

This Social Story™ was read with Danny and one of the circle of friends every day before playtimes. The approach was also combined with structured teaching as Danny also had a reminder on his written schedule, 'Remember, at playtimes put my hands by my sides when I say "Hi, can I play with you?"', to remind him of the rule and the Social Story™ content (Box 6.10).

Box 6.10 Schedule with reminder for playtime behaviour which is a sentence from a Social Story™

Monday

Morning
Morning work
Literacy
Playtime
Assembly
Numeracy
Lunch and playtime

Afternoon
Science
Art
Circle time
Home

Remember, at playtimes put my hands by my sides when I say 'Hi, can I play with you?'

Visual cue cards were also used as reminders at playtimes. These were shown to Danny by staff and peers from the circle of friends when they thought he needed reminding of appropriate behaviour (Box 6.11).

Box 6.11 Visual cue card to remind Danny of appropriate behaviour at playtimes

The class teacher decided to use the marble reward as a whole-class reward. As Danny collected marbles for appropriate behaviour, they were put into a jar and placed on the teacher's desk. At the end of the week, Danny could have the marbles during 'golden time', but in addition the whole class earned extra golden time depending upon the number of marbles in the jar. Thus Danny was rewarded for trying to remember how to approach other children at playtimes and the class were rewarded for their efforts to encourage Danny – Danny's success became everyone's success. A combination of strategies enhanced the Social Stories™ approach to improving Danny's ability to interact with his peers, including Social Stories™, circles of friends and structured teaching. This is a good example of combining strategies, involving other children in devising Social Stories™, supporting and encouraging appropriate social behaviour and developing social understanding. Note that this Social Story™ for Danny contains lots of information, including the following:

- the behaviours required
- the effect squeezing cheeks might have on others
- the consequences of hurting others in the playground
- the perspectives of all involved
- the contract and reward system.

For other individuals this amount of information would be overwhelming if presented in one Social Story™. It may be necessary to present a series of shorter stories that introduce the information incrementally (see Chapter 7).

Jigsawing, structured teaching and Social Stories™

A further possibility of combining Social Stories™ with other approaches that also focuses upon the role of peers is their use in conjunction with jigsawing and elements of structured teaching. Howley and Rose (2003) suggest that combining jigsawing with structured teaching may promote group work opportunities for pupils with ASD in school settings. Building upon this concept, it is possible to take it a stage further and enhance this suggested combination with the use of Social Stories™. The jigsaw approach suggests that it is important to create 'interdependence' of all participants involved in group work. Howley and Rose (2003) argue that this has particular relevance for the individual with ASD who can be given a task or role that is crucial to the success of their group and/or class. This may lead to other children encouraging and supporting the pupil with ASD to join in a group activity as the success of the group or class will be dependent upon all participants completing their tasks. Group work can be planned for, using the jigsaw approach, with elements of structured teaching then used to provide any necessary structure that a pupil may require: for example, a visual schedule to identify the activity and/or visual directions to break down the task into smaller sequenced steps. However, the pupil may not easily 'see' how his or her role or task 'fits' with the work of the group to whom he or she is allocated and may therefore still be operating in isolation. Social Stories™ may well provide the 'hidden' information that the pupil requires in order to 'see' how his or her role contributes to the group activity he or she is involved in. This combined approach would therefore enable the following to be considered:

1. Jigsawed lesson planning to create interdependence amongst all pupils, and allocating tasks that are of interest to and are in areas of strength of the pupil with ASD.

2. Providing elements of structured teaching to support the individual with ASD in completing his or her allocated tasks.

3.   Explanation of the overall 'picture' of the lesson and how individual tasks and roles 'fit' with the roles of others in the class through a 'cooperative efforts' (see Chapter 4) Social Story™.

For example, a school project centred on 'book week'. Each class chose a story for another class and then made a 'big book' for that class. Thomas was in a year 3 class and his class was making a book for a year 1 class. Using jigsawed planning, the teacher planned for groups of children in the class to take responsibility for different tasks: one group worked on the text, two groups worked on illustrations and another group devised 'pop-ups'. The final product, the big book, was dependent upon each group completing their task. Thomas was allocated to the group devising the illustrations in the book as this was an area of strength and interest for him. Thomas's group decided to allocate drawing the pictures to some members of the group and colouring and additional artwork to other group members. Thomas was given the role of colouring and artwork with two other pupils. Visual structure was also used to help Thomas to understand the activity, with a visual schedule that indicated his task and who he would be working with, and written instructions (work list) to remind him of key information and the sequence of the activity (Box 6.12).

Box 6.12 Work list used in cooperative group work

Book week – work list

1.   Work with Sunil and Jenny.
2.   Ask for drawings from the other children in the illustrators group.
3.   Decide who will colour which drawings and who will decorate with borders or other art effects.
4.   When finished, tell the group and ask if they have any more drawings ready for colouring.
5.   At the end of the lesson, file the drawing and illustrations ready for the next lesson.
6.   On Friday, help the group put the drawings into the book.

Ask Mr Timkins for help if needed.

In addition, the teacher wrote a Social Story™ to help Thomas and the rest of the class understand how the different tasks of each group were vital to the finished book (Box 6.13).

Box 6.13 Split Section Social Story™ combined with jigsawed planning and structured teaching

Book week at Bradley School

Page 1 (complete)
From Monday 14 June until Friday 18 June, Bradley School is having a 'book week'. Each class will make a book for another class. I am in class 5 and we are making a book for class 1.

Page 2 (complete)
Mrs Jarvis has decided the groups for book week: the writers, the illustrators and the designers. I am in the illustrators group. Jenny, Sammy, Lisa, James, Sunil and Kieran are in the illustrators group too.

Page 3 (split)
Mrs Jarvis has given the groups different tasks and instructions.

Page 3a: Writers

Write the story in your own words. Make sure the text is suitable for the age group (year 1) and is interesting to the readers. Decide upon the font and format of the text.

Page 3b: Illustrators

Use the text to draw and illustrate pictures for the book. They should be interesting and appealing to young readers.

Page 3c: Designers

Design some pop-up features for the book. Decide on your materials and how you will make the pop-ups. They need to be durable.

Page 4 (complete)
My group are drawing pictures and colouring them in and adding art effects. My part of the work is to work with Sunil and Jenny and colour in the drawn pictures and add art effects, e.g. patterns and

borders (see work list). *This is important as for the book to be finished the illustrations also need to be finished.*

Page 5 (complete)
We have five sessions, one each day, to work on the book week project. In the morning, on Friday 18 June, we will put the book together. In the afternoon we will take it to class 1 and read it with them.

As the project ran for a week, the teacher was able to plan for Thomas's involvement with the use of jigsawed planning that took into account his strengths and interests, created interdependence between the groups, and used visual structure to encourage independence. The Social Story™ provided vital information about the roles and tasks of others in the class, highlighting for Thomas and other members of the class what Gray (1998b) refers to as 'cooperative efforts'. Again, this strategy suggests that Social Stories™ can be very effective when used in combination with other strategies and in this case provided key information that gave the 'whole picture' of the activity.

Conclusion

Social Stories™ can be used flexibly in response to individual needs. Some Social Stories™ may prepare young children or individuals with ASD for more detailed social information in incremental small-step stages. Other preparatory strategies may also be useful for young children and individuals with learning difficulties, such as visual directions. In addition, using Social Stories™ in conjunction with other approaches can be effective in relation to teaching appropriate skills and behaviours, developing social understanding and involving social partners. Combining strategies, depending upon individual needs, may enhance and complement the overall approach to developing social skills and social understanding with the aim of improving social interaction for all involved. The diverse range of individual needs of those with ASD often requires diverse strategies. Social Stories™ can complement and supplement other strategies in our attempts to enhance the meaning of social situations for individuals with ASD.

Key teaching points

- Write Social Stories™ that prepare young children and/or individuals with ASD and learning difficulties for more detailed Social Stories™ at a later date.
- Use visual directions and jigs as a preparatory strategy.
- Combine Social Stories™ with elements of structured teaching to enhance meaning: for example, reminder/rule on schedule and Social Story™ to add to social understanding.
- Use Social Stories™ in conjunction with social skills programmes.
- Involve peers in drafting Social Stories™ and supporting the individual.
- Combine strategies according to individual needs.

Chapter Seven

Problem Solving and What to Do When Social Stories™ Do Not Work

Readers will by now appreciate that the process of writing Social Stories™ requires the gathering of detailed information and may be a lengthy process before completion. It can feel rather daunting when a Social Story™ fails to impact in the way intended, yet this is a frequent occurrence. Social Stories™ may appear to be simple to write, but readers will now know that this is misleading. It can be all too easy to abandon the approach as 'not working' when the first few attempts seem to fail. This chapter is therefore devoted to considering what to do when your Social Stories™ do not result in the intended outcome. Gray (2004b) provides a Social Story™ checklist (see Appendix 4) that identifies ten defining criteria that must be present for 'stories' to be called Social Stories™. This checklist should be applied to all 'stories' in order to ensure that they meet the criteria for Social Stories™. However, sometimes Social Stories™ may not be successful, even when the criteria have been applied. Possible reasons for failure are identified in this chapter, with examples. A problem-solving approach is outlined to encourage potential writers of Social Stories™ not to give up.

Why Social Stories™ might not work

There can be a number of reasons why Social Stories™ may not initially be successful and do not have the impact that was intended. It is not always possible to identify why a particular Social Story™ may not have had the effect hoped for. However, there are some common reasons for lack of success. Identifying the possible reasons may help writers to develop a problem-solving approach and to redraft Social Stories™ until they are successful.

Bossy books

One common reason for Social Stories™ to fail is a result of what Smith (2003) calls 'bossy books'. When you have identified a number of inappropriate social behaviours that an individual is exhibiting, it can be tempting to incorporate all of these within one Social Story™. This results in a list of dos and don'ts that does not meet the requirements of Social Stories™ (see Appendix 4) and is highly unlikely to have a positive impact. Stories that overuse directive sentences may be deficient in providing hidden social information that increases social understanding. Numerous directives can be overwhelming for the individual who may feel unable to meet the demands being made and may become resentful and defensive about the issues raised. This may lead them to reject the content.

Social Stories™ are more likely to be successful if directives are chosen carefully and supported by neutral descriptive and perspective sentences and the correct sentence ratio is adhered to (see Chapters 3 and 4). The wording of directive sentences needs careful thought to avoid sounding 'bossy'. Gray (1998a) suggests that Social Stories™ need to retain a neutral tone, opinion is not offered and the individual should not be set up to fail with words like 'must'. Numerous directives may result in a sense of failure for the individual and will affect their self-confidence. For Social Stories™ to be successful, directive sentences should be carefully chosen and carefully worded (see Chapter 3).

Non-literal language

The language and vocabulary of Social Stories™ are also crucial to their success. Gray (1998a) requires that language should be written so that it can be interpreted literally as many individuals with ASDs will rely on this literal interpretation. Failure to consider this aspect may mean that the intended impact is lost. Hence Gray (1998a) advocates using words like 'sometimes', 'usually' and 'often' to ensure that Social Stories™ can be interpreted literally. Other useful words that ensure literal accuracy include 'occasionally', 'rarely', 'frequently', 'most', 'many'. Words like 'always' and 'never' are avoided at all costs. If the Social Story™ does not consider this tendency to interpret language literally, it may be unsuccessful. Table 7.1 illustrates a story with too many directives (i.e. a 'bossy book'), which is also open to interpretation due to language use. This might have been written for Peter to encourage him to line up (see Chapter 5). Potential problems with this version are indicated next to each sentence or phrase.

Table 7.1 'Bossy book' with too many directives and language open to interpretation

Waiting in line: A story for Peter	*Potential problems with the sentence or phrase*
My name is Peter and I am in class 7 at Hawthorne School. My teacher is Mrs Hayes.	*Mrs Hayes may not always be the teacher. The class may have other teachers sometimes.*
Class 7 go to PE in the hall, music in the music room, assembly in the hall. Class 7 also go outside at playtimes.	*Does this mean every day? PE might be outside sometimes. Do they go outside if it's raining?*
When class 7 need to leave the classroom together, Mrs Hayes likes us to line up at the door. She likes us to be quiet. We cannot leave the classroom until we are quiet.	*Sometimes they might be allowed to leave the classroom when they are not quiet.*
I must line up. I must stand in the line quietly.	*Bossy directives!*
I must not shout.	*Problems processing 'not' – may be interpreted as 'I must shout'.*
Mrs Hayes will be very pleased if I remember to do this. She will give me a star for my star chart.	*She might sometimes forget to give the star! Will other teachers feel the same, will they give stars?*

A better version is illustrated in Box 5.3, which is presented in a more neutral reassuring way, does not make unrealistic demands of Peter and pays attention to use of language to ensure literal accuracy. This Social Story™ was illustrated by Peter to enhance meaning and for motivation.

Lack of visual cues

The importance of visual presentation is discussed in Chapter 5. Gray (1998a) suggests that Social Stories™ may be more successful if they take into account the individual's visual learning style. Howley (2001) found that Social Stories™ with an additional visual component were useful, particularly if the visual element acted as a reminder of the content of a Social Story™ for the individual. For example, a Social Story™ written for a primary school pupil to encourage him to read to an adult without shouting was supported by a number line indicating voice volumes. This was made into a bookmark and acted as a reminder of the Social Story™ content as he read.

Social Stories™ that have not been successful may be redrafted with additional visual cues which should be included to clarify meaning, to highlight important relevant information and to interest the individual. Lack of attention to this may reduce the effectiveness of the Social Story™. Box 7.1 provides an example of a Social Story™ that focuses upon information that is not appealing to the individual.

Box 7.1 Social Story™ without additional visual cues and lacking interest for the individual

Angry people at school

I attend a large comprehensive school with over 1000 students and lots of adults. At this school there are often lots of things going on, including:

- lessons
- break times
- ICT sessions
- lessons in the learning resource centre (LRC)
- lunch breaks
- sports
- other things.

Often people get angry at this school. People feel angry about different things. They might get angry about bullies, thieves, swearing or other things.

Some pupils react to people's anger by running away, shouting and throwing things. Other pupils may laugh at this behaviour and call the pupil names. Teachers might give detentions for this behaviour.

I am allowed to go to the LRC when people are angry at school. I am allowed to doodle on my doodle splat when I go to the LRC.

When I want to go to the LRC, I should try to remember to tell the LSA or teacher before I leave.

This Social Story™ was written as text only due to the pupil's excellent reading and comprehension ability. The content of the Social Story™ may not in itself be interesting or motivating to the individual. In such instances it is crucial to incorporate an element of interest. The Social Story™ in Box 7.2 was therefore redrafted to add visual cues, including a visual cue card for informing adults if he needs to leave a situation and to engage the pupil by including his interest. This pupil particularly liked expressions often found in comics where text characters are used to express a feeling; he added his own version for 'angry'. He also liked to doodle in a large notebook that he called his 'doodle splat' so this was incorporated into the Social Story™. Box 7.2 shows the revised Social Story™.

Box 7.2 Social Story™ with additional visual cues and using the individual's interests

Angry people at school

I attend a large comprehensive school with over 1000 students and lots of adults. At this school there are often lots of things going on, including:

- lessons
- break times
- ICT sessions
- lessons in the learning resource centre (LRC)
- lunch breaks
- sports
- other things.

Often people get angry at this school.

People feel angry about different things.

They might get angry  about bullies, thieves, swearing or other things.

Some pupils react to people's anger by running away, shouting and throwing things. Other pupils may laugh at this behaviour and call the pupil names. Teachers might give detentions for this behaviour.

I am allowed to go to the LRC when people are angry at school. I am allowed to doodle on my doodle splat when I go to the LRC.

splat!

When I want to go to the LRC, I should try to remember to tell the LSA or teacher, or show them my exit card, before I leave.

The redrafted Social Story™ was more successful as the pupil's interests, both in relation to visual presentation and his doodle notebook, were incorporated into the Social Story™, resulting in a more interesting and motivating product for the pupil and one which he was more likely to take note of.

Lack of individualization

Gray (1998a) emphasizes the need to individualize Social Stories™, taking into account:

- developmental age
- reading and comprehension ability

- attention span

- interests.

Insufficient attention to detail in these areas may result in unsuccessful Social Stories™. The need to design each Social Story™ for the individual is central to the approach. While off-the-shelf Social Stories™ are inspirational, it is crucial that Social Stories™ are developed for the individual for whom they are intended. Developmental age, reading and comprehension ability and attention span are straightforward to take into account and failure to do so will be apparent quite quickly. Social Stories™ that have not met these particular needs can be redrafted. For example, a Social Story™ that is too long can be rewritten as a series of Social Stories™ in order to account for the individual's shorter attention span. Box 7.3 illustrates a Social Story™ written for Anthony who lived with his mother and did not see his father. He had begun to ask men 'Are you my Daddy?' This was a huge source of embarrassment to Anthony's mother and so a Social Story™ was written to try to address the issue (Box 7.3).

Box 7.3 Social Story™ with too much detail for the individual

---

Who is my daddy?

My name is Anthony. I live at 24 Parkside Close. My mummy, Grandpa and Grandma live at 24 Parkside Close; we all live together.

I have two cousins. My cousins' names are Tim and Hilary. They live at 18 Shakespeare Drive with Uncle Gordon and Auntie Jess. Uncle Gordon is their daddy. Auntie Jess is their mummy.

Sometimes I go to play with Freddie. Freddie's mummy's name is Kate. Freddie's daddy's name is Jim.

I was born on 21 May 1995. My mummy's name is Anna. My daddy's name is Philip.

My mummy and daddy and I all lived at 8 Sycamore Road. When I was one year old, in 1996, my daddy went to live in Portsmouth and my mummy and I came to live at 24 Parkside Close with Grandpa and Grandma.

My mummy likes living with me and Grandpa and Grandma. My daddy likes living in Portsmouth. Mummy will show me a photo of my daddy.

This example provides us with a good illustration of when a Social Story™ contains too much detail for the individual to understand in one story. In addition, such an emotive issue raises many potential questions. This provides us with a good example of when it may be imperative to break down information into smaller steps and to present the information incrementally in a series of Social Stories™. A Social Story™ such as Box 7.3 is unlikely to be successful and may be overwhelming for the individual as there is too much information to process. Two Social Stories™ that provide information in smaller steps may be more effective (Box 7.4).

Box 7.4 Social Stories™ presenting information step by step

Families (1)

Families are people who are special to each other. Some families are like this:

Other groups of people may be families too.

Where is my daddy? (2)

All children have a Daddy.
    Some Daddies live with the family in the same house.

Some Daddies live in a different house.

Mummy showed me a picture of my daddy. (*photo*)
    My daddy lives in a different house and we don't see him.

These Social Stories™ provide only facts and present smaller pieces of information for Anthony to absorb. Monitoring of the individual's responses to these Social Stories™ can then inform subsequent Social Stories™ that may be required in the future.

    Finally, it is also important to take into account individual interests and incorporate these into Social Stories™. Motivational factors are essential considerations when developing strategies for teaching and working with individuals with ASDs. Individuals may lack the motivation that a neurotypical individual may experience. For example, many individuals are motivated by the desire to please others or by social praise. This may not be the case for individuals with ASDs. It may be important therefore to incorporate individual motivators into individual Social Stories™ in order for them to be of interest to the reader. This may require innovative approaches in order to ensure that the Social Story™ is motivating and interesting to the individual.

Some may respond to Social Stories™ that include a 'reward' or motivator (Box 5.5); others may be motivated by the presentation style (Boxes 5.8 and 7.2). Some will enjoy Social Stories™ that incorporate their favourite hero or character. Failure to consider motivational factors may result in a less effective Social Story™. If this seems to be the case, try to redraft the Social Story™ with motivators incorporated that relate to the individual's likes, strengths and interests.

Inappropriate aims and targets

GATHERING INFORMATION

Some Social Stories™ may not be successful because the intended aims and targets identified are not appropriate. This may arise for a number of reasons including:

- lack of information gathering prior to writing the Social Story™
- inaccurate assessment of the issues for the individual with ASD and their understanding of the situation
- insufficient information about the social information that may be 'hidden' from the individual.

This may lead to the identification of inappropriate targets and subsequently unsuccessful outcomes. For example, Howley (2001) found that a Social Story™ written for a primary school pupil to address inappropriate behaviour and an obsessional focus on who would win when playing games failed to impact upon the pupil's behaviour which was not modified in any way. This may be partly due to difficulties in identifying the pupil's understanding, due to his echolalic language, prior to introducing his Social Story™. Further observations of the pupil were required to gather more detailed information about the situation; for example, in relation to which games caused him more anxiety than others.

It should be noted that assessing the situation, including possibly any problems that are arising, and assessing the individual's understanding of the situation, is not always easy. It may be that, after gathering information and assessing the individual's understanding, targets are set that seem to be relevant and appropriate. Often it only becomes apparent that a Social Story™ has not addressed the key issues for an individual after a period of reading it with him or her. Inappropriate targets may arise for a number of reasons including insufficient information gathering and lack of information about the individual's perspective.

Despite gathering detailed information, sometimes Social Stories™ do not have the intended impact. It may be necessary to revisit the information gathered and perhaps look further in order to assess the nature of the problem that the individual is experiencing. This may mean further observations and interviewing, with focused questions to try to identify the key issues. For example, Howley (2001) found that careful questioning of lunchtime supervisors was crucial in order to develop a Social Story™ for a pupil who exhibited inappropriate playground behaviours at lunchtimes. Interviewing revealed that each lunchtime supervisor had her own rules for the playground and the pupil was not able to adjust his behaviour in response to each of the individual rules. Box 7.5 (Howley 2001, p.108) illustrates the Social Story™ that was eventually written by the speech and language therapist following detailed observations at playtimes and discussions with the lunchtime supervisors.

Box 7.5 Social Story™ that depended upon detailed information gathering in order to identify appropriate targets

Where to play at lunchtime: A story for Max

Page 1

My name is Max. I am in class _____ at _____ School.
   Usually all the children go out to play at lunchtime.
   When the grass is dry some children play ball games together on the playground, some children play on the field.

Page 2

When it is a dry day Mrs _____ or a teacher will tell me when it is my turn to play on the playground.

Page 3

When it is my turn to play on the field I can ask a dinner lady if I can play with a piece of equipment out of her bag.

    Sometimes she has:

        hoops

        skipping ropes

        stilts

        or other things.

Page 4

It is important to stay on the field when it is my turn to be on the field.

    I will have a turn on the playground another time.

Page 5

On days when the grass is wet, everyone plays on the playground.

(Howley 2001, p.108)

This Social Story™ would not have been effective if the process of gathering information had not been undertaken. It also highlights the need to gather information on a number of occasions. Observations on a single day and discussion with one supervisor would not have revealed the different rules that different supervisors were implementing each day. This illustrates the need for consistency in the use of the Social Stories™ approach. In this case, the Social Story™ introduced to the pupil was then developed in consultation with the lunchtime supervisors in order to agree some consistent rules and appropriate targets for the pupil. This helped the pupil to make sense of playground rules. In addition, the Social Story™ reminded each supervisor of ways to respond to the pupil should he need reminding of playground rules and behaviour. Used in this way, Social Stories™ can be an effective tool for sharing information and achieving consistency of approach amongst those who are involved in social interaction with the individual with ASD.

ASSESSMENT OF ISSUES FOR INDIVIDUALS WITH ASDS AND THEIR
UNDERSTANDING OF SITUATIONS

Equally important as assessing the situation from the perspectives of those
involved is the need to assess the individual's perspective. This is often
fraught with difficulties due to problems with understanding, echolalic
language and communication problems. However, it is still important to
try to see the situation from the individual's point of view through observation and discussions. Although it may be challenging for us to establish
the individual's point of view, nevertheless it is important that we attempt
to understand their perspective. Failure to do so may mean that Social
Stories™ do not work in the way intended.

Ascertaining the individual's view may be challenging but Gray's
(1994b, 1998a) Comic Strip Conversations (CSCs) offer a useful strategy
that may assist with this (see Chapter 2). If a Social Story™ is unsuccessful,
it may be possible to talk further with the individual, perhaps using Gray's
CSC technique to try to establish his or her understanding of the situation.
For example, an adolescent with Asperger's syndrome attending a mainstream secondary school was observed paying his peers to hit him on the
head with a book. Observations indicated that he appeared to enjoy the
sensory aspects of this, but that he did not seem to realize that the peers
were in fact bullying him. A discussion using the CSC technique revealed
that the pupil with ASD thought the peers were being friendly and that
when they laughed it was because that's what friends do, 'they laugh
together'. Once the individual's perspective was apparent, it was possible
to write a series of Social Stories™ to address friendships, including one
that explained that when his peers hit him on the head, took his money
and laughed, they were laughing at him, not with him, and that this is not
friendly behaviour (see Box 7.6).

Box 7.6 Social Story™ written after the pupil's view had been considered using a Comic Strip Conversation™

Friendship: Saying 'no' to bullies

I attend Southfields Secondary School. It is a large school, where
there are lots of different people. Each day usually has six lessons,
one morning break and a lunchtime and break. During lessons and

breaks I usually meet lots of different people. Some of these people are teachers, but most people are students.

Sometimes other students hit me on the head. They ask me to pay them to do this. When they hit me on the head and take my money they often laugh; they are *laughing at me*. When people laugh at me they want to make me sad or angry; it is a form of bullying.

I will try to remember to say 'no' when students ask if they can hit me on the head and ask for my money. I will try to remember that this is bullying. If they hit me on the head, I could

_____ or _____ .

If I keep saying 'no' the bullies might get fed up and leave me alone. My mum and support teacher will be pleased if I try to say no to the bullies.

I usually have regular meetings with Mrs Singh. It is important that I tell her, or my mum, of all incidences when students ask to hit me on my head and ask for money. We can then discuss how they respond when I say 'no' or do

_____ or _____ .

There are other ways to make friends. If I want to make friends with other students, I could say 'Hi, what did you do last night?' Mrs Singh might talk to me about these during social skills lessons and I can use my other social guides about friendships.

This Social Story™ would more than likely be one of a series tackling bullying issues. Whilst some individuals may find the use of CSCs helpful in discussing a situation or event, others may not. It still remains important to try to figure out their understanding of the situation through observations and discussions with people who know the individual well. In addition, other visual techniques may also be helpful; for example, video review of the situation and multiple choice or written questionnaire.

Seeking the views and checking the understanding of the individual with ASD is an important part of the process of gathering information and will help you to specify clear targets for Social Stories™. If a Social Story™ does not have the intended effect, it may be helpful therefore to explore this aspect more closely. If you can identify where the confusion lies for the individual, you can then identify more specific targets for each Social Story™.

They might not like the content!

Finally, it must be pointed out that sometimes Social Stories™ fail to have a positive impact because the individual may not like the content. There is often an assumption that Social Stories™ will be enjoyed by the individual and that they will cooperate positively. While this may often be the case, it is not always so. Writers of Social Stories™ should be aware that sometimes the hidden information being revealed in a Social Story™ may cause the individual to feel upset or embarrassed and they may then resist reading it. Sometimes the information being presented needs to be dealt with sensitively and perhaps in small step stages. Social Stories™ that focus entirely on a negative behaviour rather than emphasizing the desired behaviour are more likely to cause distress to the individual.

A young woman attending a supported work project in an office repeatedly slammed the office door very loudly whenever she entered or left the room. This was increasingly annoying to colleagues who shared the office and adjoining offices. Despite many reminders to close the door quietly, this slamming of the door persisted. Assessment of the situation and Gina's understanding led her supervisor to write her a Social Story™ to explain the impact of her behaviour on others in the office (Box 7.7).

Box 7.7 Social Story™ that resulted in the individual feeling upset

Slamming doors: A social reminder for Gina

I attend the work project from Monday to Friday.

I usually work in room 7.

Sometimes people leave room 7 to go to other rooms or to leave the building.

Sometimes when people leave room 7 they remember to close the door quietly and sometimes they close the door loudly – this is called 'slamming the door'.

Prakash and Steve do not like the door slamming because it is too loud and hurts their ears. It also distracts them from their work.

I will try to remember to close the door quietly when I leave the room.

Prakash and Steve will be pleased if I close the door quietly.

On first reading the Social Story™ with her supervisor, Gina was upset by the content and seemed astonished that she had had this impact upon her colleagues. She immediately wanted to rewrite the Social Story™ to include statements about what a bad person she was. Other individuals may respond by resisting reading the information being provided by putting their hands over their ears or eyes to reduce the impact of the information upon their feelings. If a Social Story™ does not have a positive impact, it is important to consider how the individual may feel about the hidden information that is being revealed and that it may actually make them feel uncomfortable. In such cases, careful redrafting and rewording, with smaller steps presented, may be necessary before a positive outcome is achieved. Social Stories™ that emphasize negative behaviours will need to be redrafted to change the emphasis. For example, Gina's Social Story™ could have been written with a different focus, as shown in Box 7.8.

Box 7.8 Social Story™ presented with a neutral tone that is less likely to cause upset

Social reminder: Office skills number 3, closing doors

I attend the work project from Monday to Friday.

I usually work in room 7. I am learning many new skills which will help me to find a job.

I have been successful in learning how to:

- greet people who visit the office
- answer the telephone
- file documents.

Sometimes I leave room 7 to go to other rooms or to leave the building. It is important to close the door when leaving a room. If the door makes a loud noise when someone closes it, this is called 'slamming the door'.

Prakash and Steve do not like the door slamming because it is too loud and hurts their ears. It also distracts them from their work.

I will try to remember to close the door gently so that is makes very little noise when I leave the room. Prakash and Steve will be pleased if I close the door gently.

The tone of the amended Social Story™ is more neutral and positive. Gina's achievements are acknowledged in addition to suggestions about closing doors.

Conclusion

Successful Social Stories™ are dependent upon a number of factors. Even when these are taken into account, it may still be necessary to redraft Social Stories™ several times before they are successful. Thus it is important that we adopt a problem-solving approach to the process of developing Social Stories™. This requires us carefully to consider the sentence construction and ratio in a Social Story™, the use of language, in particular relating to literal interpretation, the use of additional visual cues that may act as a reminder of the Social Story™ content, elements of individualization, including motivational factors, identification of specific goals and targets through the information-gathering process and the impact of revealing missing information upon the individual's feelings. Appendix 3 provides a checklist for checking each of these elements in order to draft and redraft Social Stories™ to improve the outcome.

Key teaching points

- If a Social Story™ is unsuccessful, don't give up but check the guidelines and redraft.
- Try adding or amending visual cues.
- Check your use of language.
- Consider individualization and motivational factors.
- Reassess the situation with further information gathering in order to set specific targets.
- Write a series of Social Stories™ to break down information into smaller, more comfortable steps.
- Consider the reactions of the person you have written the Social Story™ for.

Final Thoughts

Carol Gray's Social Stories™ technique is an innovative approach to developing social understanding and broadening the opportunities for individuals with ASDs to access and enjoy social interaction and experiences. Over the past decade the approach has been found to be helpful to professionals and parents as one effective strategy for promoting the social inclusion of people with ASDs. A real strength of the approach is the focus not only upon the individuals who have ASDs but also upon the responsibilities and responses of their social partners. Social Stories™ are most likely to be effective when care and attention are given to the following:

- the process of gathering information
- assessment of the individual's cognitive abilities, interests, motivation and learning styles
- adherence to Gray's guidelines
- monitoring and evaluating progress to inform development of the approach for each individual
- developing a problem-solving approach to the process.

The approach is versatile and responsive to individual needs and compatible with and complementary to other strategies.

It is hoped that readers of this book will be encouraged to learn more about Gray's Social Stories™ approach and to use them with individuals with ASDs and their peers as 'revealing the hidden social code' is a crucial aspect of promoting the social inclusion of all.

Checklist for drafting a Social Story™

Action	Date and notes	Progress
Identify the topic		
Gather information		
Assess individual's understanding		
Identify context, goal and set specific target		
Draft a Social Story™ (including visual cues)		

Checklist for monitoring individual progress

TOPIC	TARGET(S)
TITLE	
COMMENTS and OBSERVATIONS Record individual's responses and progress in relation to social skills, behaviour and social understanding. **SOCIAL SKILLS AND BEHAVIOUR**	**DATE and ACTIONS** *Date introduced* *Dates of readings*
SOCIAL UNDERSTANDING	*Date targets achieved or Social Stories™ redrafted* *Action*

Checklist for problem solving

Check	Action	Progress
Check the sentence ratio		
Check the use of visual cues		
Check language use		
Consider further individualization (e.g. length, language, interests)		
Consider motivational factors		
Gather further information		
Reassess individual understanding		
Does the individual need the information in smaller steps?		
Does he or she like it?		

Appendix 4

Social Story™ checklist

Directions: Compare your story to the list below, and check off all that apply. If 1 to 10 describe the story you have developed, it is a Social Story™.

1. The story meaningfully shares social information with an overall patient and reassuring quality. (If this is a story teaching a new concept or skill, another is developed to praise a child's positive qualities, behaviours or achievements.)

2. The story has an introduction that clearly identifies the topic, a body that adds detail and a conclusion that reinforces and summarizes the information.

3. The story provides the answers to 'wh' questions, describing the setting or context (WHERE), time-related information (WHEN), relevant people (WHO), important cues (WHAT), basic activities, behaviours or statements (HOW), and the reasons or rationale behind them (WHY).

4. The story is written from the first-person perspective, as though the child is describing the event (most often for a younger or more severely challenged child), or a third-person perspective, like a newspaper article (usually for a more advanced child, or an adolescent or adult).

5. The story uses positive language, omitting descriptions or references to challenging behaviours in favour of identifying positive responses.

6. The story is comprised of descriptive sentences (objective, often observable, statements of fact), with an option of any one or more of the following sentence types:

   • perspective sentences (that describe the thoughts, feelings and/or beliefs of other people)

   • cooperative sentences (to explain what others will do in support of the child)

   • directive sentences (that identify suggested responses or choices of responses to a given situation)

   • affirmative sentences (that enhance the meaning of surrounding statements)

   • control sentences developed by the child (individual) to help him or her recall and apply information in the story.

7. The story follows the Social Story™ formula:

$$\frac{\text{DESCRIBE (descriptive + perspective + cooperative + affirmative (sentences))}}{*\text{ DIRECT (directive and control sentences)}} \geq 2$$

* If there are no directive and/or control sentences, use 1 instead of 0 as the denominator.

8. The story matches the ability and interests of the audience, and is literally accurate (exception: if analogies or metaphors are used).

9. If appropriate, the story uses carefully selected illustrations that are meaningful for the child (individual) and enhance the meaning of the text.

10. The title of the story meets all applicable Social Story™ criteria.

References

Aarons, M. and Gittens, T. (1998) *Autism: A Social Skills Approach for Children and Adolescents*. Oxford: Winslow.

Agosta, E., Graetz, J. E., Mastropieri, M. A. and Scruggs, T. E. (2004) 'Teacher–researcher partnerships to improve social behaviour through social stories.' *Intervention in Schools and Clinic 39*, 5, 276–287.

American Psychiatric Association (1994) *Diagnostic and Statistical Manual of Mental Disorders* (4th edn). Washington, DC: APA.

Attwood, T. (2000) 'Strategies for improving the social integration of children with Asperger syndrome.' *Autism 4*, 1, 85–100.

Barnhill, G. P. (2001) 'Social attribution and depression in adolescents with Asperger syndrome.' *Focus on Autism and Other Developmental Disabilities 16*, 46–53.

Barnhill, G. P., Hagiwara, R., Myles, B. S., Simpson, R. L., Brick, M. L. and Griswold, D. E. (2001) 'Parent, teacher and self-report of problem and adaptive behaviors in children and adolescents with Asperger syndrome.' *Diagnostique 25*, 303–313.

Baron-Cohen, S. (1995) 'Autism and mindblindness.' In S. Baron-Cohen *Mindblindness*. Cambridge, MA: MIT Press.

Baron-Cohen, S. and Bolton, P. (1993) *Autism: The Facts*. Oxford: Oxford University Press.

Baron-Cohen, S., Leslie, A. M. and Frith, U. (1985) 'Does the autistic child have a theory of mind?' *Cognition 21*, 37–46.

Barry, L. M. and Burlew, S. B. (2004) 'Using Social Stories to teach choice and play skills to children with autism.' *Focus on Autism and Other Developmental Disabilities 19*, 1, 45–51.

Bledsoe, R., Smith, B. and Simpson, R. L. (2003) 'Use of a social story intervention to improve mealtime skills of an adolescent with Asperger syndrome.' *Autism 7*, 3, 289–295.

Bondy, A. and Frost, L. (1994) 'The picture exchange communication system.' *Focus on Autistic Behaviour 9*, 3, 1–19.

Cambridge University (2004) *Mind Reading: The Interactive Guide to Emotions*. London: Jessica Kingsley Publishers.

Chalk, M. (2003) 'Social stories for adults with autism and learning difficulties.' *Good Autism Practice 4*, 2, 3–11.

Dawson, G. and Adams, A. (1984) 'Imitation and social responsiveness in autistic children.' *Journal of Abnormal Child Psychology 12*, 209–226.

Del Valle, P. R., McEachern, A. G. and Chambers, H. D. (2001) 'Using social stories with autistic children.' *Journal of Poetry Therapy 14*, 4, 187–197.

Department for Education and Employment/Qualifications and Curriculum Authority (1999a) *The National Curriculum: A Handbook for Primary Teachers in England.* London: DfEE/QCA.

Department for Education and Employment/Qualifications and Curriculum Authority (1999b) *The National Curriculum: A Handbook for Secondary Teachers in England.* London: DfEE/QCA.

Dettmer, S., Simpson, R. L., Myles, B. S. and Ganz, J. B. (2000) 'The use of visual supports to facilitate transitions of students with autism.' *Focus on Autism and Other Developmental Disabilities 15*, 163–169.

Erangey, K. (2001) 'Using social stories as a parent of a child with an ASD.' *Good Autism Practice 2*, 1, 309–323.

Ferrara, C. and Hill, S. (1980) 'The responsiveness of autistic children to the predictability of social and non-social toys.' *Journal of Autism and Developmental Disorders 10*, 51–57.

Frith, U. (1989) *Autism: Explaining the Enigma.* Oxford: Blackwell.

Frith, U. (1991) 'Asperger and his syndrome.' In U. Frith (ed) *Autism and Asperger Syndrome.* Cambridge: Cambridge University Press.

Grandin, T. (1995) *Thinking in Pictures and Other Reports from my Life with Autism.* New York: Doubleday.

Gray, C. (1994a) *The New Social Stories Book.* Arlington: Future Horizons.

Gray, C. (1994b) *Comic Strip Conversations.* Arlington: Future Horizons.

Gray, C. (1997) 'Social Stories Unlimited™ presentations and workshops.' Unpublished workshop document.

Gray, C. (1998a) 'Social Stories and Comic Strip Conversations with students with Asperger syndrome and high functioning autism.' In E. Schopler, G. Mesibov and L. Kunce (eds) *Asperger Syndrome or High Functioning Autism?* New York: Plenum Press.

Gray, C. (1998b) 'The Advanced Social Story Workbook.' *Jenison Public Schools Morning News 10*, 2, 1–22.

Gray, C. (2004a) *Social Stories™ and Strategies in Concert: Working within the Bigger Picture.* Gray Center for Social Learning and Understanding. Unpublished training manual.

Gray, C. (2004b) 'Social Stories™ 10.0 "The new defining criteria and guidelines".' *Jenison Autism Journal 15*, 4, 2–21.

Gray, C. and Garand, J. D. (1993) 'Social Stories: improving responses of students with autism with accurate social information.' *Focus on Autistic Behavior 8*, 1, 1–10.

Gray, C. and White, A. L. (eds) (2002) *My Social Stories Book*. London: Jessica Kingsley Publishers.

Gray Center for Social Learning and Understanding (2005) 'Pictures of me.' *Social Stories™ Quarterly 1*, 1, 14–25.

Groden, J. and LeVasseur, P. (1995) 'Cognitive picture rehearsal: a system to teach self-control.' In K. Quill (ed) *Teaching Children with Autism: Strategies to Enhance Communication and Socialization*. New York: Delmar.

Gus, L. (2000) 'Autism: promoting peer understanding.' *Educational Psychology in Practice 16*, 3, 461–468.

Hagiwara, T. and Myles, B. S. (1999) 'A multimedia social story intervention: teaching skills to children with autism.' *Focus on Autism and Other Developmental Disabilities 14*, 82–95.

Happé, F. (1994) *Autism: An Introduction to Psychological Theory*. London: University College of London Press.

Happé, F. and Frith, U. (1995) 'Theory of mind in autism.' In E. Schopler and G. Mesibov (eds) *Learning and Cognition in Autism*. New York: Plenum Press.

Harris, S. and Handelman, J. (1997) 'Helping children with autism enter the mainstream.' In D. J. Cohen and F. R. Volkmar (eds) *Handbook of Autism and Pervasive Developmental Disorders*. Chichester: Wiley.

Hodgdon, L. (1995) *Visual Strategies for Improving Communication*. Michigan: QuirkRoberts.

Howley, M. (2001) 'An investigation into the impact of social stories on the behaviour and social understanding of four pupils with autistic spectrum disorder.' In R. Rose and I. Grosvenor (eds) *Doing Research in Special Education*. London: David Fulton.

Howley, M. and Rose, R. (2003) 'Facilitating group work for pupils with autistic spectrum disorders by combining jigsawing and structured teaching.' *Good Autism Practice (GAP) 4*, 1, 20–25.

Howlin, P. (1986) 'An overview of social behaviour in autism.' In E. Schopler and G. Mesibov (eds) *Social Behaviour in Autism*. New York: Plenum Press.

Howlin, P. (1997) *Autism: Preparing for Adulthood*. London: Routledge.

Howlin, P., Baron-Cohen, S. and Hadwin, J. (1999) *Teaching Children with Autism to Mind-Read*. Chichester: Wiley.

Kanner, L. (1943) 'Autistic disturbances of affective contact', *Nervous Child 2*, 217–250. Cited in U. Frith (ed) (1991) *Autism and Asperger Syndrome*. Cambridge: Cambridge University Press.

Kuttler, S., Myles, B. S. and Carlson, J. K. (1998) 'The use of social stories to reduce precursors to tantrum behaviour in a student with autism.' *Focus on Autism and Other Developmental Disabilities 12*, 176–182.

Leslie, A. (1987) 'Pretence and representation: the origins of a "theory of mind".' *Psychological Review 94*, 412–426.

Lorimer, P. A., Simpson, R., Myles, B. S. and Ganz, J. (2002) 'The use of social stories as a preventative behavioral intervention in a home setting with a child with autism.' *Journal of Positive Behavioral Interventions 4*, 1, 53–60.

MacGregor, E., Whiten, A. and Blackburn, P. (1998) 'Transfer of the picture-in-the-head analogy to natural contexts to aid false belief understanding in autism.' *Autism 2*, 367–387.

Mesibov, G. B. (1986) 'A cognitive program for teaching social behaviors to verbal, autistic adolescents and adults.' In E. Schopler and G. B. Mesibov (eds) *Social Behavior in Autism*. New York: Plenum Press.

Mesibov, G. B. and Howley, M. (2003) *Accessing the Curriculum for Pupils with Autistic Spectrum Disorders: Using the TEACCH Programme to Help Inclusion*. London: David Fulton.

Mesibov, G. B., Adams, L. W. and Klinger, L. G. (1997) *Autism: Understanding the Disorder*. New York/London: Plenum Press.

Moffat, E. (2001) 'Writing social stories to improve students' social understanding.' *Good Autism Practice 2*, 1, 12–16.

Newton, C., Taylor, G. and Wilson, D. (1996) 'Circles of friends: an inclusive approach to meeting emotional and behavioural needs.' *Educational Psychology in Practice 11*, 4, 41–48.

Norris, C. and Dattilo, J. (1999) 'Evaluating the effects of social story intervention on a young girl with autism.' *Focus on Autism and Other Developmental Disabilities 14*, 180–186.

Powell, S. (ed) (2000) *Helping Children with Autism to Learn*. London: David Fulton.

Quill, K. (ed) (1995) *Teaching Children with Autism: Strategies to Enhance Communication and Socialisation*. New York: Delmar.

Rowe, C. (1999) 'Do social stories benefit children with autism in mainstream primary school?' *British Journal of Special Education 26*, 1, 12–14.

Sainsbury, C. (2000) *Martian in the Playground*. Bristol: Lucky Duck.

Scattone, D., Wilczynski, S., Edwards, R. and Rabian, B. (2002) 'Decreasing disruptive behaviors of children with autism using social stories.' *Journal of Autism and Developmental Disorders 32*, 6, 535–543.

Schopler, E. (1994) 'Behavioural priorities for autism and related developmental disorders.' In E. Schopler and G. B. Mesibov (eds) *Behavioural Issues in Autism*. New York: Plenum Press.

Schopler, E. and Mesibov, G. B. (eds) (1986) *Social Behavior in Autism.* New York: Plenum Press.

Schopler, E., Mesibov, G. and Hearsey, K. (1995) 'Structured teaching in the TEACCH system.' In E. Schopler and G. B. Mesibov (eds) *Learning and Cognition in Autism.* New York: Plenum Press.

Schopler, E., Mesibov, G. B. and Kunce, L. (eds) (1998) *Asperger Syndrome or High Functioning Autism?* New York: Plenum Press.

Schroeder, A. (1996) *Socially Speaking: A Pragmatic Social Skills Programme for Primary Pupils.* Cambridge: LDA.

Smith, C. (2001a) 'Using social stories to enhance behaviour in children with autistic spectrum difficulties.' *Educational Psychology in Practice 17*, 4, 337–345.

Smith, C. (2001b) 'Using social stories with children with autistic spectrum disorders: an evaluation.' *Good Autism Practice 2*, 1, 16–25.

Smith, C. (2003) *Writing and Developing Social Stories: Practical Interventions in Autism.* Bicester: Speechmark.

Swaggart, B. L., Gagnon, E., Bock, S. J., Earles, T. L., Quinn, C., Myles, B. S. and Simpson, R. L. (1995) 'Using social stories to teach social and behavioural skills to children with autism.' *Focus on Autistic Behaviour 10*, 1–16.

Swettenham, J. G., Baron-Cohen, S., Gomez, J. and Walsh, S. (1996) 'What's inside someone's head? Conceiving of the mind as a camera helps children with autism acquire an alternative to a theory of mind.' *Cognitive Neuropsychiatry 39*, 893–902.

Thiemann, K. S. and Goldstein, H. (2001) 'Social stories, written text cues and video feedback: effects on social communication of children with autism.' *Journal of Applied Behavioural Analysis 34*, 4, 425–446.

Volkmar, F. R. and Cohen, D. L. (1985) 'A first-person account of the experience of infantile autism by Tony W.' *Journal of Autism and Developmental Disorders 15*, 47–54.

Volkmar, F. R. and Klin, A. (2000) 'Diagnostic issues.' In A. Klin, F. Volkmar and S. Sparrow (eds) *Asperger Syndrome.* New York: Guilford Press.

Whitaker, P., Barrat, P., Joy, H., Potter, M. and Thomas, G. (1998) 'Children with autism and peer group support: using "circles of friends".' *British Journal of Special Education 25*, 2, 60–64.

Wing, L. (1996) *The Autistic Spectrum: A Guide for Parents and Professionals.* London: Constable.

Wing, L. and Gould, J. (1979) 'Severe impairments of social interaction and associated abnormalities in children: epidemiology and classification.' *Journal of Autism and Childhood Schizophrenia 9*, 11–29.

World Health Organization (1993) *The ICD-10 Classification of Mental and Behavioural Disorders. Diagnostic Criteria for Research.* Geneva: WHO.

Subject Index

abstract concepts 59, 65
academic tasks 104
achievements, recognising 30–2, 37, 43, 47–8
activities
    choices regarding 67–8
    parental 73–5
    simultaneous 73–5
affirmative sentences 61, 64, 150–1
age, developmental 54, 132, 133
angry people 130–2
antecedents, behaviour and consequences (ABC) 33, 35–6
apologies 71, 113
Asperger's syndrome 35, 102
attention spans 54–5, 79–80, 133–5
audio Social Stories™ 96
autistic spectrum disorders (ASDs), diagnostic criteria 14–15

babies, new 66
big picture 19–20
birthday parties 85–7
booklets, picture/text 80, 97–8
'bossy books' 128, 129
bullying 139–40

cause and effect 36, 52–3
central coherence 18, 19–20
challenging behaviour 23, 30–1, 33–40
    complementary approaches to 115–20
    and sentence types 52–4
    and Social Stories™ monitoring 98–9
choice, representation of 67, 77
    activity choices 67–8
    playmates and partners 68–9

social skills and responses 70–1
circle of friends 115–21
cognitive functioning 64–6, 145
    see also social cognition
Cognitive Picture Rehearsal 26
cognitive-behavioural approaches 34
collaboration 93
    see also cooperative efforts; group work
college scenarios 113–14
Comic Strip Conversations (CSCs) 21, 40–1, 43, 99, 139–41
communication, spontaneous 111–12
complementary strategies 27–8, 75, 108–24
    circle of friends 115–21
    jigsawing 121–4
    social skills programmes 113–15, 125
    'structured teaching' 109–12, 121–4, 125
compliment paying 71, 113
comprehension ability 54, 132, 133
consistency of events 31, 138
context 32, 38
control sentences 60–1, 64, 150–1
Conversation Symbols Dictionary 40
cooperative efforts 75, 93, 94, 122, 124
cooperative sentences 62, 64, 70, 94, 150–1
CSCs see Comic Strip Conversations

descriptive sentences 45, 47–9, 52–4, 57, 63, 64, 105, 129, 150–1
detail
    focusing on 19–20, 97
    over-detailed Social Stories™ 134–5
developmental age 54, 132, 133

diagnostic criteria, of autistic spectrum disorders 14–15
directive sentences 46, 47, 49–54, 57, 64, 99–100, 105, 111, 128, 129, 150–1
domestic scenarios
    switching off washing machines 88–91
    see also family scenarios
door slamming 141–3
drawings 85–6

echolalia 136, 139
egocentrism 19
events, explaining/preparing for/reassurance about 30, 32–3, 37, 48–54, 56, 60–2, 66–8, 82–7, 102–8

fading 99–100
family scenarios
    explaining family relationships 133–5
    explaining parental activities 73–5
    new babies 66
feedback, positive 23
fire drills 105–6
first person perspective 55–6, 150
flexibility 104–5
fonts (textual) 96
friendships 68–9, 113–15
    see also peers

game winning, obsessions regarding 136
greetings 113
group work 75, 121–4

hand flapping 107–8
help, asking for 111–12
hidden information 20–1, 24, 41, 121, 143, 145
    and Advanced Social Stories™ 69, 71
    lack of information about 136
    presentation 79, 97
    sentence types and 52, 54

Author Index

To Bickley,

I hope you find this an
interesting look at our home state

Harry Straight

Bad Guys on Bulldozers

The Environmental Voice In Florida-Based Crime Fiction

Harry Straight

DEDICATION

To Kay, my everlasting grace.

CONTENTS

ACKNOWLEDGMENTS

Thanks to Dr. Maurice O'Sullivan, professor of English at Rollins College, for his inspiration, guidance and advice. And a special thanks to Larry Johnson: poet, teacher, expatriated American, jazz lover and friend. You showed me the music of words and taught me how to riff.

i

Introduction

In the late 1960s, the celebrated Florida naturalist Archie Carr set out to write a book about the wildlife and the wilderness of his native state. From the beginning, however, he ran into a problem of approach. He "immediately sensed a danger looming," he wrote. "It was that I was almost bound to fall into the trap of nostalgia and indignation, of turning this book into a diatribe against the passing of original Florida" (xv). Carr, a leading expert on Florida's wild landscape and native creatures, knew he was "especially susceptible to the disease of bitterness over the ruin of Florida–over the partly aimless, partly avaricious ruin of unequaled natural riches of the most nearly tropical state. But in my case I decided simply, 'What the hell, you cry the blues and soon nobody listens'."

Even though Carr had become a highly respected advocate for the protection of Florida's natural environment from the ravages of unchecked growth and over-development, he concluded that a "garment rendering sort of book would simply not be read." So he decided to write "mostly about what joy still remains in the Florida landscape and then just sneak in some factual tooth-gnashing every now and then when the readers might really be reading." Carr died in 1987, and the book he wanted to write, a collection of his essays titled *A Naturalist in Florida, a Celebration of Eden*, was not published until 1994.

Yet as early as 1950, "factual tooth-gnashing" about the Sunshine State's endangered environment has been a major ingredient for a handful of Florida-based writers who have found a unique way to overcome Carr's dilemma. For more than half a century, these writers have crafted compelling and highly readable stories whose themes often touched on what landscape essayist John Brinckerhoff Jackson calls "those wounds inflicted by greed and destructive fury" upon the natural environment (vii).

These stories have gained immense popularity, introducing millions of readers throughout the country and the world to the complex and vital issues of environmental survival, and at the same time, have earned these

1

writers both critical and commercial success. Yet these authors are not naturalists or scientists, politicians or even environment activists. They are, instead, writers of crime and mystery fiction.

The first of these Florida authors to have his hard-boiled hero voice concerns about the natural environment was John D. MacDonald, one of the most prolific and popular writers in America and widely recognized as the dean of American crime fiction. MacDonald and those who followed in his footsteps, most notably Carl Hiaasen, a Broward County native and *Miami Herald* columnist; Randy Wayne White, a former Sanibel Island fishing guide and columnist for *Outside Magazine*; and James W. Hall, an English professor at Florida International University; have created a substantial body of work in the crime novel genre that Rollins College professor and author Maurice O'Sullivan characterizes as "environmental noir" (22).

These "eco-mysteries," as O'Sullivan calls them, use "humanity's war on nature" as a metaphor for the corruption of both the individual and society, exploring these themes within a continuation of a tradition that traces back to the "godfathers of American noir, Dashiell Hammett and Raymond Chandler," who "created a ravaged social and physical environment as the perfect elegiac background for their tales of the bleakness enveloping the postindustrial world" (119).

The Voice

By raising the voice of environmental concern within the familiar conventions of the mystery genre, the writers of eco-mysteries tackle themes typically reserved for more serious fiction. Their novels are not just about Chandler's "simple art of murder" (1); they are about the not-so-simple art of survival; and not just the survival of the self, but the survival of the community and ultimately the survival of the species. Do a man an injustice—steal his money, destroy his reputation, seduce his wife or even murder him—and you have harmed one man. But poison the air, pollute the water, contaminate the food we eat, or otherwise tinker with the essential clockwork of the biosphere and you risk the annihilation of all life.

MacDonald's environmental voice was unequivocal on this subject. In an afterword to *Other Times, Other Worlds*, a collection of his science fiction stories, he speaks in the metaphors of biology and asks his fellow inhabitants of Earth to "think of ourselves as a virulent infection eroding this green planet even while we use it to sustain our teeming life form" and warns that we "cannot escape the consequences of our own barbarous acts by sailing off into the future. . . . We must control our numbers and guard our environment or we shall all die, sooner than we might care to guess" (167).

The Genre

The mystery novel, with its necessary emphasis on detection, is a particularly apt genre to explore ecological themes because both unraveling the mystery and understanding the complex interrelations of cause and effect in an ecosystem require an ability to separate illusion from reality. To the drivers who speed across Alligator Alley, a four-lane concrete ribbon of highway that cuts across South Florida through the heart of the Everglades, the road is nothing more than a scenic and convenient shortcut from Naples to Ft. Lauderdale. Through the eyes of the ecologically aware, however, the road carries an entirely different meaning. Here is how Hall puts it in *Mean High Tide*:

That road had been damming up the sweet, clear water of the Everglades for decades. The Glades no longer flowed as it was meant to do, filtering for a hundred miles through the rough sawgrass and scrub pine. No longer cleaning itself. And now the polluted runoff from the farms and sugarcane plantations was collecting out there, tainting the virgin water. Mercury, sulfur, lead. Some of the gar and bass and bluegills were growing third eyeballs, extra fins. Gators dying of stomach cancer, herons and gallinules with cataracts. Just another trade-off. Sacrificing Eden so the Chryslers and Nissans could race each other two abreast across the doomed remains of the state (302).

For the protagonists of these novels, the mystery of ecology and the ecology of the mystery are often inseparable. Biologist Doc Ford, the leading character in a series of ten novels by White, explains how he unravels both biological and sociological puzzles in *Captiva*:

The behavior of any organism should be understandable once external influences are deciphered. When an otherwise predictable animal behaves oddly on the tidal flats—or on the docks [he is referring to the human animal]—a little alarm goes off in my head. The inexplicable attracts me because there is nothing that cannot be explained. When the explanation is not readily apparent, I become compulsive about isolating the external influences. It attracts me in the same way that jigsaw puzzles and chess draw in similar types of people. Assemble enough pieces, make the right moves, and the reward is clarity (54).

The ecological metaphor of interconnectedness and interdependence lies at the heart of these works, constantly revealing itself in the dance between hunter and prey, villain and victim, lover and beloved. It is there in the wrestling match of logic and instinct, justice and convention, anger and forgiveness. The classic hero who must walk alone down mean streets finds himself surprisingly drawn to the comfort of community while the immediacy of the moment stands against the weight of history. Throughout it all, there is always, always, the embrace of land, sea and sky; the relentless cycle of reproduction and the entropy of death and decay.

The Villain

The villains of these novels often share two distinctive characteristics: first, they are at best indifferent to the environment or at worst aggressive despoilers of the natural world; and second, protagonists see them in ecological terms as a threat to the survival of the species, with many of the villains portrayed as genetic defects, evolutionary mistakes or an animalistic creature that represents the personification of an evil that MacDonald in *The Deep Blue Goodbye* sees as "the pustular bequest from the beast, as inexplicable as Belson" (63). MacDonald put little stock in the popular psychological theories of his day that tried to explain away the behavior of such social deviants by blaming it on a Freudian struggle in the subconscious or a childhood filled with emotional trauma. In an article for *Clues* magazine in 1980, he wrote:

There exists in the world a kind of evil which defies the Freudian explanations of the psychologists and the environmental explanations of the sociologists. It is an evil existing for the sake of itself, for the sake of the satisfactions of its own exercise. . . .For me it is less satisfying to say that this is the action of a sad, limited, tormented, unbalanced child than it is to see that this is a primordial blackness reaching up again through a dark and vulnerable soul, showing us all the horror that has always been with mankind, frustrating all rational analyses (69).

Most of the villains in the works of White, Hall and Hiaasen are of the same ilk. In Hall's second novel, *Tropical Freeze*, he describes Hespier, a Haitian hit man, this way: "Well, for one thing, he was a cannibal. He ate pieces of his hits. He made Lorraine cook stews for him' " (153).

One of White's scariest bad guys is Teddy Bauerstock, who shows no remorse after killing a small child in *Ten Thousand Islands*. A psychologist describes Teddy as extremely intelligent but having no reaction whatsoever to the suffering of others. This is a genetic "error," the doctor says, and adds "there will be more and more of these people, yet society allows their defective genes to be passed on though conjugal visits in prison!" (242).

Hiaasen, who approaches these topics through humor rather than the drama of the other three writers, nevertheless creates villains as off-center genetically as any created by his contemporaries. *Sick Puppy*'s Mr. Gash is as sick as they come, a killer who gets his kicks by listening to 911 tapes. "Mr. Gash was exhilarated by the sound of fear in human voices. Fury, panic, despair–it was all there on the 911 calls, the full cycle of primal desperation" (207).

On one hand, creating villains who are the personification of evil and who have no redeeming social value makes it easy for the hero to justify killing them. Very few of these bad guys are lead away to jail, trial and confinement; rather they are dispatched in a variety of often grisly and highly creative ways through the actions of the hero.

On the other hand, it can be argued that the elimination of these villains is not just a matter of self-defense or revenge or even balancing the scales of justice. By crafting the antagonists as threats to the very survival of the species, these writers let their protagonists take on the role of one who culls the herd. They act out of biological instinct as well as personal or social consciousness. When White's Doc Ford looks at the picture of an eight-year-old child who is kidnapped in *Sanibel Flats*, his first reaction is to want to shield him from all harm. "Perhaps the source of the emotion was some deep coding in the DNA, evolved during speciation to protect the young from marauding adults; a built-in check for the preservation of the species" (49).

White elaborates on this theme in *North of Havana*: "The realities of nature, however, cannot be argued, nor can the instincts that guide each and every successful species. Members of an animal community survive because, instinctually, they are accountable to the needs of their own species. Members that did not behave accountably could not survive–nor should they survive" (243). Hall's series character, Thorn, ponders a similar phenomenon in *Tropical Freeze*:

. . . How sometimes, as a wolf approached a herd, there seemed to be some silent transaction between hunter and hunted. The wolf halted at striking distance from the herd, seeming to ask in a voice no human could hear if there was a deer ready to die. And a deer, maybe sick, maybe just weary of the chase, separated itself from the others, answering back, all right, OK, for the sake of the herd, take me (270).

Thorn goes on to speculate that the biological instinct to protect the herd, to ensure the survival of the species, is what fuels "[a]ll cops, all heroes. A suicidal willingness to risk" (270). In other words, the kind of character who serves as the protagonist of the eco-mystery.

[*The scientific genesis of these ideas comes from a relatively recent reassessment of the works of Charles Darwin called evolutionary psychology. This new science, which first surfaced in the 1960s and 1970s, began to expand the notion of natural selection in a way that challenged the old notions of behaviorism, which is the idea that people basically act out of either fear of punishment or desire for reward. "Sociobiology" as it is often called, emphasizes our evolutionary roots, and postulates that human behavior is guided by genetics and biology to a much large degree than previously suspected. To show how writers who use ecological themes as metaphors for social behavior reflects to one degree or another the principles of evolutionary biology goes beyond the scope of this book. The books to read, however, are E. O. Wilson's* Sociobiology *(1975), Richard Dawkins's* The Selfish Gene *(1976) and an excellent overview of this subject,* The Moral

5

Animal, Why We Are the Way We Are: The New Science of Evolutionary Psychology, *by Robert Wright (1994).]*

The Place

Florida has never been an easy place to define for those who make their living telling stories. One of the ironclad rules of fiction writing (and one that is hardly ever broken by even the most innovating and daring writers) is that setting must remain subordinate to characters and plot. Sinclair Lewis put it this way: "When I want to learn about the Azores, I'll read the National Geographic, not a novel" (Conrad 83). Yet Florida seems to create for many writers an imperative of place. It refuses to be ignored. White, in a personal interview, explained "when you write about two characters and then put them in Florida, you have three characters," and more often than not that third character become a victim. Of course White, MacDonald, Hall and Hiaasen never let place overshadow people or plot, but the grand stage of Florida upon which their eco-mysteries are played out often takes on a role far beyond mere setting.

The realism demanded of twentieth century writers of crime fiction has frequently resulted in an intimate association between writer and place, from Dashiell Hammett's San Francisco, Raymond Chandler's Los Angeles and Ross MacDonald's southern California, to Tony Hillerman's American West, James Lee Burke's southern Louisiana and Elmore Leonard's Detroit. These writers evoke a specific sense of place through description, dialogue and social interaction.

Something more, however, is going on in Florida. Carl Hiaasen, in an introduction to the 1995 re-release of MacDonald's Travis McGee series, says, "most writers are delighted to achieve, on that rare occasion, a true and full sense of place—whether it's a city, a country, a valley, a jungle, the bowel of a volcano, or the bottom of the sea. MacDonald wanted his readers to do much more than see Florida. He seemed to want them to care about it as deeply as he did; celebrate it, marvel at it, laugh about it, grieve for it, and even fight for it" (viii).

These writers are not just using Florida and its ever-present environmental battles as grist for good stories; they are each personally committed to protecting Florida's fragile ecosystem against that same wanton destruction that MacDonald saw. They see the importance of this connection to the land not just as a way to make their daily life more comfortable, their commute more tolerable, their forays into what wilderness there is left more enjoyable; but as a prime responsibility as a participating member of the human species. The greater the understanding of the interconnectedness and interdependence between humans and their physical environment, the greater the understanding of that same dynamic on a sociological level.

As naturalist Terry Tempest Williams so eloquently puts it: "Our lack of intimacy with each other is in direct proportion to our lack of intimacy with the land "(64). With varying degrees of intensity, this theme runs through the work of each of these writers. Hiaasen tells us that MacDonald's "bittersweet view of South Florida was the same as my own. For me and many natives, some of McGee's finest moments were when he paused, mid-adventure, to inveigh against the runaway exploitation of the rare and dying paradise"(introduction vii).

Hall, in an essay on his own enchantment with the Sunshine State, describes his first impressions at the tender age of eighteen: " . . and while I had been on the platform of the Hollywood [Florida] train station for less than a minute, I knew with utter certainty that I had taken a mortal wound . . . .I love this place. I have loved it from the start and have learned to love it more with every passing year–all its quirkiness, its stresses, this simmering melting pot where no one wants to blend" (*Hot Damn* 1-4).

White put it this way: "Like the bulk of people who live here, I care deeply about this state. My sons are born here, my grandchildren. It's important that we talk about the people and the organizations that are a danger to the environment" (personal interview).

MacDonald, according to one critic, created a "metaphysical landscape . . . . the Florida coastline, with its butchered swamp and tacky concrete palaces," which constitutes "a moral affront," giving MacDonald "an obsessive–and inexhaustible—subject" to write about while "the really big thriller" has been unfolding, "that larger, even more ingenious work of fiction, the recent history of Florida," of which MacDonald's stories and novels "are basically incidents and chapters" (Raban, 3-D). Through Hiaasen's biting and ironic satire, Hall's redemptive power of place and White's patient and persistence science, the story continues to unfold.

Chapter One
John D. MacDonald: Godfather of the Florida Eco-mystery

When John D. Macdonald moved from New York to Florida in 1949, he had yet to write his first novel. He had, however, already established himself as an enormously prolific creator of short stories which he sold to a variety of pulp magazines. "He was not so much a writer as a writing machine" (Merrill 65). Shortly before he moved to Clearwater, a 1947 headline in the Utica *Observer-Dispatch* announced "Utican Writes 300 Stories in 20 Months." When the pulp magazines started dying out, MacDonald got in on the ground floor of a new marketing device–the small, inexpensive paperback novel. His early work was typical of the pulps, with such titles as *The Brass Cupcake*, *Weep for Me*, *The Damned*, *Cry Hard, Cry Fast*, *Murder in the Wind*, *Death Trap*, *The Deceivers*, *Deadly Welcome* and *Slam the Big Door*. They were the classic hard-boiled mysteries of the day and their often-lurid covers, drawn by artist Barrye Phillips, almost always featured a well-endowed woman in some stage of undress.

The novels sold like the proverbial hot cakes. For instance, *The Damned*, published in 1952, sold two million copies (at a whopping 40 cents apiece) (Merrill 63). In 1958, MacDonald published his first hardback work, *The Executioners*, which became an alternate selection by the Dollar Book club and went through three printings. Hollywood actor Gregory Peck liked the book so much he decided to make a movie of it with himself starring as suburbanite attorney Sam Bowden who was stalked by the villain Max Cady, played by Robert Mitchum. Hollywood executives didn't like the title, however, and changed it to *Cape Fear* (Merrill 95).

MacDonald wrote what he described as an "honest examination of how the human animal reacts to the merciless tensions of our times– physically, socially and emotionally." He told biographer and friend Ed Hirshberg "he felt he had every right to move his suspense novels in the direction of the so-called 'legitimate' novels of manners and morals, despair and failure, love and joy" (71). MacDonald would go on to publish 70 novels and more than 500 short stories. His most distinguishing device was what he called his "sociological asides," and while he took on any number of topics from the mind-numbing bureaucracy of corporate America and public education to the insanity of running air conditioners in public buildings as if they were meat lockers, he saved his most passionate opinions for "Florida's besieged environment" (Glassman, O'Sullivan 22).

Hirshberg, who writes about MacDonald's best known character, Travis McGee, and the twenty one color-coded books in which he is featured, does a good job of listing McGee's environmental "diatribes" in an essays published in both Hirshberg's biography, *John D. MacDonald*, and Glassman and O'Sullivan's *Florida Noir*. Yet the McGee books were by no means the first time MacDonald used his fiction to comment on Florida's environment.

MacDonald wrote his first novel, *The Brass Cupcake*, in 1950 when he lived in Clearwater, Florida. The book is set in the fictional Florence City, but it is typical of Clearwater and other small towns on the Gulf Coast. MacDonald describes it this way.

Before the war Florence City was a quiet middle-class resort. But the war expanded the field of endeavor. Gambling house, breast of guinea hen under glass, seagoing yachts from Havana, seventy-dollar night-club tabs for a quiet dinner for two–with the appropriate wines, of course. The bakers from Dayton and the shoe clerks from Buffalo still came down, but the high rentals had shoved them inland off the beaches, in as far as the swamps and the mangroves and the orange-juice factories. A new group had taken over the beaches. Middle-aged ladies with puffy faces and granite eyes brought down whole stables of hundred-dollar call girls, giggling like a sorority on a social welfare trip. But the rate was bumped to two hundred to cover the higher cost of accommodations and the traveling expenses. Sleek little men with hand-blocked sport shirts strolled around and made with the Bogart gestures. Boom town, fun town, money town. Rough town. Lay it on the line. You can't take it with you (13).

In his second novel set in Florida, 1953's *Dead Low Tide*, we see his first real observation on the impact of Florida's development practices on its natural landscape:

Florida, particularly along the west coast, all the way from Cedar Key to the moneyed smell of Naples, is constantly growing–not in the normal fashion of other places, with more houses going up on existing land, but the land itself growing. Shaggy dredges park in the bay flats, snarling and wheezing as they suck up mud and guck and shells and small unwary fish. The debris is piled moistly and it stinks for a time, then whitens in the sun. It is leveled and stamped down and then houses go up on it so fast they seem to appear with a small clinking sound–the way Walt Disney grows flowers (19).

MacDonald goes on for two more pages, detailing the palms plopped down into the dredged up land that last just long enough for the houses to sell before the palm fronds become a "rich tobacco brown." He talks about the "big one," the hurricane that will eventually come and blow it all away, and then he gives a long, precise, detailed description of Horseshoe Key and explains "the mathematics of made land." He tells how a developer can buy fifteen hundred feet of bayfront, dredge a series of channels that end up looking like fingers sticking into the bay, "and by god, he's got now a total of thirty-three hundred feet of bayfront" (21).

While certainly not the main focus of what are essentially crime novels, these few paragraphs illustrate that MacDonald's environmental sensitivities were well honed from the very start of his career as a novelist. In November 1959, MacDonald took his activism outside the novel when he began writing a column called Off the Beat for a small monthly magazine in Sarasota called *The Lookout*. Writing under the byline T. Carrington Burns, His first effort was in reaction to developers doing exactly what he wrote about in *Dead Low Tide*. The fiction had become fact. The newly formed Arvida Corporation, named after an acronym of the founder, ARthur VIning DAvis, began to develop five islands in Sarasota Bay, including Longboat Key, just a few humped-back bridges north of MacDonald's home on Siesta Key. Arvida's plans included dredging up the bay bottom to create waterfront property for homes and golf courses. MacDonald took Arvida to task in his magazine opinion column:

We drove out Bird Key way the other day in a sad ceremonial mood to look at where the big pines had been. After driving between the pines for so many years, it was disconcerting to have them on only one side. It gave somewhat the same feeling as walking with a pronounced limp. We parked for a bit. Lovely morning. The big dredges were contentedly masticating, while the opportunist birds awaited the goodies spewed onto the brand new land. The felled trees were disappearing with a haste we might have labeled as guilty had we not known it was merely a demonstration of Corporate Efficiency. During the days of the old bridges when Sunday traffic in season would often congeal for twenty irritating minutes, the shade of those tall pines kept many a stalled tourist from frying like a mullet in his own grease and suntan lotion"(Merrill102).

In another column in May 1960, he wields a much sharper tongue on "every zoning-buster, anti-planner, and bay-filler. . .degrading us for the sake of his own pocketbook. . .in a world so implacably conformist it seems sinful for us to lay waste to both aspects of our uniqueness, and go baying and hallooing down the cheap road to the ordinariness of other resort areas. . . .If this is conservation and snobbery, we confess guilt. . . . There is no valid justification for filling one more foot of bay. Profit is not progress" (Merrill 104).

MacDonald's columns had little effect. The dredging and filling continued as usual, but the author had the last word. According to his most recent biographer Merrill, it was this project that prompted MacDonald to write his 40th novel, *A Flash of Green*. It became the first of several MacDonald novels that examine humanity's often antagonistic relationship with Florida's environment against a backdrop of greed, corruption and morality ambiguity. For MacDonald, the bad guys more often than not rode bulldozers and operated draglines.

Green tells the story of a corrupt county commissioner who secretly plots to dredge up Grassy Bay for a housing development and a small band of citizens who rally to fight against the filling of the bay. The main character, newspaper reporter Jimmy Wing, is an observer by both occupation and nature who, like the public he represents, holds–at least initially–no strong opinions.

Wing eventually becomes seduced by Elmo Bliss, a corrupt county commissioner and de facto political boss of Palm County. As the protesters battle development of the bay, Wing finds himself drawn deeper into Bliss's scheme to discredit the environmentalists, many of whom are Wing's friends. One in particular, Kat Hubble, is the woman he secretly loves.

Wing eventually revolts and crafts his own hard-fought redemption by bringing down Bliss and his cronies. MacDonald often writes of broken characters not easily mended, and while there is some hope at the end of the novel for Wing and Kat, the bay is doomed as the developers crank up the dredges.

This novel marries the sociological world of the postmodern crime story and its iconoclastic hero to the naturalist's physical world of passionate and learned studies of landscape and nature. One of the most significant aspects of *A Flash of Green* is that it appears at a time when the environmental movement nationwide–and more particularly in Florida–was just beginning to gain attention from both the public and public policy makers (Siry 162). In 1958 Rachel Carson, a biologist and editor with the U.S. Wildlife Service from 1936 to 1952, had begun to gather data about the dangerous effects of deadly poisons, particularly insecticides, on human, animal and plant life. Her findings first appeared in a series of articles for *The New Yorker* magazine and then in her seminal book *Silent Spring*, published the same year as MacDonald's novel.

Since the early 1940s, biologists and naturalists had bemoaned Florida's transformation from a paradise into mere real estate, but public awareness of environmental issues was still in its infancy twenty years later. Shortly after World War II, "a crisis caused by a slowly degrading environment and collapsing ecosystems would become apparent," according to Leslie Kemp Poole, a former *Orlando Sentinel* environmental reporter whose master's thesis centered on the history of Florida's environmental movement. These early problems, however, were "viewed as mostly local problems. No one could see that they were merely warning signals of a greater trouble, a slow-moving disease that was eating away the very essence of the state" (23).

In 1953, John H. Storer, former president of the Florida Audubon Society, wrote a book called *The Web of Life*, designed to show "for everyone who would learn what has largely been forgotten in our machine age–how all living things fit together into a single pattern" (x). Poole explains that the fundamentals laid out by Storer were called ecology, the study of the interdependence of organisms and their environment.

"People were beginning to learn that the loss of the landscape didn't just hurt their eyes–it was affecting their quality of life," Poole wrote. "No longer could man just look at the world. He had to understand that he was part of it. When the Everglades were threatened it didn't just mean that birds would disappear. It meant that man's drinking water and his own existence in south Florida were threatened" (72).

Although the Everglades National Park officially opened in 1947, its 1.3 million acres were about half of what was originally proposed. Left out were nearly a million acres of sloughs and marshes that biologists argued were needed by the park to control water or the Everglades would not survive. Poole explains that this was "the first national park to be completely preserved as wilderness with primary consideration to saving wildlife–not to offer visitors a spectacular view" (54). However, the same year the park opened, journalist Marjory Stoneman Douglas published *The Everglades: River of Grass* in which she detailed how decades of cutting drainage ditches throughout the glades had altered the water flow so much that the land was dying, ravaged by saltwater intrusion and raging fires. "Unless people act, the fires will come again. Over-drainage will go on. The soil will shrink and burn and be wasted and destroyed, in a continuing ruin" (104).

MacDonald, who had earned a Masters of Business Degree from Harvard, had plenty of research material available to help him shape the various environmental arguments that appear in *Green*. For a vast majority of his readers, however, words such as "environment" and "ecology" and concepts such as "interdependence of species" were not exactly topics discussed around the dinner table. In addition, the environmental aspects of the novel never made it into the book's marketing literature. The back cover blurb for *Green* read:

The corrupters had taken over Palm City. Silent and deadly, like the snakes that infested the nearby swamps, they lay hidden from view, waiting for the right moment to strike. Political treachery and private greed had already softened up the town for the big sell-out. All that had to be done now was to silence a few stubborn citizens. Blackmail was their favorite weapon. . .

Inside those covers, however, MacDonald writes of the damage done to the place he called home with passion and indignation. A little more than halfway thorough the novel, we see Jimmy Wing flying back from Tampa in a small plane skirting the coastline at five thousand feet:

Stretching all the way down the coast, almost without interruption, was the raw garish night work of man, the crawl of headlights, bouquets of neon, sugarcube motels, blue dots of lighted pools. . .Wing had seen it all in a fanciful way which he had never been able to get out of his mind. The land was some great fallen animal. And all the night lights marked the long angry sore in its hide, a noisome, festering wound, maggoty and moving, draining blood and serum into the silent Gulf (192).

This is the urban wasteland of Chandler and Hammett: that "ravaged social and physical environment used as the perfect elegiac background for their tales of the bleakness enveloping the postindustrial world." Yet at the same time it is the world of Carr, Storer, and Douglas.

The novel's title itself carries a double meaning that sets the theme for the book. In a short prologue MacDonald describes a conversation between two men fishing from the end of a public pier at sundown on the Gulf Coast. The one from Indiana says, "What I want to know, do you ever get to see that flash of green?" He is talking about a rare atmospheric condition that causes the sky to light up momentarily with a flash of green at the moment of sunset. According to Florida folklore, seeing the flash is akin to seeing a falling star: make a wish when you see it and it will bring good luck. The man from Michigan, however, says the only flash of green he sees "is the flash of money you miss out on. I bought one lot for six hundred, held it for five years and sold it for three thousand. I could have bought ten. Makes you sick to your stomach" (6).

MacDonald offers two contrasting views: one emphasizing the spiritual, personal connection to the landscape and its inherent beauty and redemptive nature; the other the lust for personal gain.

The struggle over Grassy Bay is not some isolated incident made up for the benefit of MacDonald's plot. It becomes a symbol for the hallmark of Florida's growth, largely accomplished by the draining of swamp lands, marshes and bays in order to create developable land. This conflict goes beyond Florida and can be traced to patterns established at the infancy of our country. Environmental historian Joseph V. Siry writes that "historic patterns in American development of estuaries reveal conflicting assumptions concerning the use of natural resources, changing national attitudes about government-sponsored scientific research, and persistent prejudices against the least understood sections of the coast, the tidal marshes" (6).

Grassy Bay is owned by Florida's State Internal Improvement Fund and is supposed to be held in trust for the benefit of the public, but in Florida, that public often meant a handful of wealthy land developers rather than the general population. MacDonald's choice of this particular kind of environmental skullduggery represents no single isolated incident in history or some fanciful twist of fictional plot. This is exactly how most of Florida was developed.

In the 1880s, when the state's population was a mere 260,000, the state had managed to classify more than two thirds of its land as "swamp and overflow," and although much of that property turned out to be, well, if not high, at least reasonably dry, that term was used by federal and state governments as an excuse to give away more than twenty million acres of land to railroads and land developers.

The state was so anxious to bring in new people, that in 1881 it sold four million acres for 25 cents per acre to a Philadelphia entrepreneur named Hamilton Disston, who through this one transaction becomes the largest single property owner in the state. He ended up owning almost the entire lower half of the state south of Kissimmee, and he got it so cheap because he promised to drain at least half of it in order to create developable land that would in turn attract new residents and businesses.

John Rothchild in his book *Up For Grabs, A Trip Through Time and Space in the Sunshine State*, details the transaction and concludes: "[W]hat better evidence of Florida's self-perceived inferiority, its hat-in-hand attitude, its inability to distinguish substance from pose, its susceptibility to bluster in the infancy of its statehood than this 1881 deal" (29).

MacDonald's Grassy Bay deal can easily be read as a classic example of how Florida did business, not only in the past, but also in the boom of the 1950s through the 1970s when its population doubled every decade and environmental regulation was in its infancy.

In the opening pages, MacDonald finds in nature itself an apt metaphor for the novel's major conflict—the strangler fig. Kat Hubble has a conversation with her yardman who explains about a vine growing up a live oak. "This here is a strangle vine. I'll cut him off low now, and next week he lets go enough up there, I pull him down easy. Take a long long time to kill that tree, we let it go. By the time it die, all you can see is the strangle vine aholt all over it" (9)

The "strangle vine" (here used as a colloquial term for the strangler fig) represents the social and economic equivalent of Florida's unchecked growth. By the time it has finished the job; however, the thing that gives it life (the oak representing the natural unspoiled beauty of the state) has been destroyed.

The strangler fig is the first line of a thematic motif that runs throughout the book: the very quality of life that attracts people to Florida is in danger of disappearing because of that very attraction. By using the vernacular language (calling the vine "him") MacDonald foreshadows not only the struggle between the environmentalists and developers of the bay, but also the struggle between Wing and Bliss, whose personal ambitions include nothing less than becoming the governor of Florida. This plot development also reinforces the notion that Grassy Bay is a symbol for a much larger conflict. What threatens the bay also threatens the entire state. The strangler fig–like Bliss–is native to Florida. Here MacDonald implies that it is not so much outside influences or newcomers who pose the most serious threat, but homegrown men like Bliss.

Near the end of the novel, Wing manages to publish a front-page news article that details Bliss's complicity in the Grassy Bay scandal and describes in painful detail Wing's own role in helping Bliss blackmail those who opposed him.

By now it is hard to tell which is the oak and which is the strangler fig. Bliss and Wing are both diminished and locked in a symbiotic relationship by the end of the novel. Wing tells Bliss "I'll be on your back as long as we both shall live" (333). Earlier, he tells Kat his story in the paper won't stop the development of the bay, but "it will cut Elmo back down to size" (299). When Wing has his final confrontation with Bliss, he tells him "You're half the size you were last summer. And one day it will be half of that, and then halved again" (333). He has cut Bliss back just like the yard man cut back the "strangle vine."

Wing figures out that while Bliss and his partners are motivated by greed and the lust for power in their move to fill in the bay, the general public is willing to go along because of fear, fear that the tourists will stop coming, that one day they just will not show up at all:

And this hidden fear, Jimmy realized, was one of the reasons—perhaps the most pertinent reason—for the Grassy Bay project. Once you had consistently eliminated most of the environmental features that has initially attracted a large tourist trade, the unalterable climate still made it a good place to live. New permanent residents would bolster the economy. And so, up and down the coast, the locals leaned over backward to make everything as easy and profitable as possible for the speculative land developers. Arvida went into Sarasota; General Development went into Port Charlotte. And a hundred other operators converged on the 'sun coast,' platting the swamps and sloughs, clearing the palmetto scrub lands, laying out and constructing the suburban slums of the future (24)

Palm City may be fictional, but it is typical of the small towns along Florida's southwest coast such as Sarasota, Bradenton, Venice, Englewood, Port Charlotte, Ft. Myers and Naples. MacDonald also sets up Grassy Bay as an example of a trend rather than an isolated incident, showing not only its uniqueness, but also its similarity, what it holds in common with the rest of the Gulf Coast, and indeed most of the state.

Attributing these sensibilities to the author instead of the characters in the novel goes against the tradition of typical literary critique, but these observations about the environment that come through Wing's eyes and those of the omnipotent narrator are clearly those of the author. As MacDonald himself once said on this subject, "Every writer is going to put into the mouths of the people he wants you to respect opinions that he thinks are respectable. It's that simple" (Hirshberg 79).

This onrush of growth and the changes it has wrought on the environment also demands a high price sociologically. It alters the patterns of the rituals that take place there. John Brinckerhoff Jackson tells us that the expression "sense of place" is taken from the translation of a Latin term genius loci:

The phrase thus implied celebration or ritual, and the location itself acquired a special status. . . .We now use the current version to describe the atmosphere of a place, the quality of its environment. Nevertheless, we recognize that certain localities have an attraction which gives us a certain indefinable sense of well-being and which we want to return to time and again. So that original notion of ritual, of repeated celebration or reverence, is still inherent in the phrase (157-158).

MacDonald shows us that as a place's environment becomes corrupted, so do its rituals:

The more the beach eroded away, or disappeared into private ownership, the more bravely the huge highway signs proclaimed the availability of miles of white-sand beaches. As the shallow-water fishing decreased geometrically under the attrition of dredging, filing, sewage and too many outboard motors, they paid to have the superb fishing advertised, and backed contests which would further decimate the dwindling fish population. As the quiet and primitive mystery of the broad tidal bays disappeared, as the mangroves and the rookeries and the oak hammocks were uprooted with such industriousness the morning sound of construction equipment became more familiar than the sound of the mockingbird, the businessmen substituted the delights of pageants, parades and beauty contests (24).

This change of ritual is elaborated on later in the book in an analogy given of Florida's development by a former high school science teacher of Wing's:

"Every place seems to have to make the same mistake, just as if it had never been made before. The fast buck. It's an illusion, Wing. Can't they come and see and understand what's happening to St. Petersburg Beach and Clearwater? Or what's happening to Bradenton or Sarasota? This whole coast used to be a shallow-water paradise. Spoiling it is so idiotic. A friend of mine made a very neat analogy about it. Once upon a time there was a mountain peak with a wonderful view, so that people came from all over to stand on top of the mountain and look out. The village at the foot of the mountain charged a dollar a head to all tourists. But so few of them could stand on top of the mountain the same time, they leveled the top of the mountain to provide more room and increase the take. This seemed to work, so they kept enlarging the area on top of the mountain. Finally they had a place up there that would accommodate ten thousand people, but by then the mountain was only forty feet high, and suddenly everybody stopped coming to see the view. This convinced them people were tired of views, so in the name of Progress and a

Tourist Economy, they turned the flattened mountain into a carnival area, and every night you could see the lights and hear the music for miles around. They still attracted customers, but it was the kind of people who like carnivals instead of the kind of people who like beauty."

"There's more people who like carnivals," Jimmy said.

"'A fact the beauty-lovers find it hard to stomach" (189)

MacDonald certainly had plenty of examples to draw from for his image of carnivals: the high-rise hotel playground of Miami Beach, the garish commercialization of Florida's natural springs such as the dancing mermaids of Weeki Wachee Springs and the acrobatic water skiers of Cypress Gardens, not to mention the various alligator farms, snake zoos, shell factories and other assorted roadside attractions.

But his analogy in a book published a decade before Walt Disney World opened in a former cow pasture just south of Orlando is eerily prescient. Today that city's proximity to this huge "carnival" and its attendant imitators is in the minds of many the single most distinguishing factor in defining Central Florida, if not the whole state.

MacDonald also adds a subtle twist in his analogy when he says that the villagers became convinced that the reason for the fall off in business was because "people were tired of views." One of the key strategies of the developers is to convince the good citizens of Palm City that the bay is actually a pretty dismal and potentially dangerous health hazard. Bliss explains to Wing why the average man and woman will be glad to see the bay filled in.

"All the damn bird watchers and do-gooders and nature boys, they got an abstraction they've fell in love with. But the average man, you tell him that bay is a mess of mud flats likely to make his kids sick, he won't see anything pretty in it, and he won't want to save it" (93).

As Siry tells us in *Marshes*, the belief among policy makers that tidal marshes were breeding grounds for disease held sway from the late 1700s right on through to the beginning of the twentieth century (112). And while modern science has shown that coastal wetlands are well worthy of preservation, such prejudices die hard "The expansion of wisdom is a difficult task for an individual, let alone a society," Siry adds (135).

MacDonald's careful use of names also reinforces the novel's ecological themes. By using the name Grassy Bay, MacDonald evokes Douglas's *River of Grass*. Kat and its feline suggestion help reinforce the natural innocence of Kat and her passion for protecting the bay. She is threatened and despoiled by a man's blind lust just as is the bay. Wing's name is also taken from nature, but it is only a single wing–Jimmy is like a bird with a broken wing, emotionally and morally incomplete, not fully functional, and not in sync with his natural environment. The name Bliss brings to mind the adage "ignorance is Bliss."

This characteristic is reinforced when MacDonald has one of the minor characters define the bay and its importance in scientific terms. Wing goes to interview one of the supporters of the Save Our Bays group who opposes the filling of the bay. In explaining why it would be "criminal" to fill in the bay, an amateur biologist named Doris Rowell says: "We know painfully little about the world we live in. This is a living laboratory. Each new environmental fact is important to mankind." Rowell goes on to explain that the world is out of balance and we "have a plague of men." Explaining that by watching the ebb and flow of life forms in the bay, one can see how some species will flourish for a while then conditions will change and that species will die off or dwindle in population while another species becomes dominate. The same is happening with man on earth. "He is poisoning the air and waters of the earth. He is breeding beyond reason. He is devouring the earth and other creatures thereon. But it will come to an end, of course. Man has a longer cycle than do the small creatures." She also argues that those who advocate filling in the bay are demonstrating a monumental ignorance.

"It is like rubbing out one factor in a vastly complex equation. Due to the interrelationship of bird life, insect life and plant fertilization, the known characteristics of that area will change. To what? We do not know. I recognize a deity of interrelationships, of checks and balances. Acts such as this are like spitting in the face of God. It is, in essence, stupidity, nonknowing, the most precarious condition of man. Filling this bay is a part of the same pattern of throwing away everything you do not understand" (170-171).

MacDonald is careful here to put these words in the mouth of a woman who, though she means well, has a checkered past that comes back to haunt her, and in the end she suffers a nervous breakdown. She is another example of one of the broken ones about whom MacDonald likes to write.

But her environmental views are somewhat extreme and are reminiscent of environmental activist Edward Abbey, who Jackson quotes as having once said: "I would rather kill a man than a snake" (88).

The novelist is clearly advocating a particular and specific point of view about the environment, yet he also manages to give the reader examples of a wide variety of environment views—both pro and con. The intensely personal experience in connecting to nature, an experience that borders on a spiritual revelation, is found when Kat Hubble talks about the first time she realized how much she appreciated the bay.

She is out one early morning in the midst in a small boat with her husband and children, seeing the fish, the birds, the wind, all converge in a single feeling, "and that was the moment when I began to love this place" (15). She is the most sympathetic character in the book, the one without sin, and when Jimmy Wing tells her the proponents will argue that the Grassy Bay development will mean a broader tax base, more jobs and $16 million of new investment in the community, Kat counters that the bay belongs to "all of the people, all the people who don't have a prayer of every owning a home there, or making any profit off it. It belongs to all the people now living in the state and all the future generations, and this takes it away from them forever, and turns it into eight hundred pieces of private land. It's like stealing it from the public" (129).

Kat suffers much the same fate as the bay. Wing, who has become sexually obsessed with her, ends up nearly raping her, and the reader is left with the impression that Wing—who clearly represents the general public attitude—has become a victim of his own indifference and selfishness. He eventually arrives at some form of redemption and manages to get into the newspaper a story that outlines Bliss's ambition, manipulation and complicity in terrorizing those who opposed him. But Wing also must confess his own role in aiding that terror—just as the public must ultimately take responsibility for the protection of natural resources.

Bliss's ambition to take the money he plans to make on the Grassy Bay deal and finance a run for the governor's office parallels Wing's growing obsession with Kat. Bliss tells us what his own notion of bliss is when he talks about the bay. "I would sure as hell miss the money I'm going to make out of it. I'd want to lay down and cry if it went bad on me. I got to have it, and it's not an abstraction, fella. It's the most actual thing there is in the world, and I mean to have it, because I got just the right use for it" (109). Elmo's idea of heaven (bliss) is all the trappings of power:

"I want all the pretty things—like people writing down what I say, and motorcycle escorts, sirens, steaks, secretaries, dollar cigars, mahogany boats, clothes tailored to fit, my name in books, little girls fussing to pleasure me. To get it all, and keep it coming, I have to take the right-size bite at the right time" (54).

When Wing finally confesses to Kat what he has done, his shame leads him to one last act of self-destruction. He says his desire for her is "not a very romantic attachment, Kat. Not very civilized, even. Basic. Below the belt. Physical lust. Just a hell of a driving need to have you" (296). The implication of these parallel desires is that Wing's act of violence against Kat and Bliss's act of violence against the environment are both a form of rape.

Eventually, Wing manages a tentative reconciliation with Kat as she forgives him, and from that forgiveness springs some small hope for Wing's redemption, but MacDonald finds little cause for optimism for the fate of his third character, Florida.

At the end of *A Flash of Green*, Wing drives by the bay-fill project, parks his car, and walks down to the water's edge to look out at the dredges. "Both of them were working, both brilliant against the black night in the glare of their floodlights. They made a vast wet gnashing grinding roar. He lit a cigarette. He could see tiny figures moving through the lights on the furthest one" (335). The sound he describes is one of pure destruction. Wing's tiny glow of light from his cigarette is no match for the glare of the floodlights, and mankind has become "tiny" and overwhelmed by this destructive force. The novel ends with this line: "Long after he had crossed to the mainland he fancied that he could still hear the sound of the dredges" (336).

That death knell for Florida's pristine environment will echo throughout the rest of MacDonald's work, through his two other environmentally themed novels, *Condominium* and *Barrier Island*, and through the sociological asides of his Quixotic series hero, Travis McGee. It is a sound that will awaken in the generation of writers who follow—most notably Hiaasen, Hall, and White—the urge to write the next chapter in the saga of a paradise doomed by its own delight.

Chapter Two
Randy Wayne White, The Ecology of the Mystery

In the crowded bar of the Tarpon Lodge, sitting beneath a framed display of the paperback covers of seven of his novels, Randy Wayne White tries to explain why he is no John D. MacDonald. In the world of the Florida mystery writer, comparisons to the creator of Travis McGee are inevitable, and a favorable comparison is a surefire bet to tempt new readers and boost sales.

Prominent on the jacket flyers of more than one White novel is the line from the *Minneapolis Star Tribune* that claims White "has established himself as the successor to John D. MacDonald as the king of the Florida novelists." But White, who appears genuinely uncomfortable in the face of such accolades, demurs. "I know John D. MacDonald, and I admire him very much, and I can tell you, I am no John D. MacDonald. He's way more talented than me."

At the time of this conversation, White's ninth novel, *Twelve Mile Limit*, had reached No. 20 on The *New York Times* best seller list and No. 5 in the *Los Angeles Times* list. (He's currently working on his 21st.) MacDonald's literary influence on White is certainly evident in his books and White makes no secret of the homage he pays to MacDonald and other writers. Yet his relationship to MacDonald goes beyond the written page.

At the time of this interview, White lived in a pale yellow stilt house perched on top of a Calusa Indian mound on Pine Island, a bridge away from Ft. Myers, on the doorstep of the Gulf of Mexico. The rustic wooden structure, with its tin roof and wide porches nestled among the gumbo limbo trees and clumps of palms, is classic old Florida–the kind of place MacDonald would have cherished, and then bemoaned its passing at the hands of the developers.

But the high rises, condos and gated communities have yet to invade this postcard perfect slice of the Sunshine State. The sign on White's screen door asks visitors to "Please respect the writing schedule, 7 a.m. to 3 p.m.," and the bar at Rob and Phyllis Wells's Tarpon Lodge is just across the street.

Next door to the Lodge is the Mote Marine Laboratory (a convenient resource for a writer whose main character is a marine biologist), and in back of that is White's dock where he parks his dark blue twenty-one-foot Maverick flats-fishing boat with its 225-horsepower Mercury outboard, a boat he would describe in one of his novels as having the qualities of both "roadster and dragster" (*Everglades* 16). Nearly everything in this scene has made its way into White's novels. And it was from this house, sometime in the mid-1970s, that White would begin the journey into the world of John D. MacDonald.

"Two of my friends were big fans of his," White said, "read every book, and one of those friends was renting this house I now live in. We were sitting around, talking, and, I might say, drinking a bit, when we decided to get in the boat and see if we could go up to Siesta Key and find MacDonald.

"Yeah, like this was such a great idea, right? Anyway, we got there, and even then it was pretty well built up, and we didn't know where he lived. It was getting late, and it stated getting windy, and we knew we needed to be getting back soon. So we turned around, and saw a guy in an aluminum boat, and asked him, 'do you know where this guy the writer, John D. MacDonald, lives?' He says, 'sure, he lives right there.' We were right off his house. We pulled into his little, tiny harbor, and got out and he sticks his head out the door–if it had been me, I'd have called the cops–and invites us in. He couldn't have been kinder or more generous. And we ended up making a trip up there to see him and his wife about once a year, almost always unannounced."

This was the beginning of a friendship that would last until MacDonald died in 1986. Occasionally White would join MacDonald in a restaurant in downtown Sarasota where he would meet once a week with his cadre of fellow writers, including MacKinley Kantor and Richard Glendinning, to play liar's poker. "You play with dollar bills and your hand is based on the serial numbers. I'm not very quick with games and I think I won two or three times before I found out I didn't know the rules and was probably cheating. MacDonald looked at me and said: 'You did that once; don't ever do that again'."

The last time White heard from MacDonald was in a letter written on Travis McGee stationary in which MacDonald tells White that he is going up the St. Mary's Hospital in Milwaukee for heart surgery. Although doctors had told MacDonald that there was only a 5 to 8 percent risk for the operation, he came down with pneumonia after the surgery and never recovered (Merrill 219).

Three months later, on December 28, 1986, John D. MacDonald died. By then, White had already started his writing career, first as a journalist for *Outside Magazine*, an adventure magazine started by *Rolling Stone*, and then by publishing eighteen adventure novels under a pair of pseudonyms.

In 1981 and 1982, he wrote seven books using the pen name Randy Striker, all featuring a series character named Dusty MacMorgan, with titles such as *Key West Connection; The Deadlier Sex, Everglades Assault and Grand Cayman Slam*. From 1984 through 1987, using the name Carl Ramm, White wrote an additional eleven novels featuring a character called Hawker. Taking his cue from MacDonald, who used a different color in each title of his Travis McGee series, White uses the names of places to link his Hawker series: *Florida Firefight, L.A. Wars, Chicago Assault, Deadly in New York, and Operation Norfolk.*

When White started his Doc Ford novels, this time under his own name, he choose the same scheme, this time each novel's title is a place in Florida: *Sanibel Flats, Captiva, Shark River, Everglades, Ten Thousand Islands, The Mangrove Coast, The Heat Islands, The Man Who Invented Florida, Twelve Mile Limit* and *North of Havana* (a common phrase in Cuba referring to Florida.)

When asked if he had ever talked to MacDonald about writing, White said, "Not really. I like to think that, to my everlasting credit, I never told him I wanted to write novels."

White's earlier work under pen names was quickly written and quickly forgotten, and the author's own distaste for them shows up in one signed copy of *Florida Firefight* offered on the internet with the inscription "Randy White--This Book is Shitty!" Critics apparently agreed: "The plots of these novels are all too predictable: sharks, crooks, and soft pornography fill these pages. Although some readers might find escape in these novels, though-provoking images or ideas are scarce if not non-existent" (Nugent and Nugent 88).

Bad as they were, these early novels allowed White to sharpen his skills and four years after MacDonald died, White published under his own name *Sanibel Flats*, which ten years later, was selected by the Independent Mystery Booksellers Association as one of the top 100 Mystery Novels of the Century, along with Carl Hiaasen's first solo novel, *Tourist Season*, and MacDonald's first Travis McGee book, *The Deep Blue Goodbye.*

White grew up in small town America. Born in 1950, the year MacDonald published his first novel, White spent his formative years in a "little tiny village in northwest Ohio called Pioneer," he recalled. "The school I went to from kindergarten to the tenth grade had less than two hundred kids." Both of his parents and most of his relatives, however, were from North Carolina, where White spent his summers. "I was very much a Yankee part of the year and deep fried southern the other part."

His father was a World War II veteran who served in the U.S. Army's 101st Airborne, a "very tough guy" who became a highway patrolman. Both of his parents quit school in the eighth grade, "so education wasn't a big part of my family," he said.

White's appreciation for nature and his environmental sensitivities came from his mother, who "loved the outdoors, natural history, Indian lore and she liked to hunt for herbs. My great grandmother was born in Cherokee, North Carolina–I guess all that was just part of my heritage."

When White was in his junior year of high school, his parents moved to Iowa for a short time, then back to Ohio, but White stayed in the

Midwest to finish out his senior year and lived on a farm with family friends. After graduating, he "bummed around for three or four years," then came to Florida. In 1972 he got a job working as a copy editor for the *Ft. Myers News Press*.

"I kind of got bit by the writing bug," but two years later, at the age of twenty-two, he got his captain's license and started a fishing guide business out of Tarpon Bay Marina on Sanibel Island. For the next thirteen years through more than three thousand charters, he would cruise and fish Florida's Southwest Coast, learning the land and the waters as well as his trade and occasionally writing essays and stories for *Outside Magazine*.

"They kept me in the writing business. Every six or seven months, I'd do a piece for them, something for the cause." White would end up traveling the world, chronicling his adventures.

He wrote about learning Spanish in a two-week cram course in Costa Rica, finding the world's best-tasting green chili pepper sauce on an Island off the coast of Cartagena, Columbia; racing toboggans in Camden, Maine; and being chase by orangutans in Borneo. In a Key West celebration of Ernest Hemingway, White got into the boxing ring with Papa's former sparing partner, the 80-year-old Kermit "Shine" Forbes, who, with apparently little effort, dispatched White with a knockout in the third round.

White's career as a fishing guide ended abruptly in 1987 when the marina out of which he worked closed down. "I remember having a garage sale and my much adored ex-wife [Debra] and I looking for change beneath the seats of the car–that's how desperate it got." Although he was still writing for *Outside Magazine* and had in that same year published his eleventh Hawker novel, *Operation Norfolk*, White decided it was time to start a new, more ambitious, series, which this time he would publish under his own name.

In Marion "Doc" Ford, White created a hero as sophisticated and as complex as the environment he inhabits. To his neighbors who live in and around Dinkins Bay Marina on Florida's Southwest coast, Ford is a quiet, bespeckled marine biologist, content doing research on sharks and tarpons, squids and octopuses, puttering around on his Permit flats boat, collecting specimens from the tide pools and estuaries, a man whose "idea of a home entertainment center is a six-pack of beer and a dead fish" (*Sanibel Flats* 38).

Beneath this mild-mannered, Clark Kent facade, however, is a man who spent "years living a life of professional deceit" (7) as a member of a small, elite group of espionage agents, a "super-select special warfare, intelligence-gathering unit that operated at the President's pleasure and answered only to his administrators." It was privately financed, so the operatives were civilians, and thus unfettered by the normal restraints of such government-backed organizations as the National Security Agency, the Central Intelligence Agency or the Federal Bureau of Investigation. In reality, it had become "an international spy ring, deep cover reconnaissance, espionage, sabotage, political terrorism . . . and assassinations" (*Shark River* 121-122). Commander Ford himself is credited with thirteen assassinations, ten of those by his own hand, his acknowledged weapon of choice. A psychological profile of a typical candidate for this group is "a man without conscience, or at least one who had the ability to repress emotions that many believe are key to a healthy, well-adjusted human being" (124).

In each of the Doc Ford novels, White uses the theme of Ford's attempt to come to terms with his past as a springboard to explore the kinds of topics that are the hallmark of serious fiction: the search for self identity and meaning in the world; the need for love, friendship, loyalty and spirituality; the longing for a sense of community; the necessity of understanding the relationship between humans and their physical environment; and the struggle with the moral and ethical ambiguities that confront us all.

Ford constantly looks to nature to provide insight into human behavior, but his pragmatic approach and absolute faith that reason and reason alone is the path to clarity often is at odds with the world around him. Near the beginning of *Flats*, he feels no grief when he finds Rafe Hollins, one of his best friends from childhood, hung up by his neck in a mangrove thicket on a small island the two used as a playground when they were kids. He wonders about that lack of emotional reaction and remembers a friend telling him:

You've got a cold, cold eye, Ford . . .The way you study all the data trying to make it fit because you won't abide anything that can't be weighed or measured. Trouble is, some things don't fit, never will fit, but you still go plunking along collecting pieces, weighing the evidence, trying to neaten up a world that seems way too emotional and untidy (20).

Ford believes half of this assessment is "pure invention" but the part about the cold eye makes him pensive:

Maybe his eyes had grown cold; maybe he'd always been cold. Or maybe four years in West Africa, a year in South America and five years in Central America had leached away most of the emotional niceties. But Ford didn't believe that, not really (20).

The dichotomy between Ford's assessment of himself as a rational, unemotional man and his often emotional behavior lends an ironic complexity to the novels, particularly in a character who prides himself in seeing past the illusions of both his natural and social environment to seek the truth of things. When Ford explains that mangroves, when seen from a distance, give the impression "of lushness and shadow that one associates with fresh water," he calls it an "illusion."

Mangroves denote harsh sunlight, salt and sulfur. When it comes to dependence on the chemical processes of the tropics, mangroves are as basic as lightning or ozone. . . .Mangroves are creatures of muck and equatorial heat. Because of the primeval conditions in which they thrive, they are trees that seem more intimately related to the basic procedures of cellular life. It is one of the reasons that I am an admirer of mangroves. I am not troubled by illusions that I understand (*The Mangrove Coast* 13).

The illusions that Ford does not understand, however, are what drive these novels.

White gives Ford a rich heritage of literary and cultural icons. He is Ian Fleming's James Bond, trading his Austin Martin for a Chevy pickup and his license to kill for a license to fish. He is Travis McGee, uprooted from his houseboat at Bahia Mar Marina in Ft. Lauderdale and transported straight across Alligator Ally to a stilt house at Dinkins Bay on a small island just off the coast of Ft. Myers. He is John Wayne in a flats boat. And he is John Steinbeck's inimitable Doc of Cannery Row. In Ford's lover and mother of his child, we see the ghost of Ernest Hemingway and in Ford's side-kick Tomlinson, White tips his hat to English novelist and travel writer H.M. Tomlinson.

Given White's personal friendship with MacDonald, it is little wonder that Doc Ford bears more than a passing resemblance to Travis McGee. But even if White had never met MacDonald, the influence of MacDonald's work is difficult to ignore for any writer who attempts to dip his or her paddle into the same waters of the Florida eco-mystery genre MacDonald so skillfully created and dominated.

To quote one observer: "To say that John D. Macdonald is not a literary titan misses the point. . . .What he is is the best American writer of the classical genre mystery in the postwar era and possibly the century" (Glassman 12).

Unlike Ross MacDonald, who pays homage to Dashiell Hammett by simply naming his hero Lew Archer after Sam Spade's partner, Miles Archer, White pays homage to John D. MacDonald through a series of devices. Both Ford and McGee live in South Florida marinas, McGee on a house boat and Ford in a stilt house that White describes in *The Heat Islands* as "half like a boat, half like a house" (19). One of Ford's marina neighbors, fishing guide Jeth Nicholes, names his boat Jacks or Better (*Flats* 33), a not-so-subtle reference to McGee's houseboat Busted Flush.

In White's third novel, *The Man Who Invented Florida*, Ford decides to relax for a while and do some reading, "kick back with John D.

MacDonald" (234). And in one of White's more clever clues, he has Ford make a seemingly odd reference to a particular song that taps into three different cultural icons. "He stepped on the dock thinking he could use a few beers, just as in the song, wondering where he had been on that day, the day that John Wayne died' (Flats 32) The tune is "Incommunicado," written and performed by Florida-based troubadour Jimmy Buffett.

The song begins with these words: "Travis McGee's still in Cedar Key/That's what John MacDonald said." (Liner notes from album). White also used this same reference in a later work *Everglades*. As Ford idles up to his dock, he "could hear Jimmy Buffett singing about one particular harbor, and the day that John Wayne died" (17).

In addition to the similar Florida settings of both Ford and McGee, one of the strongest references to MacDonald comes in *The Heat Islands*, in which the fishing guide Jeth Nicholes, who is wrongly accused of murder, tells Ford and Ford's closest friend, Tomlinson, about seeing the green flash. "It was like a sign," Nicholes says. "That's just the way I felt, not seeing it my entire life, then finally seeing it. Like it meant something big. A great big flash outta nowhere" (69). Ford, in his usual methodical, scientific way, dismisses any symbolic meaning to the flash of green:

It has something to do with the distance sunlight travels at the earth's horizon. The light travels farther, something like that. The distance bends and separates the light, makes the sun seem visible after it has already sunk below the horizon. If conditions are just right, the yellow of the sun mixes with the blue of the sea, and it's like a chemical reaction. Volatile. Like an explosion; a flash of green. But the atmosphere has to be perfectly clear. I've seen it in other places in the world, but only twice in Florida. Once at sunrise, once at sunset, and that was years ago, before all the cars. With the monoxide fumes, you don't see it."
[Tomlinson says] "You're telling me it needs a pure canvas?"
"Well, in a way, yeah."
"O-o-o-oh, this is great. I have heard of it. Only I thought I dreamed it. The perfect metaphor. Nature's little litmus test–tells you when she's healthy by flashing you the green light..." (71-72).

By evoking MacDonald's seminal work of eco-fiction, *A Flash of Green*, White not only acknowledges MacDonald's artistry, but implies that this new series of his own work will continue the tradition of exploring the duality of "the perfect metaphor:" Florida's pristine natural environment and the ignorance, greed and indifference that threatens to destroy it.

The John Wayne reference in Buffett's song is not significant enough by itself to imply that Ford is a hero in the same vein as Wayne, and although White freely admits the homage to Wayne, saying, "He's a great American. My father admired him very much," the reference is not meant to suggest that White's own middle name of Wayne has anything to do with the actor. "I was named after Waynesville, North Carolina, the home of my mother's family." White says.

Instead, White gives the reader several references that not only give a solid link to John Wayne but in one case also circles back and makes a connection between Wayne and MacDonald. First of all, Ford's first name is Marion, which is John Wayne's real first name (Marion Morrison.) Wayne's closest friends called him Duke, a nickname also used for Ford by the man who raised him, his uncle Tucker Gatrell, (*The Man Who Invented Florida* 12).

Secondly, Ford's first love and the mother of his child is named Pilar–as is the name of Wayne's third wife. And thirdly, in *The Green Ripper*, the nineteenth McGee novel, there is a reference to John Wayne that explores an unusual aspect of the hero's character that Ford also exhibits.

To avenge the death of his lover, Gretel Howard, McGee infiltrates a terrorist training camp in California run by a cult of religious extremists who are preparing to bomb bridges, chemical plants, oil pipelines and television stations. In the climax, McGee, in trying to escape, kills two of the terrorists, and then he systematically kills the rest–eleven in all. Instead of the remorse and self recriminations MacDonald usually gives McGee when he examines his own tendencies toward violence, he gives his hero a sense of exhilaration and calls it:

". . . a John Wayne day." He goes on to describe it as "a veritable massacre. A bloodbath. Butchery. I kept the horror bottled away . . .Right now there was the high-riding pleasure of doing some difficult thing far better than you expected to be able to do it" (247-248). McGee discovers a primal emotion released by the intensity of the violence. "With the ghastly toothy grin of the skull head of death looking over my shoulder, I was intensely alive. I was alive in every thready little nerve fiber, every capillary" (248).

As MacDonald biographer David Geherin illustrates in his examination of this scene, MacDonald transforms McGee "into one of those Avenger-Revenger-Destroyer-Executioner types who go around single-handedly mopping up nasty problems they judge the government too powerless to solve. McGee's previous adventures have shown him to be temperamentally (and ethically) unfit for such a role . . ." (148). This is a description that also seems to fit Ford to a tee. In an article MacDonald wrote about his critics in the journal JDM Bibliophile, he explains that he wanted to "shake up" McGee in *Ripper*:

I am trying to open up his world a little bit, to what is going on. In the bright Florida sunshine it is difficult to believe that a flock of school teachers in Iran would pour gasoline around a movie house and incinerate 450 people, mostly children. I have indulged in a lot of social, pseudo-realism in the McGee books.

Now I wanted to try a little bit of the taste of international political realities. (11).

McGee twice refers to the slaughter as "having a John Wayne Day" (243 and 248), prompting Geherin to conclude that "the whole episode is treated like a scene from a low-budget Hollywood movie: the good guy in the white hat standing off all those black-hatted bad guys" (147). For White, however, the reference to McGee's "John Wayne day" and Ford's own namesake connection to John Wayne is less about the movies than it is about motive. In Ripper, we find a part of McGee whose nature is very similar to that of Ford's. Throughout all of the Doc Ford novels, the hero struggles to come to terms with the part of his psyche that allows him to kill without emotion. In *North of Havana*, Ford finds himself face to face with his Russian equivalent–an agent named Guis–and describes their relationship and the nature of the professional killer in biological and genetic terms:

His position, my position, were both the senseless pantomime of a vanished death dance; a pointless ceremony that was still embraced by a political theater of the absurd. For a thousand millennia we sharpened sticks or rocks into weapons and we stalked and we hunted and we killed because that is what the strongest and the fittest of us did. Those who were incapable did not contribute to the chromosomal mandate because they did not survive. It is what the genetic memory of a thousand millennia told us to do, what it still tells us to do (169).

Ford could easily be describing McGee in *a*. Later, when Guis has Ford in his sights and asks Ford if he would kill his opponent if the situation was reversed, Ford says, "No. . . Because I grew up" (173). Ford wants to believe he has evolved into a different kind of man. Yet in subsequent novels, Ford is drawn back into the world of the professional assassin and is finally forced to admit to himself that there is something about those "John Wayne days" that are irresistible.

In *Twelve Mile Limit*, Ford encounters another fellow traveler, this time an unabashed admire of Commander Ford's, a ruthless madman named Curtis Tyner, who operates his own little assassin empire in the rain forests of Columbia. Ford is forced to enlist Tyner's help to rescue friends (and a lover) of Ford's from white slave traders. Tyner is the kind of man who collects the shrunken heads of his vanquished enemies; a man Ford cannot imagine being anything like in any way. When Tyner asks Ford why he prefers to use his hands to kill his targets, Ford answers:

He knew too much for me not to answer–and it would have seemed an infidelity to the person I hoped and believed I'd now become: the quiet biologist who loved to work in his lab, the guy who delighted in sunset beers with his many friends back on Sanibel Island. . .I let myself think about it for several long beats before I said in a more reflective voice, "I chose that way, that method because. . . because it was more. . .because it was more personal "(284).

Tyner misunderstands Ford, believing that his answer means that Ford enjoys the killing. Later, when Ford finally catches up with the last of the bad guys, we discover that he prefers to kill in such an intimate way because of his own sense of guilt.

His final words to his victim are "I'm sorry" (311). However, when Ford is safely back at Dinkins Bay, he comes to the realization that he cannot ignore that biological imperative to play the roll of the one who culls the herd, the roll of professional assassin.

"I had seen myself in another incarnation, and my name was Curtis Tyner. As much as I'd fought the truth, I'd proven it true. As much as I hated the truth, I now had no choice but to acknowledge it. It was not an easy thing to live with, yet I would have to find a way to do exactly that for the rest of my life" (313).

When Ford sets aside his emotions and picks up his gun, he could very well be saying exactly what McGee says at the onset of his killing spree in *Ripper*: "For this caper, I am the iceman"(238) Here, Ford is McGee.

Of course Ford is not just an assassin; he is also Doc, that "quiet biologist who loved to work in his lab, the guy who delighted in sunset beers with his many friends. . . ." And for the genesis of that character, White turned to one of his favorite authors, John Steinbeck.

Ford runs a "small company called Sanibel Biological Supply, selling marine specimens, alive or preserved, to schools and research firms around the county" (*Captiva* 3). Doc in *Cannery Row* is "the owner and operator of Western Biological Laboratory" which sells "the lovely animals of the sea" and "for the students there are the sharks with the blood drained out and yellow and blue color substituted in veins and arteries, so that you may follow the systems with a scalpel" (369).

Over a period of years "Doc had dug himself into Cannery Row to an extent not even he suspected. He became the fountain of philosophy and science and art . . . Doc would listen to any kind of nonsense and change it for you into a kind of wisdom. His mind had no horizon—and his sympathy had no warp . . . Everyone who knew him was indebted to him" (371).

Back at Dinkins Bay " . . .there was beer and consoling conservation to be had at Ford's stilt house. Ford became the trusted dispenser of first aid, wisdom, reluctant medical diagnoses, and unwilling advice on everything from love to law to broken timing chains . . . His rapid climb to position in the community surprised no one more than Ford . . . ."(*Sanibel Flats* 7). White is by no means a plagiarist. But in terms that Ford would surely understand, a DNA test of both biologists would prove paternity beyond a reasonable doubt. When asked who his literary influences are, the first word out of White's mouth is "Steinbeck." The second is "Hemingway."

In *Flats*, White introduces Pilar Santana Fuentes Balserio, the wife of the president of the fictional Central American country of Masagua. She is Ford's lover and will eventually take over the country after rebels kill her dictator husband, whom she had married at the age of "twenty-one, abandoning an already brilliant academic career at the Universidad de Costa Rica to fulfill a marriage contract arranged by her father" (100).

She becomes an expert in the government, the power behind the throne, and both the military and the people "loved and admired her." (103) At the end of the novel, she helps save Ford when he goes back to Masagua to rescue the kidnapped eight-year-old son of his friend. White manages to use the name Pilar to evoke both John Wayne and Hemingway, whose novel *For Whom the Bell Tolls* features a Spanish peasant girl named Pilar who, like White's heroine, gains control over a weak husband and leads his followers into battle.

The book takes place during the Spanish Civil War and is considered by critics to be one of Hemingway's best novels. In a scene that is often cited as a one of the best examples of Hemingway's descriptive style, Pilar tells American Robert Jordan the story of how the rebels captured a group of fascists and executed them by beating them to death and throwing them over a cliff. (118-138) In *Flats*, White crafts a similar scene in which a sadistic rebel leader Zacul, who heads the ultra-leftists group El Dictamen, tortures his captives and throws them from a cliff (261). At the very end of the novel, Ford learns that Pilar has given birth to his son.

By paying homage to writers such as Hemingway, Steinbeck and MacDonald, and to such cultural icons as John Wayne and his most creative film director John Ford (who shares the same surname as White's hero) White creates a character whose fictional heritage in one of great storytellers. At the same time, by setting great stories against the backdrop of Florida's environmental struggles, White continues in the tradition set by MacDonald and carried on into the twenty-first century by Hall and Hiaasen.

In *Everglades*, Ford makes the comment: "As a marine biologist I am also, necessarily, an environmentalist" (208). This statement hardly comes as a surprise to anyone familiar with White's Doc Ford series. From the very first pages in which Ford appears, White reveals a world of human and biological ecologies that serve as complimentary metaphors which he skillfully integrates into the story. When Ford describes his home base in *Flats*, he is describing a sociological ecosystem: "All marinas are more than the sum total of docks and property, bait wells, ship's stores, and receipts. They are communities; ephemeral colonies with personalities as varied as the individuals who form them" (7). In *The Heat Islands*, Ford recovers a dead body from the water, and while he waits for the Coast Guard to arrive, he looks down into the shallows and sees a multitude of creatures, and then says "the bottom was alive, one continuous interconnecting cycle, everything going on simultaneously and without pause; egg, sperm, death and decay; all obliquely keyed by tides and heat and a million years of having survived" (4).

The description of what Ford sees beneath the surface of the water serves as a metaphor for the complex relationships in a marina, and by extension, the wider world in which he lives. The dead body that sets in motion the mystery of the novel becomes part of that same "interconnecting cycle," of "egg, sperm, death and decay." In *Flats*, when Ford is on his rescue mission in Central America, he again observes the biological interconnectedness of an ecosystem in a search for frogs:

"It was the mating season, and several of the females had smaller males clinging to their backsides. That made Ford search for something else, and it didn't take him long to find the glutinous deposits of frog's eggs stuck to the undersides of the leaves. Some of the eggs had already matured into tadpoles, and the viscid masses hung in the light like icicles, dripping life into the water below . . .where two–no four–cat-eyed snakes waited, feeding on the globs of tadpoles in a frenzy. Ford watched the snakes feeding, taking an odd pleasure in knowing that this same drama was going on all around him; the same cycle of copulation, birth, and death; the same earnest theater being played out by jaguars, dung flies, tapirs, leaf-cutter ants, crocodiles, boas, and men throughout the millions of acres of jungle darkness (197).

White again uses those same images of eggs, birth, death and the endless cycle of reproduction. By using these observations, White reinforces the plot of the story since Ford wants to put the poison from those frogs into the soup served to the rebels who not only have kidnapped the boy but also are destroying the ecology of the mountainside in their search for Mayan relics.

In the final battle with the rebels, White marries the drama of the "earnest theater" of the tide pool to the same struggle for life and death among the jungle's two-legged creatures with a single, striking simile when he sees: " . . . a Soviet gunship, its blades folded like wilted petals, rockets clinging to its underbelly like eggs on a gravid crab" (234)

The frog poison leads to a particularly horrific death for most of the rebels, but Ford and the boy survive. Not only has White used the ecology of the jungle pond to reflect and illuminate the life and death struggle of the characters in his novel, but he also creates a Dantesque poetic justice for the villains who are dispatched by an element of the very ecosystem they are trying to destroy.

Here White elaborates on a theme explored by MacDonald in his novel *Condominium*, which centers on a massive hurricane that destroys most of a small key off the Southwest Coast of Florida. One of the retirees who live in the Golden Sands Condominium, Thelma Mensenkott, gets into the habit of going into a small tangle of natural growth next door to the condo. She has become somewhat of an amateur naturalist, thinking of herself as an objective observer, but that feeling begins to change:

> She relaxed and in the next few magical minutes she became part of what she saw and heard and smelled. She sat amid a complex unity, an exquisitely balanced pattern of interwoven, interdependent life forms. Around her was a veritable furnace of birthing and dying, a soft roaring of consumption, consummation, growth and contest, the heats of decay, the ripeness of blossoming. At first she was only a witness to the life around her, and then she became aware of herself, of her body, as part of it too. Within her was a ferment of microorganisms, dreadful combat, birthing of cells, and the gases and stinks of decay. She was a miniature of the miniature world around her, caught up in life rhythms independent of thought and mood. She was a furnace within a furnace, another strand in the complexity, a growing churning dying part of all wildness. This sense of unity was a revelation which shook her. She knew she had never felt at home in her body because she had never clearly identified herself with all the processes of life and death. She was a life form supporting within herself billions of smaller life forms dependent upon her for food and shelter just as the live oak under her rump was haven for spiders and moths and bugs under its skin of bark. She would die as would the tree, and their substance would fuel and provision other life forms in a chain too complex to ever comprehend (139).

Developers eager to build a new condominium come in early one morning and strip this small jungle bare, which nearly destroys Thelma. This act is also a key factor in the destruction of the entire island when the hurricane comes, because the bare stretch of land opens the way for tidal waves to gain a foothold and eventually bring down the condominium and wipe clean the entire island, killing dozens of people. The message of *Condominium* is that the consequences of abusing the environment and not understanding our complex relationship to it will ultimately lead to disaster.

MacDonald's "veritable furnace of birthing and dying, a soft roaring of consumption, consummation, growth and contest," becomes White's "egg, sperm, death and decay." Thelma's realization of the "sense of unity" between herself and this biological process leads her to understand that she was part of an intricate scheme of things "too complex to ever comprehend." White reinforces this point in the head note to his first Doc Ford novel with the lines from a poem by Edna St. Vincent Millay, "Whether or not we find what we are seeking/Is idle, biologically speaking."

The notion that nature is essentially indifferent to humans is the crucial component in the science of ecology and is one of the linchpins of our modern secular society, yet its Darwinian heritage makes it all the more disturbing because it runs counter to the long-established Christian theology which sees nature as something placed on earth for the service of mankind. In 1967, historian Lynn White Jr. published a groundbreaking and controversial paper in the journal *Science* that laid much of the blame for our current environmental predicament upon the doorstep of Christianity. In that paper White says the message we have gotten from Christianity is:

> that we humans are uniquely created in the image of God, a quality which cuts us out from the rest of creation, making us not only separate but special, and that our role on this earth with regard to the rest of God's creation is to dominate and subdue. Hence, because of these background assumptions, humans feel 'we are superior to nature, contemptuous of it, willing to use it for our slightest whim'. Hence, Christianity not only allows for the anthropogenic exploitation of nature that has resulted in our environmental crisis, it also sanctions and enforces it (Nelson 203).

Randy Wayne White's novels go straight to the heart of these conflicting ideologies of man's relationship to his environment. Ford's antagonists believe they are, as Lynn White, Jr. says, "superior to nature, contemptuous of it, willing to use it for [their] slightest whim," yet Ford is able to defeat them largely became of his understanding of what O'Sullivan calls "the complex nexus of organisms that we constitute." It is this understanding that gives Ford the ability to uncover the truth and clarity needed to survive, and ultimately, triumph.

In most of the Ford novels, the bad guys are developers, driven by greed and the lust for power, and the act that sets the story in motion is often some form of environmental affront.

In *Flats*, Ford sets out to rescue his friend's kidnapped son, encountering along the way a bloodthirsty, psychotic revolutionary; a corrupt county sheriff, a mysterious Mayan artifact and his old lover Pilar. He not only brings Rafe Hollins's son back alive, along the way he manages to wipe out the terrorists in a small Central American country, help put his lover back in the Presidential palace as the spiritual leader of her people (as well as get her pregnant) and almost as an afterthought, cleans up a corrupt pack of bureaucrats and developers who created an island "smothered with a stalagmite jumble of condominiums and the bleak geometrics of planned housing" (122).

The crime that sets all this in motion is a singular attack on the environment. The developers of the fictional Sandy Key order Rafe, a pilot by trade, to spray a deadly poison over the entire island in order to kill the mosquitoes. The outlawed chemical spray also kills thousands of birds, fish and small animals. When Rafe threatens to expose the developers in a desperate attempt to raise ransom money for his son, they try to kill him.

The developer is a classic Florida eco-mystery villain:

Before becoming sheriff of Everglades County, DeArmand had been involved in pyramid schemes. Herbal Foods; Rags-to-Real Estate–two scam corporations disguised as multilevel marketing companies. They bought late-night television time to drum Herbal Foods distributorships and their get-rich-quick real estate course to poor schmucks who never stopped to think: If these people are making so much money selling health food and real estate, why do they want competition from me? DeArmand had been investigated for tax fraud, mail fraud, and conspiracy to defraud the public, but had always found a way to buy his way out. When the quack food business got too hot, DeArmand and his partners pooled the rich profits and bought an island in Florida: Sandy Key (120).

White creates an ecological symmetry here that contrasts the man-made chemical poison and its indiscriminate destruction with his own use of the natural poison of the frogs in a surgical strike against the terrorists.

In *The Heat Islands*, the dead body Ford discovers is Marvin Rios, a greedy marina owner who made a fatal miscalculation by using dynamite to stun fish in hopes of winning forty thousand dollars in a tarpon tournament he himself was sponsoring.

Again, White gives us a good dose of nature's ability to devise a punishment that fits the crime. Rios, we learn on the last page of the novel, was beaten to death by a 400-pound tarpon. Rios "had experienced this creature for what it really was: unyielding, instinctive, and elemental . . . .Ford had a brief mental image of Rios, the night of the storm, lying terrified beneath a tarpon while that fish pounded him to death, trying to find its way back into the water. . . " (307). Along the way to helping prove his friend Jeth Nicholes had nothing to do with the death of Rios, Ford makes observations about the spawning habits of the tarpon (119), the lack of ethics and morals of a Legislature run by attorneys (152) and in the best tradition of Travis McGee, offers a history lesson of Florida:

. . .a chaotic thing built upon thin layers of human endeavor that are covered or quickly absorbed by more thin layers, then forgotten entirely. Because Florida has always appealed to the provisional and the transitory, what has gone before and what inevitably must come have never been of much interest. Which explains many of Florida's ills, and also why Florida has always been the nation's tackiest, glitziest state (230).

Greed-driven developers who twist the law and plunder the environment get plenty of ink from White, but he also singles out short-sighted, power-hungry elected officials, well-meaning but ineffectual bureaucrats and environmental activists who distort their cause for personal gain.

White offers no easy answers. Ford gives thoughtful and well-reasoned arguments on both sides of such complex issues such as the consequences of Florida's net fishing ban (*Captiva*), the destruction of the rainforest in Panama (*The Mangrove Coast*) and a proposed powerboat ban to save the manatees along the waterways of the Southwest Coast (*Twelve Mile Limit*).

On the question of how to stop powerboats from killing manatees, Ford observes: "Most of us are eager fans of the environment, until its maintenance threatens to inconvenience us," and he raises the question, "What is necessary maintenance? And what is symptomatic of very human and predictable attempts by government and nonprofit bureaucrats to expand their power?" The problem for a scientist such as Ford is that "the line has become so broad, so gray, that I sit way, way back and gather all the information I can before choosing sides in any environmental debate"(9).

White believes that "you still see developers as villains, but they don't have free reign anymore, not like they did in MacDonald's day." Today, he says, "It's a new game. It's absolutely insidious. The big corporate industries and environmental groups both will use any scientific fact to support their own cause. They are now doing what the old private industries used to do, like the tobacco industry saying that tobacco is not addictive. That's what I'm trying to take on. The title 'environmentalist' used to have great respect. But now there's been so much misinformation put out by both sides."

In *Limit*, White puts these opinions in the mouth of a Dr. Frieda Matthews, a biologist who was fired by the Save All Manatees group because her findings did not support their claim that the manatee population was dwindling:

"I used to think that I was as radical and green as the come. Not anymore. . . . lately I've been meeting more and more so-called environmentalists who aren't really pro-environment. What they are is anti-human. Anything that has to do with people, they hate. They want to rope it all off, exclude everyone—except themselves, of course. They're enviro-elitists, not environmentalists" (78-79).

White elaborates on this theme in a long passage in his following novel, *Everglades*:

...what is now known as the "environmental movement" began in 1962 with the publication of Rachel Carson's *Silent Spring*. It is a fact that at that time, America's natural resources were in terrible shape. The Great Lakes were so polluted they were unsafe for swimming. Our rivers were such cesspools of chemicals and petroleum waste that they caught fire and burned. In industrial cities, all six of the most dangerous air pollutants tracked by the EPA measured off the scale. Private enterprise and a profit-minded government were slowly killing an entire continent. The environmental movement deserves full credit for changing that.

Half a century later, though, what was once a movement has now become the very thing its founders battled. So called 'environmentalism' has become a profit-driven, power-hungry industry in which private political agendas are more important than biological realities, and monetary objectives excuse any perversion of scientific fact (207).

Ford goes on to tell a story that White swears actually happened.

A few months back, I was talking with someone familiar with Mote Marine, the organization I'm now doing contract work for. He told me that Mote had received an official letter of protest from PETA (People for the Ethical Treatment of Animals) that condemned Mote for housing and studying jellyfish. I'm paraphrasing, but there was a line in the letter that read, "These magnificent creatures should be allowed to roam free in the wild." That a national "environmental" organization could pen a letter so stupid, so childishly ignorant of the species which they referenced, is not just sad, it is frightening. Unthinking extremists have taken possession of what was once a noble title, Environmentalist, and they are destroying our credibility, just as surely as they are giving credence and power to people who use sad phrases such as environmental wackos (207).

Ford finds those same environmentally extreme attitudes among the state and federal officials who are charged with protecting the Everglades. The novel centers around the scheme of Bhagwan Shiva, a murderous religious con-man-turned-developer who wants to make a deal with the Seminole Indians to build casinos and a huge housing and commercial complex on the edge of the Everglades.

As if turning the Glades into another parking lot is not enough, he also plans to set off explosive charges near the proposed site to create a small earthquake. The reason? He wants to win over the Seminoles by predicting the quake, thus proving him to be a prophet like the great Indian leader Tecumseh, who had predicted the worst earthquake in American history in 1811.

When Ford and Tomlinson first see the beginnings of this new development, Casino Lakes, the land is nothing but parched earth, scraped clean by the bulldozers that wiped out two hundred acres of cypress trees. Ford explains how they could do this without getting any permits:

"What could be happening here . . .is what's becoming a sophisticated developer's device. It's so tough to get permits to build anything, developers know it's going to take them months, even years before they'll get the okay on a project. So they've figured out they'll actually save money by going ahead, building anyway, then paying fines later with inflated dollars. There's a whole generation of bureaucrats out there who behave as if people in the private sector are enemies of the state. Which is just idiotic. So it's become like a war–and everybody is losing" (109).

Everglades was published in June 2003, and the tenth in the Doc Ford series. As we have seen, in this novel White gives us a much more subtle and complex view of Florida's environmental problems than in his earlier work. It is Ford himself, however, who goes through the most profound change, one that harkens back to our first introduction to Ford in the opening pages of *Sanibel Flats* and one that has been consistently foreshadowed throughout the series.

As *Everglades* opens, we find Ford with his "own dark cloud hanging over him. Too many bad dreams, too many bad and haunting memories. Too many good people lost" (54). While each of the Ford novels can stand alone, here it is helpful to remember how we left our hero at the end of *Twelve Mile Limit*, where Ford realizes that he had seen his true self in the face of the sadistic professional assassin Curtis Tyner. "As much as I'd fought the truth, I'd proven it true. As much as I hated the truth, I now had no choice but to acknowledge it. It was not an easy thing to live with, yet I would have to find a way to do exactly that for the rest of my life" (313).

In *Everglades*, his black mood has put Ford "in the worst shape of [his] life" (23), recognizing in himself "an uncharacteristic slide toward clinical depression. [He] kept fighting it, kept thinking that one day, the feelings of guilt and dread would dissipate . . .." He had gained nearly twenty pounds, stopped his normally rigorous exercise routine and his "increasing dependence on alcohol was symptomatic" (54).

Ford's physical and mental deterioration and his struggle for survival become metaphors for the environmental damage done to the Everglades. In what appears to be a flight of whimsy, White has Tomlinson coax Ford into an expedition to search the Everglades for "what some Floridians call the Swamp Ape, or Skunk Ape, which is the tropical version of Big Foot or the Abominable Snowman" (59).

Of course Ford does not believe for a moment that such a creature exists, but he likes to humor his friend, who produces dozens of newspaper articles and research that show that as far back as the late 1500s, missionaries reported seeing a " '. . . giant man, befouled by a body of hair, running away into the swamps' "(60). Tomlinson explains that the peak of the sightings, however, came in the early 1970s "'when construction was booming in Miami and Lauderdale, everything expanding west into what was then the Everglades. The bulldozers and draglines were draining the edge of the big swamp, scraping it bare, taking away all the cover. The River Prophet had to move around, maybe for survival . . . or maybe to investigate the damage being done to the biosphere' "(60).

Although this scene is primarily played for humor, this primitive creature of the swamps, this River Prophet who is forced by modern civilization to change his habits to survive and who is someone who Tomlinson sees as a protector of the wild, is a lot like Ford. The pressure of the government to force Ford back into the role of the assassin and his own, dark, primitive genetic imperatives that respond to that pressure are mirrored in the Swamp Ape.

Ford sees this kind of elemental, instinctual creature in his own psyche when he is forced into a fistfight with some of Shiva's henchmen. In past novels, when Doc is forced into a confrontation, he is circumvent, calculating, and careful not to show too many of his skills acquired in his past life as an assassin. In *Everglades*, however, that past comes boiling up to the surface with a vengeance:

I experienced an internal transformation that I've experienced before. I've come to despise the transformation . . . and to fear it. In the brain is a tiny region called the amygdala, a section of cerebral matter so ancient that some scientists refer to it as our 'lizard brain.' Its purpose is to insure survival, and all the complicated emotions and behaviors which survival implies. It is here that our basest of instincts thrive: sex, fury, flight–the earliest markers of more than a hundred million years of adaptation and survival. It is here that our atavistic dread of snakes is passed from generation to generation. In this small, dark place lives the killer that is in us all. The modern portion of our brain has built up around that lizard brain, like a walnut cloaking a seed. However, when sufficiently stimulated, there can be an electrical transfer of behavioral control from the modern, rational brain to the cave-dwelling primate that hides within. (148).

Ford becomes the Swamp Ape. And when he finally snaps out of it, it is like he has "awakened from a nightmare . . .. People who suffer seizures, I suspect, are familiar with the stares I received. Violent criminals, too" (150). This transformation that Ford undergoes is the first hint of a much more powerful one yet to come.

These changes Ford undergoes are part of a recurring theme of rebirth, reincarnation and re-invention that runs through all of his novels. He first steps onto the stage in *Flats* being mistaken for the resurrection of the Mayan god Quetzalcoatl. Ford attends Rafe Hollins's funeral only to later stumble across him alive and well and having sex with Ford's girlfriend.

In *The Man Who Invented Florida*, the old Seminole Joseph Egret escapes from a mental hospital, dons the Halloween costume of a skeleton and believes he is dead. In the same novel, Ford's uncle Tucker Gatrell claims he has discovered the fountain of youth–after his horse drinks from a sulfur-water well and then grows back his testicles.

Tomlinson nearly dies in *Captiva* and lapses into a coma. Ford, believing his friend will never recover, leaves his home on Dinkins Bay vowing never to return. He is camping on the coast of Australia when he hears a radio broadcast that a miracle has happened–Tomlinson is stuck with lightening and is back among the living.

And in *The Mangrove Coast*, an old friend who Ford thought had died in Vietnam comes back to life in one of the most satisfying and surprising endings in modern fiction.

White also shows us that Florida itself is a place of renewal, a place where people come to reinvent themselves, and its environment is one of constant renewal, with a tenacious power to cleanse itself.

Throughout the series, Ford has tried to reinvent himself by shaking off his past life as a government assassin. In *Everglades*, however, he finds himself still on the payroll, a consequence of seeking the help of his old organization in the rescue mission of *Twelve Mile Limit*.

"Unfortunately, once one has participated in a violent, clandestine life, one cannot simply shed it like a skin, or leave it behind like a former job or an old house" (*Everglades* 250). When in the midst of trying to help Sally Minster, a childhood girlfriend whose husband was murdered by Shiva, Ford gets the offer of an assignment to kill an international terrorist. He hardly hesitates: "Know what? Yes. That one's a real possibility" (252).

As soon as he agrees, however, Tomlinson brings him bad news. A private detective who was helping Ford protect Sally is found murdered and Sally is kidnapped by Shiva's psychotic henchman, Izzy. Ford immediately blames himself–he had refused when the detective had asked Ford for help to work surveillance on the girl's house. Ford finally hits bottom: "That night, something inside me snapped. Something within the core region of my brain. It was ignited by a growing, withering pressure without vent. Intellectually, emotionally, I felt the scaffolding that defines me fracture, then break" (265).

He spends the rest of the day and most of the night getting drunk, he "snapped. . . . In that isolated space between what I was, and what I had become, the stranger within spoke for the first time: You are insane" (268). Then, he seems to verify his conclusion: he hops on a sailboard and as the moon disappears behind a cloud, races at twenty miles an hour past the mangroves. As he sails through a school of mullet, he sees a shark.

"In this brackish mangrove lake, it was almost certainly a bull shark judging from its girth. It was the fish that I'd traveled the world studying. It was the fish I often used as an excuse for clandestine work" (270). The shark is the lizard brain of Ford's past, the Skunk Ape, the darkness in Ford's soul that has brought him to this place, this time. Ford, the predator, becomes Ford the prey.

Knocked off the board, flailing around in the water, Ford is "drunk and disoriented . . .. too fat, too winded, too slow. . . .That's when something in [his] brain ruptured once again. It was the same sensation: A flashbulb exploding behind [his] eyes" The lizard brain takes over and in a "cold and loathing fury," Ford shouts " 'Fuck it!'" and charges the shark.

"In my crazed state, there was a single, stabilizing truth that fueled my rage: Why run? We are both predators". He dives head first with both fists extended, fully expecting to die in the jaws of the shark. But the shark isn't there. "It was swimming away at top speed. Spooked" (272).

The encounter brings Ford to a defining moment. "For the last many years, I have been at odds with my own past. In my previous life, in what I think of as my former life, I'd been required to demonstrate what I prefer to define as extreme behavior."

Ford was ashamed of what he had done, even though reason and logic told him it was all done under a legally binding mandate, he felt guilty. But then he realizes he had absolutely no reason to be ashamed and "it was a transcendent moment." In the battle with the shark, Ford saw his true self. "I am predatory by nature. I also like to think that I am ethical, kind, selective and generous. But, at the atavistic core, I am a hunter, a killer" (274). He is McGee the iceman.

Ford's encounter with the shark is a baptism and rebirth–a particularly apt symbol in a novel where the villain is the guru of the Church of Ashram who is holding his final service on Easter Sunday, complete with an earthquake and a scene in which all Hell quite literally breaks loose.

Ford will enter the water five more times in the novel, and each time is another kind of baptism. First, he begins the slow reversal of his physical deterioration, running three miles, and then a long swim in which he twice vomits up seawater. The baptism with the shark purged his soul of guilt and shame; the swim begins the process of purging his body of months of neglect. Then Ford races across the Everglades to rescue Sally Minster, trapped in the back of a U-Haul truck full of explosives timed to set off an earthquake at the climax of Shiva's Easter service. Ford arrives at the truck just in time to rescue Sally, but in order to prevent the explosives from detonating; he is forced to drive the truck into Lost Lake, a nearly bottomless sinkhole that connects to an underground river that runs to the sea.

This third baptism purges the Everglades of a catastrophic threat, and deep in the bowels of the lake Ford sees what at first he thinks are sharks, but realizes they are tarpon, saltwater fish that swim the underground river, a sign the Seminoles believes signals a healthier Everglades.

In another elegant stroke of poetic environmental justice, Shiva is swallowed up by a sinkhole created around his outdoor amphitheater by a series of small tremors sent off by explosions planted by the guru himself.

". . . .The sinkhole created by a series of explosions had collapsed into the underground river–the Long Key Formation. The river had swept Shiva's body along beneath sawgrass, swamp, mangrove fringe and all of Florida Bay, before jettisoning him into open sea."

Just as Ford had vomited up the sea water in his efforts to restore himself, so too has Florida purged itself of what had been trying to destroy it. Once again White gives us an image of a Dantesque Hell, Shiva sucked into the bowls of the earth by the very Everglades he had threatened. The Seminole leader Billie Egret had a single word for it: "Reciprocity" (312).

The last time Ford goes into the water is in the final scene in the book when he and his girlfriend Dewey Nye are vacationing on a private beach on St. Martins in the French West Indies.

Ford, however, has an additional agenda. He tells Dewey he is going for swim, won't be gone for more than an hour, then straps a knife to his right calf and sets out to swim across the bay and assassinate a terrorist name Omar Muhammad. Ford is back on the payroll of his government's secret service, and for the first time since he made his entrance in the opening of his first novel, he is going to kill a man simply because it is his job. He has come full circle, embracing the man he swore he no longer was, accepting his biological and genetic destiny as the one who culls the herd, and White leaves his readers with the one question on their minds that all novelist love to hear: What happens next?

Chapter Three
James W. Hall, The Redemptive Power of Place

In the September 1996 issue of *Outside* magazine, Randy Wayne White published a satirical column that was supposedly based on a fishing trip out into the Atlantic Ocean with friend and fellow author James W. Hall, whom White describes as "a highly regarded poet and author of such best-selling eco-thrillers as *Gone Wild, Bones of Coral, Under Cover of Daylight,* and *Buzz Cut.*"

Hall thought he was taking White out for a dolphin fishing expedition. But for White, the object of the trip was not to hunt crafty denizens of the deep, but to see just how seasick Hall gets after White conducted a little experiment that included a night of ingesting massive amounts of spaghetti, followed by a breakfast of chocolate-chip cookies and White's insistent smoking of some rather odorous Nicaraguan cigars.

The results were not pretty. In a collections of essays published under the title *Hot Damn*, Hall called White article "scurrilous" (12). "Let's just say that the article's general subject was seasickness and it reflected badly on me, and ninety-nine percent of the facts in it were unfactual." Hall waited patiently to get his revenge and he finally talked White into another sea voyage–this time in Randy's boat out into the Gulf to see Cabbage Key, just south of White's home on Pine Island.

Hall had been hearing "rousing stories about the quaint inn on Cabbage Key" for more than thirty years," the inn itself portrayed in nearly mythic strokes. The walls were said to be papered with thousands of dollar bills, and "the ancient mahogany of the bar etched with the names of famous writers" (11).

Hall writes eloquently about his visit to the heart of old Florida–the Calusa Indian mounds behind White's tinned-roof cracker house and a visit to Useppa Island, home to a mansion built by Baron Collier back in the early 1900s, the scene of many a gathering of the rich and famous such as the Roosevelts, du Ponts, Rothschilds and Rockefellers.

He goes on to describe the trip to Cabbage Key where "yes indeed, the walls are papered with dollar bills and the beer is flawlessly cold and the people are eccentric and polite and love to unspool their yarns. And the aura of mystery novelist and playwright Mary Roberts Rinehart still hovers above the charming inn that she helped design as a private residence some sixty years ago" (14-15).

Suddenly, Hall writes, his desire to seek revenge on White seemed "cheap and small, withering in my breast like the last shreds of daylight on the distant horizon" (15). Once again, Hall had been seduced by the redemptive power of place, a particular place he calls "sweet Florida, what a sensuous and libertine land" (3). In many ways, this small essay contains all the essential hallmarks of Hall's mystery novels. Almost all are set in South Florida, rich in tropical intrigue, often colored with historical research and steeped in an abiding affection for place and the people who, in Hall's words, "are shaped by the land or the water that dominates their lives"(O'Brian).

Hall's love affair with the Sunshine State began in his senior year in high school, 1965, when he left his hometown of Hopkinsville, Kentucky, to attend Riverside Military Academy in Hollywood, Florida. Traveling by train, he watched the brown and scraggly winter landscape of Tennessee and Georgia slowly give way to a "Shangri-La."

The palm trees began to thicken, the greens grew lush . . . Suddenly I was standing beside the tracks looking at a sky dense with extravagant birds, white and huge with lazy wings, long orange legs trailing.
I remember taking my first breath of rich subtropical air. There was something sweet and spicy in the breeze–that warm macaroon aroma with an intoxicating undertone of cinnamon that seems to waft directly from some secret Caribbean island. That afternoon I breathed in a lungful of air I have yet to release (2).

Hall carries this passion for place into his mystery novels, where the shadowy elements of classic noir play out under the brilliance of the tropical sun, and the promise of redemption is nurtured by the landscape but seldom achieved by characters haunted by the darkness of their own souls.

For Hall, "setting is more than just neutral backdrop" (O'Brian). With its mythic roots of the eternal fountain of youth and its reputation as a magnet for those who wish to shed their past and reinvent themselves, Florida has often served as a backdrop for fiction, but Hall wants his characters to "react to the landscape and have them describe it as a shaping force. The stories could not have been written in a different location" (O'Brian).

In writing on his website about his first novel, *Under Cover of Daylight*, Hall recounts how moving from Miami to Key Largo in the early 1980s influenced his choice of material:

When I began to work on *Under Cover*, I was enthralled with Key Largo. The light, the birds and water, the endless sky. I wanted to write the kind of book I'd always cherished, Travis McGee novels and works by Chandler and Hammett, and Ross MacDonald, Robert Parker and Elmore Leonard. But I also wanted to use the Keys as my backdrop and to make that place as much of a character as the people in the novel.

The only role of a "shaping force" played by Hall's hometown of Hopkinsville was to compel him to leave as soon as possible. "I fled her narrow streets and scrubby fields forever" (*Damn* 21). He felt trapped in "a world of narrow-mindedness and conformity. No future there for a kid with big dreams" (41). However, the town's gloomy public library, with its ornate Old South architecture, was to be one of those places that proved to be a significant influence on this young writer-to-be.

At the age of ten, his only ambitions were "muscular achievements on hash-marked fields or gymnasium floors" (18) – the library was the last place he would have chosen to spend a summer afternoon. But his mother started dropping him off there while she went shopping, and it was here he would discover that books "were about adult things. Strong emotions, extreme behaviors, the inside stuff of a work I had never imagined existed. . . . I suddenly realized that novels could fill one with heart-pounding fear as well as lip-smacking lust" (20). Hall was hooked.

He had picked up a book at random, and there on the first page was a description of a nude woman's body. She was dead, of course, the book turned out to be a British mystery, and the librarian steered him to Sherlock Holmes, Dickens, Hardy and Joyce. He fell in love with Lawrence Durrell and John Fowles, Faulkner and Steinbeck. When the young athlete read Hemingway's novels of boxing and other intensely competitive exploits, he "started to picture the unspeakable–that I might someday learn the craft of writing well enough to create the very things I so dearly loved to consume" (21).

His father, a local realtor in this town that sat just across the state line from Nashville, was probably the one who introduced Hall to the natural world. Years after retiring, he would write letters to his son that were "always full of natural descriptions of the weather, the changing seasons, the trees and flowers and birds" (43). Although young James had demonstrated an inclination for things literary, his father, an alumnus of the Citadel in Charleston, S.C., had hopes for a military career for his son and after sending James off at the age of seventeen to Riverside Military Academy; Hall's father helped him secure an appointment to the Air Force Academy in Colorado.

But after a season in the Sunshine State, Hall developed a terminal case of sand in his shoes. He told his parents he wanted to give up his free ride at the Air Force Academy and instead attend Florida Presbyterian College, (Now Eckerd). "I convinced my parents that a small religious campus represented a safe haven for a young Christian man in the dangerous '60s," he told Brewster Robertson in a 1996 interview in Publishers Weekly. "Truth was, I'd seen the college catalogue and it was full of pictures of coeds in shorts" (2). Florida continued to work its magic on the Kentucky boy from the hillbilly small town.

I did four glorious years of college in the charming and soporific Saint Petersburg of the sixties. On holiday I explored the west coast, the Keys, camping at starkly primitive Bahia Honda, building bonfires on midnight beaches, discovering out-of-the-way taverns that served cheap pitchers of beer and spectacular cheeseburgers, bays where fish jumped happily into frying pans, and unair-conditioned piano bars in Key West where writers huddled in the corners and talked the secret talk. I had never felt so at home (*Damn* 3).

At Eckerd, Hall honed his writing skills, particularly his poetry, under the tutorship of English professor Peter Meinke, winner of the Flannery O'Connor award for poetry. The summer before his senior year, Hall got a scholarship at the Breadloaf Writer's Conference and convinced the editor of the Antioch Review to accept for publication his poem "The Lady from the Dark Green Hills."

When he graduated from Eckerd in 1969, he left Florida to pursue a master of fine arts degree at John Hopkins and then out to the University of Utah for his doctorate. "I entered Utah as a poet and graduated a fiction writer. It was an aspect of my writing life that I almost didn't recover from. I fell under the influence of the fabulists like Donald Barthleme, Vonnegut—those far out books of the '60s (Robertson 3). After serving what he calls "a bleak exile in snowy latitudes" he returned to Florida in 1973 in search of a teaching post. He had to do a series of odd jobs, including landscaping, while he waited, but he never applied for anything outside of Florida. Finally he got an offer to teach at Florida International University and ended up living his dream, camped out in a stilt house in Key Largo, writing in his spare time. In his essay about how he came to this southernmost state, he writes:

I kidnapped a boy from Kentucky and transplanted him in paradise, and he grew up to write books that sing the praises and mock the dizzy and perilous follies of this gaudy corner of the nation. I love this place. I have loved it from the start and have learned to love it more with every passing year–all its quirkiness, its stresses, this simmering melting pot where no one wants to blend (4).

Hall had found a home, yet success as a novelist proved elusive. Although he had published four books of poetry and a collection of short stories, his first four attempts at novel writing ended up in the delete file. "Those books failed because I imagined I was better than I was. I was a poet. I had virtually no concept of conflict and thematic movement" (Robertson). By 1984 his failed novels and deteriorating marriage to his college sweetheart drove him to what he called a profound mid-life crisis.

"I was seriously entertaining thoughts of going back to Kentucky to join my father's real estate business" (Robertson).

Instead, he decided to spend the summer in a decidedly un-academic way, working in a bait-and-tackle shop in Key Largo and reading crime novels at a record pace, almost one a day. As an English teacher and poet, he had become what he calls an "intellectual snob, talking down to my students about books like *Gone with the Wind* and *From Here to Eternity* "(Robertson), but since those first days of discovery in the Hopkinsville public library, he had never gotten over "the sinful pleasure of reading stories about crime, adventure, the chase, the hunt, the unraveling of a deviant mind"(*Damn* 228).

Spending those lazy South Florida days in the company of Dashiell Hammett, John D. MacDonald, Sue Grafton, Elmore Leonard and the like, brought Hall to an epiphany.

"I suddenly came to realize that these books affected me in a powerful way. . . .This new sense of freedom allowed me to take a new direction. That's when I decided to write *Under Cover of Daylight*" (Robertson). Hall sold the book to W. W. Norton & Company and got a ten thousand dollar advance with a modest first printing of five thousand. "To everyone's surprise," he says, "the book got good reviews from *Kirkus Review* and *Publishers Weekly*, prompting a larger than usual advertising campaign from Norton and sales that were "three or four times more than anyone dreamed," (Robertson) Hall said.

Publisher's Weekly wrote that "Hall, who is also a poet, makes place and climate as important as character in building the powerful effect of this accomplished novel" (Amazon.com) and the *Library Journal* called it "a great first novel" (Amazon.com).

Published in 1987, *Daylight*'s success launched Hall's career as a mystery writer and the switch from the somewhat rarified academic atmosphere of poetry to the commercial grit and grime of crime novels was a transition that Hall readily embraced. Interviewers, however, inevitably asked him about that change in a tone of voice he describes as somewhat akin to asking: "'So, Jim, you used to be on the Supreme Court and now you're a personal injury attorney. How could you have let that happen to yourself' "(*Damn* 226)? Hall's short answer is that he did it for the money, but on a more serious level he offered this defense of the genre:

I sometimes tell those who ask the dreaded question that, in fact, I still do write poetry. It's just that these days the poetry goes from margin to margin rather than down the middle of the page. But in the back rooms of my secret heart, what I really want to say is: What I'm doing now–these novels I'm writing–demands more from me, challenges me artistically in ways that poetry never did . . . writers of suspense novels have never forgotten their Dickensian responsibilities. From Hammett and MacDonald to Grafton and Leonard, it is our suspense writers who have kept alive complex plotting and rousing good yarns. Mystery novelists are practically alone in preserving rich regional settings, authentic patterns of speech, and three-dimensional minor characters. It is our crime fiction that looks square in the malevolent face of the violence and corruption that are so rife in our society. Our novelists of suspense are indeed the only group of writers today who consistently fulfill Tom Wolfe's view of the novelist's true responsibility: to write works with a wide social scope that are populated by people of all classes and to tackle the great moral and political issues of the day. (228).

Hall may privately bemoan the fact that by writing crime novels he has forever removed himself from being in the running for the Flannery O'Connor award for poetry–since the publication of *Daylight* he has hardly written any—(*Damn* 226), and his defense of the genre could certainly be viewed as self-serving; but in each of his novels, Hall has obviously tried to hold true to both the letter and the spirit of Wolfe's edict.

Hall's work also embodies the same moralistic themes that lay the heart of MacDonald's writings: a belief that people must accept responsibility for all these acts that affect the lives of others. Hirshberg concludes his 1985 biography of MacDonald with a defense of that moralism.

What MacDonald almost invariably tries to do is to depict the view of reality in which two choices always exist, thereby illuminating effectively and conscientiously and faithfully the real moral dilemmas that beset the human spirit. If the mark of greatness in a writer of fiction is to create this kind of illumination–as I believe it is–then that mark is on John D. MacDonald (111).

When Hall tells us he wants his characters to "react to the landscape and have them describe it as a shaping force" (O'Brian), he is talking about how a sense of place molds and informs the moral structure of his characters. For Hall–indeed for all of these writers of eco-mysteries–this notion is not just some academic exercise or pre-determined formula for creating a commercial success; it is the author's own epiphany of place being transfused into his work. Hall finds his true self in Key Largo and transforms himself from the academic poet and professor into a writer of eco-thrillers in which MacDonald's "moral dilemmas that beset the human spirit" are often anchored literally and metaphorically in a landscape that both Hall and his characters inhabit.

In *Daylight*, Hall introduces Thorn, a man with no first name whose identity and character are formed from the very onset of his birth by the Florida Keys. "He's a simple guy, a little grumpy sometimes, who mainly wants to be left alone," Hall writes in his website description of the novel. "I thought of him as Travis without a houseboat and without even the semblance of a job. He's no knight errant, just a guy who fishes for a living and scrapes by in a kind of Walden Pond existence."

While he was working on *Daylight*, Hall had become enthralled with Key Largo and the kind of local residents who were tough enough to eke out a living on that coral rock, people who came there "to escape something or other. The law, the pressures of the mainland. Something... He's a tough guy with a lyrical love for the water and the sky and the birds of the Keys. He's who I'd be If I didn't write books."

In the beginning of the novel, we learn that Thorn was born on July 5, 1947 (which makes him the same age as Hall) at Homestead Hospital on the mainland. His mother and father, Quentin and Elizabeth Thorn, are driving home, little Thorn twenty hours out of the womb, "still four hours left to get him back to the Keys so he'd be officially, by local custom, a Conch." So important was this custom that Thorn's parents had stolen out of the hospital after midnight against the doctor's wishes "to give the boy roots. Maybe roots was wrong. Suction was a better word. This island didn't grant much purchase.. . .Conchs had suction. They could hold on to places where no roots could burrow in" (23).

They never make it. A drunk driver named Dallas James forces them off the road and they both drown in Lake Surprise with only baby Thorn surviving. The drunk gets off, goes free.

The novel opens nineteen years later, July 1966, with a scene in which Thorn tracks down and kidnaps James and forces him to drive off into the same lake. It is an act of murder and revenge, and Thorn's struggle for redemption takes him through his first serious love affair with a women named Sarah who turns out to be the very daughter of the man he killed, a women set on her own path of revenge.

Meanwhile, Thorn must also deal with the murder of his foster mother, Kate Truman, a charter boat captain and environmentalist who works behind the scenes to buy up endangered land threatened by greedy developers. Thorn gains purchase, but he pays a high price, no amount of daylight can wash away the darkness of his own guilt.

His connection to the landscape and the sea that surrounds it are indeed powerful shaping forces in his life, forces that become both gift and curse. The unintended consequences of his parents compelling drive to give their newborn son a meaningful connection to place ends their lives and sets Thorn down a dark passage. Yet their deaths and Thorn's murder of the drunk driver steer Thorn into an even more symbiotic relationship with his environment.

After the murder of Dallas James, the nineteen-year-old Thorn retreats into a near-hermit's existence for the next twenty years, living in a one-room, unpainted, plank-floored, stilt house just twenty feet from Blackwater Sound, a "quiet bay rimmed with mangroves. His coral and limestone dock ran out a hundred feet into about two feet of water at high tide" (75). It sits four hundred yards down a gravel road from U.S. Highway 1. "If anyone wanted a peep of him, they'd have to pole into the flats off shore."

This physical isolation of Thorn's living space mirrors his psychological isolation from the rest of civilization and becomes both refuge and prison. For the past twenty years on the day of the anniversary of his parents' death, he returns to Lake Surprise to sit beside the bay. "Twenty years," he thinks. "It sounds like a jail term. Twenty to life. That was about the sentence he might've expected if he'd turned himself into the sheriff" (23). After falling in love with Sarah, Thorn begins to reconsider this self-imposed prison term.

Thorn's sense of self is rooted in this natural world, attuned to the pull of tides, the wind and the clouds. For nearly a decade, he made a living as a bonefishing guide, coming back to the Keys after a three-month stint at John Hopkins University, "nineteen and with about nineteen years of experience on the flats. Baptized out there. Knew how to be quiet and blend in. For ten years he tried to learn how to take money from strangers who know how to do neither" (74).

Thorn eventually gives up guiding and concentrates on tying fishing flies. It is an art he never attempts to intellectualize. "It was a kind of voodoo" (73). Thorn even calls the bonefishermen "priests. They thought like priests. It meant whatever they thought they kept to themselves. When they did talk, they all talked alike, quiet as dust floating in church. And they had eyes burned hard and transparent by the sun off shallow water, from tracking ghosts with a ten-ton pull" (73-74). But Key Largo is not all bonefish, beaches and mangroves:

Right now it all looked wretched to Thorn. There were just a few survivors of the old days, wood-frame house with tin roofs and cisterns and cupolas, stranded between the Pizza Huts and the skin diving shops and the shell stores that had mounds of queen conchs piled high out front. A haze from deep-fat fryers hung over the cluster of franchise restaurants. Even the steady sea breezes couldn't seem to wash the air of that smell. . . . billboard after billboard urging drivers forward through the tackiness to Key West. . . .everywhere there were shadows where there had never been shadows before. The oldest things still standing for a hundred miles around were the people. And all but a handful of them were new arrivals, retirees so used to the shopping centers and vast parking lots back home, in fact, so proud of their malls, so quick to describe to the Conchs what luxuries the rest of America was enjoying that defectors had been showing up everywhere (114-115).

By contrasting Thorn's bayside Walden Pond with the garish and ravished landscape of touristville, Hall sets up a parallel between the psychological conflicts that confront Thorn and the physiological conflicts that beset the Keys, foreshadowing the events that force Thorn to step out of his idealized role that one friend describes as "'the Gandhi of Key Largo, a loincloth and sandals and [only] one burner'" on the stove that works (42). He is drawn into the battle over a condominium project that his foster mother, Kate, fights against. Her efforts to buy up the land before the developer can seal the deal result in her death, and Thorn is once again caught up in a cycle of violence, justice and revenge. *Daylight's* environmental themes are reminiscent of MacDonald classic *Flash of Green:* Grassy Bay becomes Port Allamada, a thousand-unit, 400-acre condominium community with "shopping centers, banks, a couple of marinas, a golf course. Fifteen miles of internal roads, its own sewage plant" (46). Each work has its developers singing the promise of economic prosperity and new jobs and the passionate but out-numbered opposition, arguing about intangibles such as beauty and nature. The arguments and attitudes of county commissioner Elmo Bliss in *Green* are the same as those of Port Allamada's developer, Philip Grayson.

"I hear nothing from these people but how I'm single-handedly wrecking the Keys. . . ."If it weren't for men like me, this state would still be paying its way with roadside freak shows. Sure I make a buck on this and that. But you tell me something. When was the last time one of those people got out a machete and took a stroll through that land they're in such a hurry to protect? When was the last time they went out there in the swamp and played with a butterfly? They don't give a shit about any butterflies or mice. They're just as selfish as the next guy" (175).

Now here is Bliss.

All those damn bird watchers and do-gooders and nature boys, they got an abstraction they've fell in love with . . ... When the average man goes to look at nature, he wants something going on, like a porpoise coming ten feet up out of the water to eat a fish, or like pretty girls underwater, sucking air from a hose and eating bananas. There's nothing going on in that bay they can look at. But the goddam do-gooders got this abstraction they look at. They like the idea of nature being left the hell alone. Boy, it never is left alone. Never. Not when there's a dollar you can make out of it." (*Green* 93)

Daylight even has an environmental heroine named Kate to remind us of Kat in *Green*. And just as Bliss argued that Grassy Bay was nothing but a swamp filled with disease and families should be scared to let their children near it, we have in *Daylight* the issue of wood rats, a particularly scruffy and decidedly uncute creature designated by the federal government as an endangered species, "its last major stronghold in America was in the hardwood hammock where . . . investors wanted to build Port Allamanda" (46). Kate tries to put the issue into perspective:

"When are you going to be ready to draw the line? When will it be that someone will walk into a room like this and say, 'I'll trade you a library, I'll trade you a couple hundred temporary jobs for your last lobster'? Is that when you'll say no? Not lobsters. We like lobsters. Or make that sailfish. . . .this year it's wood rats. And you say, yes, we'll part with our wood rats. We'll take the library. We got bills and taxes, so we'll take jobs. Next year what'll it be? And five years from now. . ." (50)?

Of course it would easy to conclude that Hall's first novel drew directly on MacDonald's classic, but the similarities of environmental elements can just as easily be ascribed to the ubiquity of such events in Florida. Not that much had changed in the twenty-five years between the publication of *Green* and *Daylight*. Hall needs only turn to the pages of his daily newspaper or spend a few days attending the county zoning board meetings to come up with plenty of fodder that resembled the fight over Grassy Bay.

What is interesting is that in subsequent novels, Hall never returns to the traditional growth issue of pristine land raped by bad-guy developer. Instead, he focuses his environmental sensitivity on issues of a much larger scale. Even in *Daylight*, the environmentalist Kate has already done much more to preserve the natural landscape and protect it from developers than any of the characters in a MacDonald novel. Kate and her husband, Dr. Bill, had invested in land all over the Keys and owned something called Vacation Island, an upscale resort that was worth millions of dollars. Kate had taken the profits and had begun buying up land to save it from the developers. Sarah, Thorn's lover and young lawyer who was helping Kate, explained it this way:

"One of these [developments] would get into trouble, miss a couple of payments. Or the Sierra Club, the Audubon Society would get the investors so bogged down in suits and court cases the owners would get tired or nervous waiting, making payments, till the building can get going again, and Kate would step up, make them an offer, either buy it outright or buy into it and keep increasing her share until she had it. All sub Rosa, of course. She's fighting these places publicly with the wildlife groups, and undercover she's trying to buy them out. Soon as she owned a place, the hammers stopped."(133).

Thorns own view of nature is not so romantic. After Sarah tells him that all this property is his now, left to his care after Kate died, Thorn looks at the half-built development and says, "'you caught this one a little late. Land's been cleared, buildings built. I mean, it doesn't seem like this qualifies as saving a place' "(134). His reaction surprises Sarah. "'I thought you living like you do, close to nature, you'd just see it automatically. I thought you'd see it' "(134). Even the plight of the wood rats fails to engage his emotions or his intellect (47). McGee preaches with an advocate's passion, Doc Ford makes his case through the logic of science and experimentation. Thorn, however, simply reacts and stubbornly resists attempts to sentimentalize the landscape.

In another scene, a friend tells Thorn about his son's cancer: "'Used to be, living down here, eating fresh fish, good clean air, people lived to be older than rocks. But gone are the days, Thorn. All the shit coming down lately, it's as bad as living in Miama[sic]' "(145).

Thorn replies, "'People say it was, but I sure don't remember it ever being a paradise'. " Nature is no guiding light for Thorn. When he sees a frigate bird suspended over the bay, looking to snatch a mullet from the mouth of a gull, the allusion of thief and predator, the metaphoric link to Kate's killers, are unmistakable. Yet Thorn simply observes that this is "survival of the shittiest," and adds, "Just the kind of thing that discouraged Thorn from counting too much on nature to guide the way" (215).

He is an environmental anti-hero, intelligent but not an intellectual, driven more by instinct and a moral code cobbled together as much from his own pain as from his upbringing. He is not one to ponder his place in the grand scheme of nature; that task is left to Hall, the novelist, who tells Thorn's story not just in action, plot, and personal relationships, but also in the metaphoric language of a natural world.

When Sarah tells him he lives "at Walden Pond" (42), it references the headnote of the novel, taken from Henry David Thoreau's *A Writer's Journal*.

There is a calmness of the lake when there is not a breath of wind; there is the calmness of a stagnant ditch. So it is with us. Sometimes we are clarified and calmed healthily, as we never were before in our lives, not by an opiate, but by some unconscious obedience to the all-just laws, so that we become like a still lake of purest crystal . . ..

These contrasting images of the lake and the ditch are the novel's central motifs, defining Thorn's inner struggle to rise above that "stagnant ditch" where his parents died and he took his own revenge on the man responsible for their deaths. Thorn longs for the "clarity" of the still pond, and ultimately finds it and his own redemption at the end of the novel, where he is immersed in that same Lake Surprise, waiting to see if Sarah will kill him in another round of revenge, or forgive him and prove that their love is the stronger force.

The novel's opening line echoes this theme: "Standing in front of his dresser mirror, the young man pointed the revolver at his reflection" (14). (Why the novel starts on page 14 is unclear.) The reflection in the mirror is akin to the calm surface of a lake, and the twin images of Thorn, who is only referred to in the opening chapter as "the young man," foreshadows the protagonist's central moral conflict: how he comes to terms with his own act of murder and revenge.

Can he ever really leave behind the stench of guilt from that "stagnant ditch?" Was his killing of Dallas James an "unconscious obedience to the all-just laws," an Old Testament commandment of an eye for an eye, or was it just murder? Is living an isolated life enough of an act of true contrition or simply the act of a coward?

Thorn is aptly named, representing both his hero's role as a thorn in the side of his enemies, and the more complex issue of a man facing a thorny dilemma—no matter which way he turns, the consequences of his moral decisions are going to inflict sharp and constant pain, it is the dilemma of classic noir fiction and film. By using this quote from Thoreau to strike the first thematic chords of the novel, Hall begins the process of revealing how place and landscape shape his characters.

"And so it is with us. . ." Thoreau writes, and Hall gives us Thorn, whose own life is as still as the surface of the lake, but beneath that surface is turmoil. "For years he'd stayed hidden away in the woods, the action in his life happening deep inside" (74).

As Thorn begins his search for redemption, we also see a change in the character of Lake Surprise. The first two times it is mentioned are as scenes of death: Thorn's parents, then Dallas James. The third and fourth times we see it in the context of Thorn's relationship with his lover Sarah. After the first chapter, which describes the nineteen-year-old Thorn's murder of James, the second chapter opens twenty years later, with Thorn bringing Sarah to his annual visit to the lake on the anniversary of his parents' death.

In the murder scene, as Thorn watches the cops pull James and the car out of the lake, the lake is "calm. It went from black to gray to green" (20), full of blood and death, the lake becomes Thoreau's "stagnant ditch."

When Sarah strips naked and wades out into the water for a swim, she cannot coax him in. He thinks: "Would she swim so easily there if she knew the blood that water was spiked with? Thorn has shuddered when Sarah first grazed her toe across it, but he'd said nothing. He had not been able to touch that water himself for twenty years" (22).

Just as Sarah disturbs the surface of the lake, she also disturbs the calm surface of Thorn. Before Sarah, Thorn's quiet, withdrawn life in the woods was "enough. The silence. The reading. The food. The weather. The bonefish strikes. But now that wasn't. He was starting to feel a hunger. Lately he'd found his eyes drifting up from the desk, looking off" (74).

Thorn is no longer the boy in the mirror. That duel image from the first line of the book is revisited as Thorn sits on the shore and watches Sarah. ". . . [H]e was here, serving his indeterminate sentence, his hard time out among the innocent. Very cruel, very unusual. And this was visiting day at the penitentiary. Mr. Thorn to visit Mr. Thorn" (26). Sarah, too, turns out to have a secret identity. Sarah Ryan the lawyer and Thorn's lover is actually Sarah James; daughter of the man Thorn has killed. Even Kate, the woman who raised Thorn has a hidden identity he only discovers after she is killed. Her environmental activism is well know to Thorn, but her project to buy up endangered lands to save them from development, something she has been doing for years, has been kept from Thorn.

At the end of the novel, after tracking down the man responsible for Kate's death (who in an ironic twist is shot to death by Sarah), Sarah forces Thorn to return to Lake Surprise at gunpoint, and this time, the lake is no "stagnant ditch," reeking of blood and death, but clear to the bottom, where Thorn can see the "turtle grass bending with the incoming tide" (285).

Nature has cleansed itself. Sarah tells Thorn to "take everything off" and get in the water, forcing him to shed his old identity, his old self. This is Thorn's final baptism in the waters that were both his penitentiary and salvation, and now, possibly, his death chamber. Facing what might be his final moments on earth, he finally lets go of his past in a scene that speaks in the voice of connection and belonging, of discovery and loss.

He wasn't feeling detached anymore. . . .He wanted badly to tell her what he saw now. That they were joined. By thin, invisible umbilicals, hooked together. Every pinprick made the other wince. Her stricken face, the panic in her eyes at what she might do, was a replica of his face. Her exhalation came with his inhaling. Twined. Something more powerful than love binding them. It was a marriage consecrated . . . by a lifetime of regret and loss and anger. (287).

Earlier in the novel, when Thorn first discovers Sarah's secret, he has a similar feeling of connection, one that he expresses in a biological metaphor that is reminiscent of MacDonald's description of Thelma Mensenkott's feelings toward nature in his novel *Condominium*, "The sense of unity was a revelation which shook her, . . .she sat amid a complex unity, an exquisitely balanced pattern of interwoven, interdependent life forms. . .a ferment of microorganisms, dreadful combat, birthing of cells, and the gases and stinks of decay"(133).

Thorn thinks:

Sharing the same air, breathing in, breathing out. All that air, all those molecules endlessly passing between us, along streams of air, connecting us, converting us. In this hothouse, this closed system, breathing in the expelled breath of men long dead, breathing out molecules that will outlive us. Caught in a plot too complex for any one mind to hold. Quentin and Elizabeth [Thorn's parents] breathing out, Dallas James breathing in, Dallas exhaling, Sarah inhaling. Thorn standing beside the water fountain, trying to breathe (224).

The sun sets, the cover of daylight is drawn away, and "Sarah's shadow fell onto him;" she is his revenge personified and it is that deed of revenge that has blocked out the sun and filled his life with darkness. She is the Thorn in the mirror, pointing the gun.

He wants to tell her that "they were halves of one whole, depending on the other. If he sank below the surface, she would be dragged down too" (287). As Thorn swims toward the very spot in the lake where the killing was done twenty years earlier, the water becomes "thicker than water, warmer than water," an image that conjures up the blood of the dead.

Thorn had sought salvation, redemption, forgiveness, some kind of peace through his penitent visits to this spot, but he knew now that "that pain had not changed him" (288), it was Sarah and her love that changed him. She "skinned out of her clothes and was standing naked now, holding the pistol by her side." She, too, much shed her past, become naked, newly born.

She throws away the pistol and slips over the side of the skiff. The last line of the novel reads: "Thorn released the breath he'd been holding and pushed ahead against the swelling tide toward her" (288). This is the final baptism, a literal and metaphorical washing away of sins, as he swims toward her, he is swimming toward his own self, the young man who stood in front of the mirror, the self that stuck like a thorn in his side, the self he now embraces and in doing so finds salvation. Here, in this final scene, the tacky, overdeveloped, overcrowded, ravaged and trumped up landscape of Florida gives way to a paradise, if for only a moment, but a paradise that still holds within itself the redemptive power of place.

Hall never intended for Thorn to have a life after *Daylight*, but publishers at Norton found out that Warner would pay more money for paperback rights for *Daylight* if Thorn returned as the hero of Hall's next novel. Hall balked, telling the folks at Norton that he was already one hundred thirty pages into what would become *Tropical Freeze* (1989) and that his new hero was completely different from Thorn (Robertson).

But the character proved to be a strong seller for Hall, and after appearing in his first two novels, he showed up in five more, 1994's *Mean High Tide*, 1996's *Buzz Cut*, 1999's *Red Sky at Night*, 2002's *Blackwater Sound*, and 2003's *Off The Charts*. He even makes an appearance as a minor character in 1995's *Gone Wild*.

By 2012, Thorn had been featured in 12 out of 18 Hall novels. In 1998, he made an effort get away from Thorn. He dropped his agent of ten years, Nat Sobel, and switched publishing houses from Delacorte to St. Martin's Press—and his new agent, Richard Pine, got him a reported $1.7 million, three-book deal for what Pine then called "non-Thorn, non-Florida - focused thrillers" (Quinn).

Hall may have been able to put Thorn aside for a while, but he could not abandon his beloved Florida. Both 1998's *Body Language* and 2000's *Rough Draft* still take place in Florida, and two years later, Hall debuts *Blackwater Sound*, with both Thorn and the Keys once again taking center stage, making a shambles of Pine's predictions. Other non-Thorn fiction includes are *Paper Products*(1990), a collection of short stories; *Bones of Coral*(1991), *Hard Aground*(1992) and *Forests of the Night*(2004).

Hall has struggled with Thorn from the very beginning. "I'd never really intended to write a series with one character," he writes on his website description of his third novel, 1991's *Bones of Coral*, his first non-Thorn novel.

"I'd always liked series characters like Travis McGee and Spencer and Lew Archer and Sam Spade, but I never pictured myself as that kind of writer. I certainly would have given Thorn's personality a lot more thought at the outset if I'd known I was going to be living with the guy indefinitely." Both *Coral* and the following novel, 1993's *Hard Aground*, were Thornless and suffered from lackluster sales.

Hall tried to abandon Thorn again in 1995's *Gone Wild*, a novel that featured a female protagonist who was caught up in a global scheme to sell endangered species on the black market. Hall's editor at St. Martin's, Jenifer Weis, told him she loved what he had done with the story, but it needed Thorn, so he was back, this time a secondary character, but still the hero who saves the day. The decision to keep Thorn alive proved profitable– Hall's next novel, *Tide*, with Thorn back in the driver's seat, was a bestseller.

In the *Publisher's Weekly* interview in 1996, Hall says he did not see Thorn as genre fiction. "Genre fiction is stuck in a loop of the same conflict and resolution. Poetry was a great training ground for writing about the interior life. Now I see my novels as a process of evolution and expansion of my inner self. As my interests and perceptions change, so do Thorn's" (Robertson).

We see a hint of those changes materialize in Hall's next novel, *Buzz Cut* (1996), which takes Thorn off the Keys and puts him on a cruise ship tracking down a crazed killer who has taken the ship hostage. The story not only takes Thorn out of his natural element, but it also focuses as much on Thorn's friend Sugarman as it does on Thorn.

In *Body Language* and *Rough Draft*, Hall switches to female protagonists and when Thorn finally does return to the scene in *Blackwater Sound* and *Off the Charts*, we find him sharing double billing with Alexandra Rafferty, the heroine first introduced in *Language*. While Hall tells us Thorn is changing, what ends up in the novels is a character who remains substantially the same throughout–Thorn seems to not grow a day older, and even though his rustic beach house is both blown up in one novel and burned to the ground in another, we know he will rebuild, never leaving the idyllic spot at the junction of sand and sea, still tying flies, still grumbling about the ever-changing landscape as development camps out on his doorstep, ever the bachelor required by the genre. The stuff of Hall's plots, however, are by necessity constantly changing, with new villains of ever increasingly weirdness, locations that range from Thorn's backyard, to North Florida beaches to the tropical coast of Central America. What remains constant throughout Hall's novel is his continued use of landscape and ecology as a shaping force for his characters.

In setting a natural scene, Hall infuses his descriptive powers with poetic sensibilities. "Out in the western sky a few wispy cirrus clouds sprang from the horizon like the fine sprigs of hair curling off the neck of an elegant woman" (*Charts* 70). In *Blackwater Sound*, Hall describes a game fish this way: "The marlin was the color of the ocean at twenty fathoms, an iridescent blue, with eerie light smoldering within its silky flesh as if its electrons had become unstable by the cold friction of the sea" (1). As skillful as he is with these kinds of standard literary components, it is in his environmental voice and its symbiotic connections between his characters and their physical surroundings that mark his true craft.

In his second novel, *Freeze,* Hall builds these connections in a way that allows him to make environmental observations that range from the ravage of the landscape to the very intricate turns in the weather, in ways that enhance both character and plot. In the beginning of the novel, Thorn is sitting in a bar, chatting up a pretty tourist lady and she tells him that after a scuba dive off the reefs she is "shocked by the decay of the coral and the degrading of the water. The damn locals were doing a lousy job of protecting the ecology. This place was a national treasure, and they were letting it get ruined" (14). Despite a healthy dose of irony in putting this complaint in the mouth of a member of that tourist horde that contributes substantially to the damage of the reef, this small scene at first seems like a typical eco-thriller aside. Hall, however, is just starting to construct his intricate framework of connection. Thorn has no reaction to her diatribe. Instead, he leave the tourist bar and ends up at a place called Papa John's Bomb Bay Bar, a hangout for the locals where he encounters a group of long time shrimpers, and this is what he sees:

They were in their sixties, and there was still a pioneer gristle in their faces. But the flesh on their arms was loose, their fingers thick and clumsy with gout or arthritis. Thorn knew these shrimpers, and he knew their sons. They were paler than their fathers, less hardy specimens, men whose only calluses came from golf or tapping buttons. . . These men who had done every rough and difficult thing a man might expect to do in the Keys. Everything but replace themselves (16-17).

These are the "damn locals" the tourist lady blames for the deterioration of the coral reefs, but what Hall is telling us is that the deterioration of the men and their lifestyle is no less important than that of the reefs, and in fact, much more important. In this symbiotic relationship between the shrimpers and the sea from which they earned their livelihood, a degrading of one results in the degrading of the other. Hall then goes on to add the element of genetic decline, the kind of toughness needed for their species to survive had not been passed down to their sons, implying that just as the coral is threatened with extinction, so too are these men and what they represent. Destroying the environment destroys those who depend on it for life. Six chapters later, Hall introduces us to Papa John himself. "A Conch, sixty-three nonstop years on the islands" running his bar in Key West, "making some smuggling runs, pot, rum, Uzis once, always on the lookout for a place with the fishing camp feel that Key West had lost" (57). Papa John found that place in Key Largo, but now, after living there for fifteen years, he is as discouraged as any MacDonald character with the way things have changed in the Keys.

The hot tubs and wooden decks, pastels had arrived. Fancy stores were festering along the highway, full of plastic geegaws you wouldn't believe. Turning shit into chic. Everybody trying to snag the tourists on their way to Key West. Now the island was full of fern bars with brass railings and speakers seven feet tall. Bars with names of tropical fruits, Mangoes, Pineapples, Papayas. And the tourists dancing the night away while some guy did his Jimmy Buffet calypso imitation. All of them thinking this is the real Key Largo. Hey, let's boogie. It bothered the fuck out of him (57).

Papa John is a genuine Keys character, but he is not one of the good guys, and it is through him we finally meet Ozzie Hardison, a thirty-two year-old born loser who drives an ice cream truck for a living, and whom Papa John wants to mentor, to serve as his father figure, to get him hooked up on a life of crime. But Ozzie "wasn't at all what Papa John had had in mind. He was a Florida Cracker for one thing. Worse than an ordinary redneck. You couldn't teach Crackers anything. They had undescended brains" (56).

Ozzie turns out to be one of the major bad guys in the novel and he has all the qualities of those "less hardy specimens" whom the old shrimpers sired. When Thorn looks at Ozzie he is "looking into those lightless eyes that were a shallow as the eyes of a fish. The brain behind them probably only a bundle of tropistic impulses. Feed, screw, run" (266). When Ozzie asks Thorn what he looking at, Thorn says: "the decline of Western civilization." Hall has created a metaphoric linkage that runs from a complaint about the deterioration of the coral reefs to their human counterparts in the shrimpers to the specific characters of Papa John and Ozzie. When Thorn goes up against Ozzie and friends, he is symbolically fighting against the deterioration of both the physical and human landscape of the Keys.

The novel's plot takes its theme from Florida's well deserved reputation as place to start over, a place to reinvent oneself, to find a new identity. The villain is an ex-DEA agent named Benny Cousins who smuggles rich cocaine dealers into the country and gives them new identities, only instead of sending them off to live the good life in Palm Beach or Aspen, Benny kills them and buries them under the royal palms in his front yard.

Thorn's childhood friend Gaeton Richards is an FBI agent working undercover in Benny's organization and when Gaeton's cover is blown, Benny kills him. Thorn sets out to find Gaeton's killers with the help of Gaeton's sister, Darcy, the local TV weatherwoman. And it is in Darcy that we see a counterpoint to the environmental degradation depicted in its association with Papa John, Ozzie and Benny.

Darcy's connection to the physical world around her is almost mystical, a hypersensitivity to the weather.

As usual she had an early hint of it, something like the tartness of green apples in the back of the throat, a quiet burn in the sinuses. It was something no radar could trace and no normal person would even give words to. But it was her work and the nearest thing to a gift she had. . . It was the weight and color of the air, the taste in her lungs, the vibrations her bones could hear, the odor of light. Weather moved through her as if she were permeable, and she extracted from the currents their messages, whispers of where they had come from, where they were headed (48).

When Darcy finds out that Cousins has killed her brother, she sets out to destroy him by pretending to be a criminal on the lam, and approaches Cousins about setting up a new identity. She takes on the role of the one who culls the herd and she sets up this analogy in a conversation with Thorn about the Melaleuca trees in the Everglades.

. . . in a lightning storm the melaleucas, because their bark is so papery, they catch fire very easily. The fires spread to the hardwoods, but the melaleucas don't burn down themselves. They're too waterlogged. They have the insides of a cactus. . .they're overrunning the Everglades. When someone goes to chop one of them down, the tree senses it somehow and puffs out a million spores . . .Somebody has to do something, Thorn. . .I want to see Benny dead, Thorn. I do, and I don't much care how (227-228).

This is no tourist complaining about the coral reefs, this is a passion for the environment and the will to turn that passion into action. Just as the melaleucas corrupt the Everglades, Benny Cousins and those like him corrupt the human environment, and both destructive forces need to be eradicated. When Thorn speculates about why people don't take up environmental causes any more, why no one will fight for the trees, he blames it on apathy and boredom, a lack of the long view.

Thorn had begun to believe it was because there was a drop in the population of grandchildren. When people stopped having kids, it rippled everywhere. It got harder to care about what happened in the middle of the next century when nobody you loved would be alive then. To hell with the long view (235).

The number one imperative for the survival of the species is to procreate, to pass on those genes that ensure survival. Once again, the eco-thriller puts the battle between good and evil into a biological and environmental context.

Darcy and Thorn become lovers, of course, a development that is almost demanded by the genre, but here Hall also reinforces that notion of naturalist Terry Tempest Williams that "Our lack of intimacy with each other is in direct proportion to our lack of intimacy with the land "(64). This connection to the land, and in Darcy's case to the atmosphere, serves as a metaphor for plot twists in the novel. When Gaeton is about to die, he wonders how he ended up staring down the barrel of Benny's gun:

He had imagined this moment, pictured it in different ways. But never like this. It was Ozzie. Poor stupid Ozzie stumbling into it. That unpredictable swirl of weather that fouled up even Darcy's forecasts. You could see the big patterns, shifts in the jet stream, fronts, and make probable calls based on them, but it was the little local dips and eddies in the atmosphere that might just lash up a tornado that would scatter a mobile home park. Hard as hell to see them forming (111).

Just as Thoreau tells us in the head note to *Daylight* "and so it is with us," Hall uses those small, random "little local dips and eddies" in the natural world to reflect twists and turns in the lives of his characters, and when the final resolution comes, and Darcy, Thorn and his friends are gathered around his dock on a day when "that last arctic cold front had scrubbed the atmosphere clean and left a crystalline ping in the air"(319), Thorn sees himself and his friends moving in new directions. In the final paragraph of the novel, he pays homage to the redemptive power of place.

And though Thorn knew the carbon dioxide fumes and the methane and ozone and all the rest of it had not been blown very far away, and though he was certain the pollution was already beginning to mount up again, still, for a while, the sky would be fresh. And for those few days he and Darcy and Sugarman and Jack and the rest of them would be able to feast on that good rich air, breathing again the way they were always meant to breathe"(319).

Those toxic fumes are the Bennys and Ozzies of the world, an ever-present threat, but occasionally the good guys win, and the "crystalline ping in the air" reminds us of Thoreau's "still lake of purest crystal," and "breathing again in the way they were always meant to breathe" becomes Thoreau's "unconscious obedience to the all-just laws." As Hall moves from book to book, sometimes in the company of his alter ego Thorn, and sometimes with new inventions of character, those observations of Thoreau's continue to resonate.

A toxic landfill in *Bones of Coral* hides secret chemical wastes that may have caused unusually high disease rates in Key West. When hero Shaw Chandler, a Miami paramedic, returns home to the Keys to investigate the murder of his father, he reacquaints himself with his old high school lover, Trula Montoya, a victim of multiple sclerosis, an illness most likely caused by the illegal dumping of biological warfare chemicals in the landfill.

At the center of the novel's plot is a limestone and coral quarry about the size of a small house with a five-foot wide channel connecting it to the bay. It is here where Chandler first sees Trula, swimming nude, with her pet dolphin, and it is here at the bottom of the pit where the evidence lies that will ultimately solve the mystery of who is responsible for the dumping of the toxic waste. The image of the pool with its link to the bay is strikingly similar to Lake Surprise in *Daylight*. For Trula, it is a place to renew her bond with the natural world, a place to heal. Once again we find Thoreau's "still lake of purest crystal", and the landfill, which in the climax of the novel is described as "that rough sea of rubbish and decay" (303), is the stagnant ditch.

For Hall, the land, the sky and the water are essential elements of his stories; elements whose unique qualities define both the place and the characters whose lives are shaped by them. As Shaw Chandler drives down from Miami, he sheds his artificial Miami self and becomes once again "a Keys guy" (32), describing the land as a place where "the light seemed purer . . . no smog to filter the UV's out. And the air was thickened by the ocean, a vegetable odor with a faint trace of decay" (32), a phrase that foreshadows the decay of the landfill and the decay of those lives it has affected.

Florida, and particularly the Keys, are intimately connected to the sea, "there was no escape" from it, "you worked with it, played with it, made love with it, slept with it, Always the ocean. Always its pressure in the ears, its rippling light, its haunt" (32). This was Chandler's birthplace, an "outpost for the unstable, maladjusted, the just plain insane" (33). Here, more than anywhere else in Florida, the landscape becomes character, a character that can influence and shape the lives of others as surely as a parent, a lover or an enemy.

If they weren't insane when they came, they turned out that way. They became islanders, devolved creatures. Creatures with both gills and opposable thumbs. Lower and higher forms intertwined. Still walking upright, but beginning to fall into a hunch. A thing with two hearts. One that beat in tune with the rhythms of the nearly forgotten land, one heart that obeyed only the primitive metronome of the ocean. . . .That island made you crazy (33).

Hall's environmental voice speaks loudest when addressing humanity's perversion of nature. In *Red Sky at Night*, an obsessed doctor searching for ways to ease the pain in the stumps of the legs he lost in Viet Nam ends up slaughtering dolphins so he can extract endorphins from the dolphins' spines and use it to heal that pain. The irony is that the dolphins he butchers are already being used to heal. A half hour spend swimming with them can smooth out brain waves, increase neurological function and even "shrink tumor mass" (4), Thorn learns in the opening chapter. When Thorn confronts the doctor in the climax of the novel, he puts it this way:

". . .those eleven dolphins were making hundreds of people feel better, a little at a time. Lessening their pain, making some pretty shitty lives tolerable. How do you work it out in your head, Bean, that the pain in your missing legs is more important that all that" (363)?

The horror of this affront on nature, depicted in graphic detail in the novel, is all Hall needs to make his point, and outside of a few comments about "dolphin radicals" (58) who want to shut down facilities where the sick and injured can swim with the dolphins; there is no need for philosophizing or editorializing.

In an earlier novel, *Mean High Tide*, Hall has Thorn stop an environmental catastrophe that could have worldwide impact–an act that makes the draining of swamp to build condominiums pale in comparison.

A former trained assassin for the U.S. military, Harden Winchester, hatches a plot of revenged against the man who wooed away Harden's wife–he plans to let loose in the ocean a mutant breed of fish called the red tilapia, a fish that reproduces "'so fast, they're so aggressive, they'll beat out all the other fish and it wouldn't be long, maybe a year or two, before they start to strangle the whole damn ocean, strangle it with themselves' " (267).

At the climax of the novel, Thorn has to resort to dropping explosives into the river leading to the ocean to stop the red tilapia, a solution that will unfortunately kill all the living creatures in the water for miles around, "the snakes and alligators, the frogs, the turtles and river otters and raccoons, manatee and spoonbills, night herons, the snowy egrets, ospreys" (395). Thorn wishes he could find a less harmful solution, but he cannot, "no matter that he considered these river creatures his biological equal, their lives as rich and sacred as any two-legged mammal's on the shore, there was no other way to proceed" (394). In the end, he "killed a million fish that night. A few million other things. And filled the dark with unforgivable thunder" (395). Like Jimmy Wing in MacDonald's *Flash of Green*, Thorn gets a lecture from an impassioned scientist on the intricate connectedness of nature.

"You know how the story goes, Thorn, right? The hip bone's connected to the thigh bone. I clap my hands in Florida; a sparrow falls out of its nest in Hong Kong. You know the story. Every little thing you do has effects you'll never see. Effects no one understands. We start playing around with Mother Nature, shipping a fish from its natural habitat to some other place, bad things can happen" (307).

This is the image in the mirror of nature that reflects the meat and bones of the eco-thriller, characters that skew nature's delicate balance get the same results in their own lives and "bad things can happen."

Not all of Hall's novels feature some massive threat to the environment, but even in those that focus on other issues, Hall manages to cast his characters in ways that illustrate essential themes of eco-fiction. The ecological metaphor of interconnectedness and interdependence that Thorn finds in his fight to stop the red tilapia surfaces in a later Hall novel, *Off The Charts*, as sociological metaphor.

Thorn, his lover and friends, are literally swimming for their lives while chased by a madman intent on killing them. Thorn's every instinct was to turn back and face the villain, abandon his friends and do mortal combat with evil, but it is a "bad instinct formed by a lifetime of isolation. A man living alone could do as he pleased, follow his codes, develop his eccentric routines, his peculiar addictions" (328). As the quintessential loner of classic noir crime fiction, he would take any risk he chose because it did not endanger the lives of others. But now Thorn has become part of something greater than himself.

To live within a group required a limberness of spirit, an absolute need to compromise and adjust. Subordinating his maverick urges to the needs of the common good. . .it ran contrary to every inclination Thorn had acquired over the years, but as he knifed through the water, he found him self. . .adjusting his natural willfulness to the needs and wisdom of the group (329)

As White's Doc Ford states in *North of Havana*: "members of an animal community survive because, instinctually, they are accountable to the needs of their own species. Members that did not behave accountably could not survive—nor should they survive" (243).

Hall's villains, like those of White, are also shaped by the landscape and the environment, but it is at a genetic level, a skewing of the genes that creates the kind of evil that MacDonald describes as "existing for the sake of itself, for the sake of the satisfactions of its own exercise" (*Clues* 69)— and all three authors resist the temptation to blame society for these evils.

In *Body Language*, the heroine Alexandra Rafferty tracks a serial rapist whom psychological profilers theorized was trying to reconstruct moments of abuse he'd witnessed as a child, "acts of violence against his mother he was helpless to prevent" (24). But Rafferty calls that a "far too neat an explanation. "Just as likely" the killer was acting on "the twisted commandments of some crazed inner voice" (24). Hall elaborates on this theme in *Tide*.

With a clever enough lawyer, a string of professional experts, even the most horrendous acts could be justified. Every culprit could be made to seem a victim of one brainwashing or another, a helpless casualty of negative conditioning. Poverty, race, drugs, sexual abuse. The great escape clauses of the age. But as far as Thorn was concerned, all that was bullshit. Only conduct counted. Behavior was everything (289).

Behavior was everything. In this single three-word sentence, Hall encapsulates the quintessential theme of the eco-thriller, the biological imperative of the species to ensure its own survival and the corresponding necessity to protect and nurture the physical ecology of that species' environment. Just as the survival of the species is driven by genetics, so too, is the counterforce of evil that works against it.

Tinkering with the genetics of the red tilapia turns that species' natural drive to reproduce into a weapon that destroys all other life in its environment. That same theme is mirrored in the character of Sylvie Winchester, Harden's daughter, a femme fatale whose own sexuality is as genetically twisted as the tilapia. She "wasn't a woman, normal or otherwise," had plenty of sex but "didn't crave a baby" and in fact, even by the age of twenty-five, she had "never even had a menstrual period. . .No fat accumulated, her breasts never budded, her hips stayed narrow. Sylvie, the girl with no sex. Yet somehow certain men found her irresistible" (31-31).. She thinks of herself as a "brand-new evolutionary development. Sylvie, the missing link, an early stage of what was coming. Neither sex. Sexless" (32). Unable to conceive, she is symbolic of the ultimate threat to the species. If this is what is coming next, then there is no question that the human race is doomed. Thorn not only has to stop the red tilapia from spreading, he has to stop Sylvie as well.

Hall takes these eco-themes of survival and their biological imperative of the cycle of birth, growth, decay, death, copulation and reproduction, and brings them all together in a single novel, *Buzz Cut*. Villain Butler Jack, who has what Hall calls a "mania for etymologies", is given a chance to riff on all of these themes as he constantly recites the meaning and origin of words. He hijacks a cruise ship in a scheme to take revenge on his parents and plots to crash the cruise ship into a Liberian supertanker filled with enough crude oil to "cover every beach in Florida an inch deep" (102). Again, we see this dismissal of pop psychology's excuses for bad behavior, only this time; it comes from the mouth of the villain himself.

There had been blood, yes. There had been murder and violence and the ugliness of death. Yes, it was true. These things were true. But that didn't mean he was insane or psychopathic or had lost touch with the difference between right and wrong, good and evil. He knew exactly what he was doing. You could be bad and not be psychopathic. You could be a villain without being nuts. That was hooey. That was bullshit. Result of too many temporary insanity defenses. These days no one could commit a crime without some lawyer calling them insane (224).

Butler Jack's theory of evil is that it is absolutely necessary, because it kept "good from growing too powerful. Saving the world from turning white and pure and sterile. Evil stirred the pot, kept it percolating. Without it there was no change, no movement, no growth, nothing" (225). This is MacDonald's evil justifying itself, its own existence. It is also an interesting take on the necessities of the novel because certainly from a novelist's point of view, evil is necessary for those very same reasons, it not only stirs the pot, it stirs the plot. Hall continues to give the reader parallels between the ecology of the mystery and mystery of ecology. When Thorn begins to figure out the complex relationship between Jack and his family members and his scheme, Thorn explains this process by using a simile drawn from his relationship to nature.

The revelations coming to him as such revelations always had. Staring at the camouflage so long, his eyes had grown weary, gone out of focus, then there it was, the shape that had been hidden so artfully was now standing out in full relief. It was the way he spotted bonefish through the bright sheen of sunlight on the surface of the water. His eyes becoming relaxed, easing the glare (345).

From Jack, the reader gets a short lesson in the history of the word "climax," tracing its roots to Greek klimax, meaning ladder, moving higher step by step, then he links it to the moment of sexual peak and finally to the moment of revelation in narrative, a story, "all prior moments leading to this. Romance, foreplay, copulation, climax, afterglow. Sex and story, climbing ever higher" (363). The sexual connection takes us back to the biological imperative to ensure survival of the species. In the case of Butler Jack, Hall begins to build a climax that will ultimately defeat Jack by going directly to the heart of his own reproductive abilities. The good guys repeatedly hit the bad guy in the nuts. Butler Jack riffs on that word:

Nuts. Crazy, or passionate. A devotee, a fan, as in "sports nut." And the coarse slang for testicles, of course. All the words growing out of the Dutch noot or the German noos meaning the kernel of a hard-shelled fruit. All the slang spinning out of that, the testicles' resemblance to acorns or walnuts, only soft and vulnerable. Having in common with acorns, beyond the size and shape, that they were also full of life, the seeds of the new tree. The storage place for new existence. Eggs and nuts. The association with passion sprang from the copulatory connection with seeds and sperm. Crazy following from that passion. Extreme passion, copulatory madness. Nuts (297).

Jack is driven by this passion; a life long lust for Monica Sampson, the daughter of the man his mother had married after his biological father has skipped out. Even her name rings true to theme, Sampson, phonetically identical to the biblical strongman emasculated by a woman. This is the trigger that sets the entire novel's madness in motion. Jack's obsession becomes his downfall when he discovers that Monica, who promised Jack at the age of twelve that she would wait for him forever, took another lover and was no longer pure.

In a rage, Jack kills that old boyfriend, but not before the victim knees Jack in the balls. Then Thorn's old friend Sugarman turns out to be half brother to both Jack and Monica, and it is Sugarman who gives Jack his second pounding, kneeing him in the groin over and over in a blind rage.

The old lover and Sugarman are symbolically (and also quite literally) destroying the villain's capacity for reproduction, culling the herd. Jack dies by being electrocuted by his owe bizarre device, a stun gun wired to his fingertips that he uses to disable his victims. When the current hits him, it "seemed to gather in his nuts and pulsate. . . .Electricity seeking safety in the dirt. Negative charge seeking positive. Positive seeking negative. Nature always wanted to be zero. To be quiet and still and dead and empty and neutral" (370).

What Jack describes is the principal of entropy, the tendency in the universe that seeks an imagined state where every atom is equally distanced from another and all movement ceases, a force that moves toward decay, death, decomposition, moves from a state of order to a state of disorder. The one force in the universe that counteracts that death march is life, the joining of egg and sperm, seed and earth, growth, complexity building upon complexity, nature spitting in the eye of physics. For eco-warriors such as Thorn and Doc Ford and even that old knight errant McGee, the best way to ensure the survival of the species is to kick evil square in the nuts.

Chapter Four
Carl Hiaasen, Eco-terrorist in a Clown Suit

When Carl Hiaasen was eleven years old, living in his hometown of Plantation, Florida, on the outskirts of Ft. Lauderdale, he heard about a new kid in the neighborhood. His name was Travis McGee and he had just sprung to life in the pages of John D. MacDonald's novel *The Deep Blue Good-by*.

"Imagine the kick in discovering a clever action novel set in one's own hometown," Hiaasen writes in the introduction to the 1995 reissued of the novel. "McGee and I ran on the same beaches, rambled the same roads, fished the same flats, ate at the same seafood joints, and avoided the same tourists" (vi). For Hiaasen, MacDonald was more than just a literary influence; he was a kindred spirit, sharing the same "bittersweet" view of South Florida, the same outrage against the "runaway exploitation of this rare and dying paradise" (vi).

As both a reporter and columnist for the *Miami Herald*, Hiaasen would come to inveigh against the same villains in real life that MacDonald targeted in his novels: "greedhead developers, crooked politicians, chamber-of-commerce flacks, and the cold hearted scammers who flock like buzzards to the Sunshine State" (vii). When Hiaasen began writing fiction, he took his material from the headlines and back stories of the daily news that chronicled the misuse and abuse of his home state, and through the element of satire and the succinct poetry of profanity he has crafted a theme that runs throughout all of his novels that can be summed up in the words of his favorite character, ex-Florida governor Clinton Tyree, better known as Skink: "Fuck with Mother Nature and she'll fuck back' "(*Stormy Weather* 224). Little wonder that Hiaasen's most recent collection of columns was published under the title *Paradise Screwed* (2001).

There is an old adage that says, "all politics are local," and for Hiaasen, the most important battles, both political and environmental, are those on the homefront. While readers can find White's Doc Ford in such exotic settings as Cuba, Columbia, Panama, the Bahamas, Singapore and even the remote coast of Australia, Hiaasen's characters never set their sandals outside Florida.

Hall writes of massive affronts to the environment such as toxic waste dumps, dolphin slaughter, and mutant fish that could kill off an entire ocean of creatures and giant oil spills that threaten to poison beaches along the entire East Coast. Hiaasen, however, prefers to limit his attacks to the bad guys on bulldozers. The villains in his novels are interchangeable with the characters he writes about in his newspaper columns: the slick hustlers who pave over paradise, greasing the palms of corrupt bureaucrats and politicians, the shameless promoters who worship at the feet of the Great God of Growth.

In *Tourist Season* (1986), a crazed newspaper columnist becomes an eco-terrorist and along with a Seminole Indian chief, a fake Cuban radical and a washed up pro-football player, sets out to scare all the tourists out of the state. *Double Whammy* (1989) features a scheming televangelist who tries to build a development of twenty-nine thousand lakefront condominiums on top of an old land fill—the results of which ends up killing thousands of imported bass which immediately turn belly up when he puts them into his toxic lakes. In *Native Tongue* (1991) a theme park mogul who turns out to be an ex-Mafia snitch now in the witness protection program plans to build a golf course and housing development on the last patch of green in the Keys and dump his sewage onto the only living coral reef in the United States. South Florida's sugar industry, often called Public Enemy No. 1 by environmentalists, gets tangled up in *Strip Tease* (1993) when it takes millions of dollars in federal tax subsidies while at the same time secretly opening vast tracts of cane acreage for future development of condominiums and golf resorts.

The list goes on. *Stormy Weather* (1993) centers on the aftermath of Hurricane Andrew and the devastation it caused in South Florida because of shoddy construction and code enforcement officials who were paid to look the other way. A developer's scheme to bribe his way into gaining permission to build on an unspoiled North Florida barrier island is the villain of 2000's *Sick Puppy*. A lottery winner fights to save an Eden-like forest from becoming a strip mall in 1997's *Lucky You*, and in Hiaasen's Newbery Honor winner *Hoot* (2003), a ten-year-old eco-warrior sets out to stop a pancake house from being build on land inhabited by burrowing owls.

It is only in 2002's *Basket Case*, that the threat presented by over-development takes a back seat. Even in Hiaasen's early non-fiction book, *Team Rodent, How Disney Devours the World*, the theme returns to his favorite territory: how money and power and its accompanying greed corrupt the real Florida. Disney has created what Hiaasen calls a "sublime and unbreakable artificiality" (80) . . ." To do what [Disney CEO Michael] Eisner's Team Rodent does, and do it on that scale, requires a degree of order that doesn't exist in the natural world. Not all birds sing sweetly. Not all lakes are blue. Not all islands have sandy beaches" (79).

Hiaasen comes by his environmental sensibilities by right of birth. Unlike MacDonald, White and Hall, who all came to Florida as immigrants, Hiaasen is a second generation native. As *Native Tongue*'s character Joe Winder says to the theme park mogul, "'you'll never understand . . . because you weren't born here. Compared to where you came from, this is always going to look like paradise. Hell, you could wipe out every last bird and butterfly, and it's still better than Toledo in the dead of winter' "(370). Almost from the day he was born in 1953, Hiaasen has stood witness to an ongoing transformation of wilderness into parking lots. In the introduction to his first collection of columns, *Kick Ass* (1999), editor Diane Stevenson describes the impact of growth on Hiaasen's hometown.

Plantation sits on the westernmost edge of Broward County, bordered by the Everglades and swamps, the "perfect environment for an idyllic boyhood" (xv). By 1960, Broward's population has more than doubled, and almost one-third of the state's population was concentrated on its Southeast coast. With an average of 700 to 1,000 new people arriving in Florida every day, the impact on the environment was substantial, requiring 300 acres of green space to be paved over each day for "subdivisions, streets, schools, and shopping malls" (xv). In addition, by 1990, more than forty-one million tourists were making their annual trek to the Sunshine State, each requiring their own little share of new parking spaces, motels, entertainment complexes, restaurants, each sucking down their share of the fresh water and each dumping their waste into the septic tanks, lakes, rivers and the ocean.

Between 1922, the year Hiaasen's grandfather moved down from North Dakota to open up the area's first law firm, and 1990, almost 75 percent of all current development was being built. During that same period, "at least five animal species disappeared completely, and a significant number of others were greatly reduced as their habitats either vanished or were poisoned by agricultural runoff or toxins like mercury" (xv-xvi). The Everglades, meanwhile, had been reduced to half its size.

Growing up in Plantation was "as close to being in a wilderness as you could get," Hiaasen recalls in a 2003 interview with a Scottish newspaper. "There were creeks and woods and pastures, every week we used to go out exploring to the west of town, riding around the dirt tracks on our bikes. And every week there'd be some new development that would look like a bomb had gone off and some bulldozers had just come in and flattened the place" (Robinson). He and his friends would sneak into the development site and pull up surveyor's stakes. "'We didn't know what else to do. We were little and the bulldozers were so big,'" he told Stevenson. Hiaasen characterizes the roar of the bulldozers as the sound of money, because "'greed is the engine that has run Florida ever since there was a Florida' "(xvi). He told *People Magazine* in 1991 that his boyhood haunts he loved so much were now "in the middle of mall hell" (Grant), adding that he had seen "very little that had happened in Florida to give me much faith in the human race. Somebody's got to stand up and scream bloody murder."

"Angry" is a word you see in almost every interview with Hiaasen–and there are hundreds of such interviews. He has written 20 novels (including three early works co-written with former *Herald* editor the late William Montalbano and four young adult novels) Most of these are bestsellers, and two have made it to the big screen: *Strip Tease*, was turned into a Hollywood box office bomb with Burt Reynolds and Demi Moore, and *Hoot*, his first young adult novel.

His works have been translated into twenty-eight languages and have sold more than 30 million copies worldwide. Standing up and screaming bloody murder about the ravages that unbridled growth has visited upon his beloved Florida has not only made him rich and famous, but it has also given the eco-mystery its most outspoken environmental voice.

In an interview on ABC's "Good Morning America" show shortly after publishing *Tourist Season* in 1986, he told the audience "there's nothing wrong with Florida that a force-five hurricane wouldn't fix," a statement that prompted Miami Mayor Xavier Suarez to complain in a letter to the *Herald* that Hiaasen "displayed a one-dimensional, exponential hatred of South Florida" and owed an apology to "the entire human race" (Weeks).

No apology was forthcoming. Instead Hiaasen started writing columns for the paper that Stevenson characterizes as "uniquely venomous, wickedly funny satire" (xx). Until *Season* was published, Hiaasen had been writing investigative stories for the *Herald*, including one which ultimately stopped the construction of a development called Port Bougainville in North Key Largo that would have added nearly sixty thousand people to the fragile mix of the islands, the largest development every planned for the Keys. Writing *Tourist Season* was a way for him to vent his frustration and anger and to relieve the stress of these months-long investigations. It was a kind of "psychotherapy" for him (Robinson). Hiaasen said, "'the novels were always, to my mind, something I did on the side, just to work out these demons. Then you end up profiting from it. And in my own defense, the one way I would rationalize it is that it does get the gospel out' " (Robinson).

Hiaasen's love affair with the fourth estate began at the age of four, when he learned to read using the *Herald*'s sports pages and maps of Florida. His father bought him a typewriter two years later and he taught himself how to pound out his own sports stories, which he handed out to the kids in his neighborhood. At Plantation High, he started an underground newsletter *More Trash*, poking fun at teenage culture and occasionally taking a few jabs at the teachers and administrators (Grant). He never wanted to be anything other than a journalist and he attributes the strong moral sense of right and wrong that permeates his work to his coming of age in the 1960S.

He told Stevenson it was a time of the " 'complete end of innocence' " as he witnessed the assassinations of president John F. Kennedy, his brother Robert, and civil rights leader Martin Luther King. From the peace movement and growing disillusionment of the Viet Nam war to the corruption of the Nixon White House that lead to Watergate, it was " 'a poisonous time,' " he says. " 'It seemed to me there was so much wrong in the world. I felt such outrage for so many years over those things happening that it wasn't a hard thing to carry into journalism' "(xvi).

Hiaasen attended Emory University for two years, and then transferred to the University of Florida where he earned a degree in journalism. After a two-year stint as a general assignment reporter for Coco Today (now USA Today) he joined the *Herald*'s Brevard County bureau, working on the same turf he had covered as a ten-year-old with his homegrown newsletter. He eventually moved on to a job as a feature writer for the paper's Sunday magazine, and in 1979, joined two-time Pulitzer prize winner Gene Miller's investigative team (Stevenson xix), working on such stories as the Port Bougainville project on North Key Largo, dope smuggling in the Keys, and an expose of doctors who did drugs, raped and cheated their patients and botched routine operations so badly that patients died.

Hiaasen thinks of himself as an old fashioned journalist whose job is, in the words of *The New Yorker* magazine's press critic A.J. Liebling, "to comfort the afflicted and afflict the comfortable" (Herring 34). He describes his column in similar terms:

You just cover a lot of territory and you do it aggressively and you do it fairly and you don't play favorites and you don't take any prisoners. It's the old school of slash-and-burn metropolitan column writing. You just kick ass. That's what you do. And that's what they pay you to do (*Kick Ass* head note).

Hiaasen's novels are basically his columns on steroids: behind the exaggerations of satire, the twisted plots and a cast of characters belonging to what syndicated humor columnist Dave Barry calls "the Bunch of Florida Wackos Genre" (Dorsey 1), his books are a serious plea for sanity in an insane world where the environment is just another commodity to be bought and sold to the highest bidder, used and abused, then tossed out on the trash heap like an empty can of Budweiser.

In the world of Carl Hiaasen, desperate times call for desperate measures. The hero is often an outlaw, whether he is a ten-year-old boy who vandalizes a construction site that threatens to destroy the habitat of burrowing owls or a demented newspaper columnist who takes to feeding tourists to alligators and kidnapping the Orange Bowl Queen. The question Hiaasen poses is just how far one can take this business of eco-terrorism. Is protecting what little is left of Florida's pristine environment really worth the taking of innocent lives? Of course, to Hiaasen's protagonists few are really innocent–certainly not the bribe-wielding developers, or the fat cat lobbyists or the graft-greedy politicians or the dope dealers or the scam artists. Even the tourists themselves are tarred with the same guilty brush; they are offenders by their very presence. Hiaasen the citizen, the newspaper columnist and author, denies that he actually advocates such lawlessness in the name of saving the environment.

"My characters have done certain things that I wish I would have done, and I can say that they've done certain things that I know have been done in real life. But most of what I do is venting; the legal outlets are always preferable" (Sutcliffe). Yet these extremes, while done in the fictional context of a satirical novel, serve to illustrate two principles: first, that the protection of the environment and the punishment of those who abuse it is the prime directive for the human race; and second, those "preferable" legal outlets often fall far short of doing the job.

Hiaasen can make his reader laugh with a scene in which a passionate defender of the environment kills the president of the Miami Chamber of Commerce by choking him to death with a toy rubber alligator, but it is an uneasy laugh, one that forces the reader, who by now may be quite sympathetic to the eco-terrorist's cause, to take a second look at what is a very serious issue. The job of a satirist is to "blend a censorious attitude with humor and wit for improving human institutions or humanity" (Harmon and Holman 461). Hiaasen does just that.

Tourist Season, his first and one of his most popular novels, is the best example of a character taking the defense of the environment to an outlandish extreme. Skip Wiley is a Miami newspaper columnist who becomes so incensed with the over-development of Florida that he decides to form a terrorist group with the aim of scaring all the state's tourist into stampeding back home.

The first person he kills is Sparky Harper, the president of "the most powerful chamber of commerce in all Florida," (6) who is choked to death with a toy rubber alligator, dressed in typical tourist garb complete with a flowered baggy shirt and Bermuda-style shorts, then stuffed in an apple-red Samsonite Royal Tourister. Harper is described as a "proud pioneer of the shameless, witless boosterism that made Florida grow" (29). He is the symbol of all that Wiley finds disgusting and morally reprehensible about the snake-oil mentality of those who sell out paradise for a quick buck. For Wiley, it is open season on tourists, hence the book title's double meaning.

When the police start to question whether there really is a terrorist group kidnapping and killing tourists, the powers that be tell them to back off. Explains Sgt. Al Garcia:

"It's the start of the tourist season. . . Snow birds on the wing, tourist dollars, my friend. What's everyone so afraid of? Empty hotel rooms, that's what. A gang of homicidal kidnappers is not exactly a PR man's dream, is it? The boys at the Chamber of Commerce would rather drink Drano than read El Fuego [the name of Wiley's organization] headlines" (75).

This is the same fear that Jimmy Wing talks about in MacDonald's *Flash of Green* as being the driving force behind the dredging and filling of Grassy Bay in order to build a new development, ". . . and so, up and down the coast, the locals leaned over backward to make everything as easy and profitable as possible for the speculative land developers" (24). Wiley wants to reverse the process:

"We're gonna empty out this entire state. . . Give it back to the bloody raccoons. Imagine: all the condos, the cheesy hotels, the trailer parks, the motor courts, the town houses, fucking Disney World–a ghost town, old pal. All the morons who thundered into Florida the past thirty years and made such a mess are gonna thunder right out again . . .the ones who don't die in the stampede" (*Season* 103).

Wiley had tried to obtain his objective through one of those "preferable" legal outlets, his column, one of which is a particularly striking example of Hiaasen's theme of Nature's ability to strike back at those who "fuck" with her.

What South Florida needs most is a killer hurricane, sudden and furious, an implacable tempest that would raze the concrete shorelines and rake away the scum and corruption . . . (293).

In a case of life imitating art, Hiaasen himself would make the same suggestion during that ABC interview to promote the book. (See earlier reference). Later in the novel, Hiaasen drops comfortably into his own column-writing mode when he takes several paragraphs to tell the early history of Fort Dallas, the mid-1800s settlement that would eventually grow into Miami.

In describing the early founders of the city he notes "their inventiveness and tenacity and utter contempt for the wilderness around them would set the tone for the development of South Florida. They preserved only what was free and immutable–the sunshine and the sea–and marked the rest for destruction, because how else could you sell it" (315)?

Once again, we are reminded of MacDonald's observations about the Grassy Bay project: "Once you had consistently eliminated most of the environmental features which had initially attracted a large tourist trade, the unalterable climate still made it a good place to live" (*Green* 24).

Wiley's last column takes up three whole pages in the novel and is a classic Hiaasen rant against over-development, nearly indistinguishable from the sentiments he had expressed in more than fifteen hundred columns he has published in the *Herald*.

. . . Most of us born here were always taught to worship growth, or tolerate it unquestioningly. Growth meant prosperity, which was defined in terms of swimming pools and waterfront lots and putting one's kids through college. So when the first frostbitten lemmings arrived with their checkbooks, all the locals raced out and got real-estate licenses; everybody wanted in on the ground floor. Greed was so thick you had to scrape it off your shoes. The only thing that ever stood between the development and the autocracy was the cursed wilderness. Where there was water, we drained it. Where there were trees, we sawed them down. The scrub we simply burned. The bulldozer was God's machine, so we fed it. Malignantly, progress gnawed its way inland from both coasts, stampeding nature (*Season* 329).

The destruction of the wilderness Wiley talks about in his column takes concrete form in the climax of the novel when Wiley is holed up on Osprey Island, an outcrop in east Biscayne Bay about five miles south of the Cape Florida lighthouse. Abandoned by its original inhabitants, it has long since gone back to nature and is described by Wiley as one of the last stands of paradise, complete with a fresh water spring, no beaches, just fifty-three acres of hard coral and oolite rock but rich in mangroves, buttonwoods, gumbo-limbo, sea grape and mahogany, a haven for raccoons, opossums, wood rats, wood storks, blue herons and even a bald eagle.

Of course the island is doomed. Meanwhile, Wiley has kidnapped Orange Bowl Queen Lara Lynn and plans to have her–and himself–blown to smithereens when the developers clear off the land with a massive load of dynamite. Wiley reasons that the eagle, the wood storks and the rest of the animals have "no real value" to the developers. " 'Weighed against the depreciated net worth of a sixteen-story condominium after sellout, the natural inhabitants of this island do not represent life–they have no fucking value' " (364).

What has value, however, is the beautiful Lara Lynn who as Orange Bowl Queen represents everything the tourist industry–and by extension the entire population of Florida–values the most. And if she has to die for Wiley to make his point, then she will, for the first time in her life, he says, become "truly part of the natural order" and then maybe "the good people of Florida will finally appreciate the magnitude of their sins' " (367).

Hall makes this same point when Thorn in *Mean High Tide* is forced to kill all of the living creatures in the estuary to keep the plague of red tilapia from being loosed on the world.. Thorn "considered these river creatures his biological equal, their lives as rich and sacred as any two-legged mammal's on the shore.. . . No time to sort the good creatures from the bad . . . .The blameless would have to die" (294)

Wiley, like Thorn, does not see his role as evil, but as a necessary means for restoring the balance of nature. His viewpoint is that the choice between human life (the girl) and life of the creatures who inhabit the island is really no choice at all. If one is threatened, both are threatened because they are dependent on each other, in order for humans to survive, so too must the environment.

Yes, the good people of Florida will not miss a few birds or raccoons when the island is blasted clean of every living thing, but what Hiaasen is asking the reader to consider is where do you draw the line, when to make the choice to stop destroying the environment? How much is enough?

The girl is finally rescued, and Wiley chooses to die on the island instead of return and face a trial and prison. No one rides to the rescue and this is the only one of Hiaasen's novels in which the part of the environment at risk is destroyed. In each of his other works, the good guys always win, but *Tourist Season* has a disturbing darkness about it, a villain who fights for the environment and loses.

At the end of novel, Brian Keyes, an ex-newspaper reporter and friend of Wiley's, rescues Laura Lynn and speeds away from the island just moments before the explosives are set off by remote control. As they watch Wiley climbing a tall pine in an attempt to scare off the eagle before the island explodes, they hear the warning signal from an offshore barge where the developers had set up their gear to trigger the explosives. The signal is "the most dolorous sound that Brian Keys had ever heard" (378).

The scene is reminiscent of *Flash of Green's* ending, where Jimmy Wing hears the "vast wet gnashing grinding roar"(336) of the dredges digging up Grassy Bay, a sound that lingers in his ears on the long drive back to the mainland. Osprey Island and Grassy Bay share the same fate and these sounds of destruction from dredge and barge are metaphoric alarms for all of Florida's vanishing wilderness.

Wiley may have been killed off in *Season*, but he is reincarnated in six other Hiaasen novels as the character Skink, an ex-Florida governor who walked off the job out of frustration and disappeared into the Everglades. He dines on road kill and generally plays havoc with those who tend to screw around with Nature.

Hiaasen never wanted to create a series character along the lines of Travis McGee. "I said, in the first place, I'm not John D. MacDonald. I'd give anything if I could write that way, out of that guy's head, again and again, but I can't. I get bored," he told interviewer Jay Lee MacDonald. Although Skink has now appeared in *Double Whammy*, *Native Tongue*, *Stormy Weather*, *Sick Puppy*, *Skinny Dip* and *Star Island*, his creator says he has to be careful not to use him too much because he "does sort of tend to come on stage and start dominating, and he really is out of control at this point." (Jay MacDonald).

Skink is Wiley if he had lived and stopped killing innocents. They both started out on as passionate defenders of the environment, working within the system to effect change (Wiley as a newspaper columnist and Skink as a politician) but their outrage turned them into outlaws who also share the same twisted penchant for creative mischief when it comes to poking a finger in the eye of tourists, developers, crooked politicians and assorted henchmen.

White's Skunk Ape in *Everglades* serves very much the same symbolic purpose as Skink and Tomlinson's theory of why there the number of reported cities of the creature had peaked during the 1970s, sounds very much like he is talking about Hiaasen's governor. "'That's when construction was booming in Miami and Lauderdale, everything expanding west into what was then the Everglades. The bulldozers and draglines were draining the edge of the big swamp, scraping it bare, and taking away all the cover. The River Prophet had to move around, maybe for survival . . .or maybe to investigate the damage being done to the biosphere' "(60)

The eco-outlaw appears repeatedly in Hiaasen's works, each one popping up like an improvised riff on the same theme. In *Native Tongue*, we not only find Skink, but also Joe Winder, an ex-newspaper reporter who takes a job as a public relations flack for the Amazing Kingdom of Thrills, a theme park rival to Disney World located on North Key Largo. Like Wiley, Winder finally has had enough and goes over to the dark side, only in Hiaasen's satires; the dark side is the right side, the domain of the eco-terrorist.

In *Double Whammy*, protagonists R. J. Decker, (nicknamed Rage by his ex-wife) is a former newspaper photographer turned private eye who, like Winder, teams up with Skink and sets out to bring down a televangelist/developer and a sugar plantation owner who literally would kill to win a bass tournament. *Sick Puppy's* Twilly Spree, who inherited millions from his real estate mogul father, begins his own little eco-war early on in life when he sets out to teach litterbugs a lesson and ends up as Skink's sidekick in undoing a developer's scheme to bribe and murder his way into covering Toad Island with condominiums.

Hiaasen even gives us a miniature version of Skink in his children's boot *Hoot* (2003).

Mullet Fingers is a ten-year-old runaway who lives in an abandoned ice-cream truck inside a junkyard and sets out to save the borrowing owls that inhabit a development site for a pancake house. When he tries to enlist Roy Eberhardt into joining his crusade, he chides him by saying: "You're sayin' it's a lost cause, right? Come on, Tex, you gotta start thinkin' like an outlaw" (170).

Skink makes his debut in *Double Whammy*, Hiaasen's second novel, as former Florida governor Clinton Tyree, a Florida native elected in the mid-nineteen seventies. He was a shoo-in with his rugged, six-foot, four-inch good looks, a Hollywood smile, a resume that included a winning career as a college football player and service in Viet Nam where he once had been lost behind enemy lines for sixteen days with no food or ammunition. The only thing wrong with Tyree was that he turned out to be that rarest of breeds, a completely honest politician.

When developers who had contributed handsomely to his campaign got their eye on a pristine coastal wildlife preserve and tried to bribe the governor into greasing its passage through the legislature and Cabinet, Tyree promptly had them all arrested by the FBI.

But Florida, being the development haven it is, could not long tolerate such honesty and Tyree ended up losing all of his battles. Although he was lauded by the public and the press, his political enemies found it easy to out maneuver him. The final straw came when the Cabinet voted to sell the Sparrow Beach Wildlife Preserve to developers for twelve million dollars and the principal shareholder in the new development turned out to be none other than Tyree's trusted lieutenant governor. Tyree walked off the job that day and disappeared.

Skink is at least partly based on a childhood friend of Hiaasen's, he told *People Weekly* in a 1991 interview. Clyde Ingalls and Hiaasen used to hunt and fish together and the author remembers how that Ingalls "was particularly angry about the fact that every time we'd go out West (Brevard), there'd be a new bulldozer doing something to some place we knew." Ingalls committed suicide at the age of seventeen. "You can't have someone close to you die that young and not have it affect you," Hiaasen said.

If place becomes a character in Florida's eco-fiction, then Tyree is a character who embodies place. He is the Everglades, the wilderness, the moral soul of the landscape. He even gets himself tied to a bridge pier in the middle of Hurricane Andrew just so he can experience the force of nature at its most violent, in a very real sense, becoming one with the land.

Skink represents the last stand between Florida's pristine environment and the encroaching development. In *Tourist Season*, Brian Keyes travels out to the edge of the Everglades in search of a condominium project that Wiley had written about in one of his columns. As he walks along a dike that separates the wetlands from the development, Keyes "marveled at the contrast; to the western horizon, nothing but sawgrass and hammock and silent swamp; to the east, diesel cranes and cinderblock husks and high-rises. Not a hundred yards stood between the backhoes and the last of South Florida's wilderness" (86).

In *Double Whammy*, Skink stands on that same dike and says: "This dike is like the moral seam of the universe . . . Evil on one side, good on the other" (281). Stevenson in her introduction to *Kick Ass* writes that it is against this backdrop of moral clarity that "events play out in Hiaasen's novels and columns, the moral landscape making almost tangible certain basic and universal values," such as loyalty, friendship, trust, honesty and "never surrender our belief in those values, or to anyone who would violate them for personal gain." As Hiaasen himself puts it: "'You try to be a good citizen wherever you live. Plant mangroves and don't piss in the water' "(xvi).

One of Skink's most defining characteristics is that he dines on road kill. He turns the evil of a civilization that destroys the wildlife into the good. The raccoons, the snakes, the possums–all fulfill their natural place in the scheme of the universe; instead of being left to rot in the sunshine, they become sustenance for their defender, Skink. The road is like the dike, the moral center where man and Nature meet.

Man will always win the battle between bumper and Thumper, but Hiaasen makes sure that Nature gets plenty of chances to turn the tables. In *Whammy*, Skink sets up a confrontation between Dennis Gault (the bass-fishing sugar plantation owner who will cheat and even kill to win) and Queenie, a world-record size bass that Skink has raised almost by hand. Gault hooks Queenie, but after an epic battle, the giant bass eventually pulls Gault overboard where he is promptly cut to ribbons by the prop on his seventeen-foot bass boat. To Skink, this is perfect justice because:

"Confrontation is the essence of nature . . .the rhythm of life . . .In nature violence is pure and purposeful, one species against another in an act of survival . . .All I did to Dennis Gault . . .was to arrange a natural confrontation. No different from a thousand other confrontations that take place every night and every day out here, unseen and uncelebrated. Yet I knew Gault's instincts as well as I knew the fish. It was only a matter of timing, of matching the natural rhythms. Putting the two species within striking distance" (317)

This is exactly the same argument that Wiley uses when he feeds a condominium widow named Ida Kimmelman to a giant North America crocodile affectionately named Pavlov, a rare species of which there are only about thirty left.

"This is not murder," Wiley declared, "it's social Darwinism. Two endangered species, Pavlov there and Mrs. Kimmelman, locked in mortal combat. To the victor goes the turf. That's how it ought to be . . .' " When Brian Keyes protests that this is not a fair fight, Wiley answers: "'Fair? There are nine million Mrs. Kimmelmans between here and Tallahassee, and thirty fucking crocodiles. Is that fair? Who has the legitimate right to be here? Who does this place really belong to? ""(115) This is an essential question for the eco-terrorist and one to which his enemies never seem to get the right answer.

Two kinds of villains populate Hiaasen's novels: the first are certified wackos like Mr. Gash in *Sick Puppy*, a hit man hired to scare off the opposition to the development of Toad Island. He gets his kicks from listening to 9-11 tapes, the more suffering and horrible the better. Another example is Chemo in *Skin Tight*, a petty criminal turned hit man whose face was so damaged in an electrolysis accident that it looked like "somebody had glued Rice Krispy's to every square centimeter of his face" (52). After getting his hand bitten off by a barracuda, he grafts a battery powered Weed Whacker to it (158).

In *Stormy Weather* we meet Lester Maddox Parsons, whose racist parents affectionately named him after the former governor of Georgia "best know for scaring off black restaurant customers with an ax handle" (95). [An historical note: although the ax handle became a symbol for Maddox, he did not actually rebuff the African American customers with one—he used a pistol. The ax handles were wielded by those in the crowd behind him (Associated Press).]

At the age of seventeen, Parsons earned the nickname "Snapper" after a game warden that caught him trying to hot-wire a tractor slammed him in the jaw with a shotgun. The blow permanently knocked his jaw "approximately thirty-six degrees out of alignment" (96).

The physical deformities of these villains represent the physical corruption of the landscape inflicted by the second kind of villain: the congressman, the developer, the lobbyist, the theme park owner, who are much more insidious and dangerous because they masquerade as upstanding citizens. As critic Julie Sloan Brannon says, "The physical deformity of killers like Chemo and Snapper is so outrageously grotesque that they stand out from the usual riffraff. Their amorality is simple, straightforward, and unmasked" (*Crime Fiction & Film in the Sunshine State* 62). In Hiaasen's world, they are not as dangerous as those upstanding citizens who "operate in a corrupt society that demands amorality, and they all feel that they are doing nothing more than pursuing the American dream, South Florida-style" (62).

One of the best examples is the lobbyist Palmer Stoat (think shoat, as in small pig). Hiaasen describes him this way:

"The trouble is, he sort of checks his moral compass at the door and that's what gets him . . .In the end he'll do anything for a buck for anyone with a buck. He just doesn't see that he's doing anything wrong; he doesn't think about the consequences. That's what I was trying to get across. It's different from having a villain who is skinning people and eating their brains" (Jay MacDonald).

Stoat is hired by Robert Clapley, a newcomer to Florida and the land development business, who Stoat correctly deduces is "a Yuppie ex-smuggler with a gold chains, a deep-water tan, diamond ear stud and a two hundred dollar haircut" (40). Clapley has to bribe both a Miami legislator and the governor in order to get the state to build a new bridge over to Toad Island. To avoid any nasty complications from the state's environmental protection agency, Clapley orders his construction crew to bulldoze over and bury thousands of toads that inhabit the island.

He also cons the few island residents and protesters into believing he will "preserve the natural character of the barrier island" by signing something called a mitigation agreement, a program that required Clapley to plant three new trees for every one tree uprooted during the construction process. What he fails to reveal, however, is that the agreement does not compel Clapley to replant the trees on Toad Island–he can simply replant them anywhere else in Florida–such as in far away Putnam County where he happens to own "nine hundred acres of fresh-cut timberland that needed replanting . . .the architect of the mitigation scam was none other than Palmer Stoat" (62)

These mitigation schemes are not some exaggerated imaginary device thought up by Hiaasen, they are frequently used in granting development rights in Florida. Clapley and Stoat end up killing each other in a bizarre hunting accident while trying to shoot a rhino on an exclusive hunting preserve in Ocala. The rhino will have nothing of it and ends up turning the tables on his hunters in a classic Hiaasen comeuppance in which nature takes her revenge.

If Hiaasen's characterizations sound a little far fetched, consider the real life case of J. Ben Rowe, subject of a Hiaasen column dated January 30, 1992. Rowe made headlines when he decided to go for a little hunting trip in the north Florida woods and bag himself a black bear. Never mind that the Florida black bear had been declared an endangered species in 1974 and animal rights groups had been petitioning Florida's Game and Fresh Water Fish Commission for years to ban those kinds of hunt. What really got Hiaasen's goat was that Rowe himself was one of the five members of that very same commission, which is charged by law with protecting Florida wildlife. Rowe claimed he killed the bear for "educational purposes" (Ratzkin).

Carl Hiaasen's books are literarily transparent, with little of the complex and multi-layered symbols one finds in "serious fiction," or even in the popular works of his eco-mystery contemporaries such as Hall, White or MacDonald. While his critics applaud his environmental gusto, his comic inventiveness, his fully developed characters and taut plots, they occasionally find fault with his excesses. *Kirkus Review* concluded that in *Tourist Season*, "real feelings would be intrusive–even about ecology and the rape of Florida. Everything is sacrificed to a news-hound humor that is as forced as it is cynical" and of *Native Tongue*, they said, it was "madcap and sometimes quite funny, but strained as well, with the action often so absurd as to leach realism and thus lacks suspense."

If Hiaasen is more preacher than poet, it is a choice gladly made. "'These novels have always been a form of therapy for me,'" he told *Entertainment Weekly*. "'I write them to vent. After 20 years of journalism, of being ruled by the notebook, I can finally make the stories go the way that I want.'" And if those stories sometimes seem a little messy, self-indulgent or just plain weird, then it is only because this is the reality of Florida as seen through Hiaasen's critical eye.

Still, no matter how much he rants and raves, he would never pack up and abandon his beloved Florida. In a recent interview, Hiaasen was asked why he chooses to make his home in the Keys since so much of its original beauty and wilderness had been wiped out. He answered, "you don't walk out on a dying friend"(Robinson). It was a good line, but one he had used before. In *Sick Puppy*, Twilly Spree asks Skink if he had ever thought of moving out of Florida. Skink answers: "Every single day, son," confessing that he had even gotten so far as to buy an airline ticket to the Grenadines but could not bring himself to get on the plane. "It felt like I was sneaking out the back door on a dying friend" (304).

That is the beauty of reading Hiaasen. You never know for sure where the reality ends and fiction begins, and if that is excess, then it is the kind of excess that is the very stuff of which Florida is made. Here, "there's no such word as 'enough'," he says. "It's how may more people can we cram in and how much can we sell them and how much beach can we cut up into little tiny pieces and tell them this is their little piece of paradise . . .Basically, it's the operating mechanism of a cancer cell" (Sutcliffe).

Florida is too far gone for chemotherapy, what is needed here is radical surgery, the eco-terrorist on a rampage. Hiaasen's writing will never be a cure for the ailing landscape, for far too much has already been lost, but for Hiaasen and his legions of fans that bleed along with him for the plight of a paradise plundered, an Eden lost, a steady dose of his novels just might ease the pain.

Chapter Five
What Doesn't Kill You Only Makes You Stronger

In September 1985, John D. MacDonald agreed to sit down in his living room for an interview with the host of a television program called Library Edition. After the camera was turned off and the lights dimmed, he started talking about readers, reading and nonreaders. The host, Jean Trebri, who was also the executive director of the Florida Center for the Book, found MacDonald's observations so compelling that she urged him to write an essay on the subject for the Center for the Book in the Library of Congress. The result of that effort was published in early 1987, shortly after MacDonald died in December 1986. The writer had struggled for months to find a way to approach the subject. "I could not make the essay work," he wrote, "and I could not imagine why. I must have done two hundred pages of junk"(*Survival* 42). Then Trebri asked, "why didn't I use the device of a conversation between McGee and Meyer. Why indeed . . ." MacDonald found the answer in fiction. The result is a succinct thirty pages of the final piece of fiction he was ever to write and the final chapter in the saga of that old tarnished knight Travis McGee and his erudite hirsute sidekick Meyer.

In *Reading for Survival*, MacDonald reiterated a theme that permeates his work, and one that would be taken up by the writers who followed in his footsteps, particularly those who turned their talents to a passionate defense of the environment. It is a plea against ignorance and stupidity, selfishness and greed, a plea for the survival of the species couched in the device of an entertaining and enlightening work of fiction. The theme of the essay, MacDonald writes in the head note to *Survival* is:

. . . The terrible isolation of the nonreader, his life without meaning or substance because he cannot comprehend the world in which he lives. The best way to make my words fall usefully upon deaf ears is to use such colorful language that it will be quoted, sooner or later, to a great many of the nonreader.

In the form of a Socratic dialogue between Meyer and McGee, the essay leads up to a simple question posed by Meyer: "So why are we doing such a poor job surviving as a species, Travis" (22)? Meyer begins this line of thinking by speculating on how the earliest humans learned to survive. The roving hunters of half a million years ago lived in small groups moving from shelter to shelter following the herds. The key to staying alive was knowledge–knowing which of the hundreds of plants and trees were useful or harmful. "Never eat the fruit of this bush. To heal a cut, crush the leaves of this plant and tie them to the wound with a length of vine" (15).

He learned how to track animals, how to read the weather signs, how to avoid snakebites and the fangs of the saber toothed tiger. Knowledge was the essential tool for survival and memory was the only device for storing that knowledge. As the world became more complicated, more sophisticated, man had to invent writing as a way to organize, store and retrieve the knowledge needed to survive. The realities of the prehistoric world were limited to the senses, what could be seen, heard, smelled, tasted, felt. Today's realities include far more than that, "'histories of nations, cultures, religions, politics, and the total history of man–from biology to technology' " (23).

For humans living in such a complex environment, the key to survival is reading, Meyer adds. "'Complex ideas and complex relationships are not transmitted by body language, by brainstorming sessions, by the boob tube or the boom box. You cannot turn back the pages of a television show and review a part you did not quite understand. You cannot carry conversations around in you coat pocket' " (25). (*Remember, this was written long before digital cable TV, DVRs and smart phones.*)

Meyer quotes statistics saying that more than sixty million American adults cannot read well enough to fully function in society, "'to understand a help-wanted ad, or the warning label on household cleaners, or an electric bill . . .' " (25). (That number today is about thirty-five million, according to the Adult Literacy Service website.) The nonreader, Meyer argues, is just as unprepared for survival as the ancient man who wanders off from the group and is attacked by wild animals. "'These are our realities,' " he says. " 'If we –as a species rather than as an individual–are uninformed, or careless or indifferent to the facts, then survival as a species is in serious doubt '" (24).

It is only through reading–and reading a wide range of diverse material–that we stand any chance at all. Just as ancient man needed the ability to discriminate between the nourishing fruit and the poisonous one, we need to be able to distinguish between the scam artist and honest merchant, to look behind the curtain at the man who would be wizard, to separate fact from propaganda, politics from policy. And when the siren call of growth promises painless prosperity, we need to ask at what cost.

The eco-warriors of this genre all are voracious readers, and whatever the differences between Doc Ford, Thorn and Hiaasen's characters, sooner or later each of them will pick up something by MacDonald. Skink may live in the Everglades and eat road kill, but he always had a stash of books close at hand. " 'You should've seen,' "Winder says in *Sick Puppy*, " 'there were hundreds in here. Steinbeck, Hemingway . . . García Márquez in Spanish. First editions! Some of the greatest books every written' " (305).

For more than half a century, the writers of Florida's eco-fiction have spoken in many different voices to tell the continuing saga of a once-pristine land nearly loved to death.

John D. MacDonald teaches that even tough guy heroes of action novels can have a soft spot for the environment, and he showed us how to occasionally pause and take a good hard look at the natural world around us, to see what it can teach us about not just how to survive, but how to endure, and ultimate triumph.

Randy Wayne White demonstrates how science and biology could serve the novelist's cause, marrying the mating rituals of tarpon to the genetic disposition of a hired assassin or paralleling the habitat of the tide pool to the social ecology of the community.

For James W. Hall, the pull of place becomes the gravitational field around which all life orbits, with his characters forever shaped by the landscape, and the landscape forever shaped by his characters.

Carl Hiaasen wraps his rage in a rubber chicken, and between the laughs, uses the wickedly effective blade of satire to lay bare the foibles and follies of a species that dares to bite the hand that feeds it.

Some critics will say these writers are only crafting an obituary, spinning out elegies for a lost cause. But if there is one thing that these works illustrate, it is that the landscape, given even the slightest chance, can be every bit as hard-boiled as the heroes who risk their lives to defend it.

Novelists are by nature hopeful, because if they were not, there would be no reason to write. For the writers of Florida's eco-fiction, the compulsion to raise the environmental voice in defense of what was, is by necessity, a hope that it will be again, and as long as they and those who follow them continue to write, there will be readers to read, and with each book opened with anticipation and consumed with quiet pleasure, the human species gains a little bit tighter foothold on the bedrock planet earth. How could it not?

WORKS CITED

Books

Brannon, Julie Sloan. "The Rules Are Different Here: South Florida Noir and The Grotesque." *Florida Noir, Crime Fiction & Film in the Sunshine State* (Bowling Green State University Popular Press, 1997. 47-64.

Carr, Archie. *A Naturalist in Florida, A Celebration of Eden.* New Haven and London Yale University Press, 1994

Chandler, Raymond. *The Simple Art of Murder.* New York: Balantine Books, 1972.

Conrad, Barnaby. *The Complete Guide to Writing Fiction.* Cincinnati: Writer's Digest Books, 1990.

Douglas, Marjory Stoneman. *The Everglades: River of Grass.* Rev. Ed. Sarasota, Fla.: Pineapple Press Inc., 1988.

Geherin, David. *John D. MacDonald.* New York: Fredrick Ungar Publishing Co.: Inc. 1982.

Glassman, Steve & Maurice O'Sullivan. *Florida Noir, Crime Fiction & Film in the Sunshine State.* (Bowling Green: Bowling Green State University Popular Press, 1997.

Glassman, Steve. "West Comes East." *Florida Noir, Crime Fiction & Film in the Sunshine State.* (Bowling Green: Bowling Green State University Popular Press, 1997. 5-18.

Hall, James W. *Under Cover of Daylight.* New York: W. W. Norton & Company, 1987.

- - - . *Bones of Coral.* New York: Dell Publishing, 1991.

- - - . *Mean High Tide.* New York: Dell Publishing, 1993.

- - - . *Hot Damn.* New York: St. Martin's Press, 2002.

- - - . *Hard Aground.* New York: Delacorte Press, 1993.

- - - . *Rough Draft.* New York: St. Martin's Press. 2000.

- - - . *Off the Chart.* New York: St. Martin's Press, 2003.

- - - . *Blackwater Sound.* New York: St. Martin's Press, 2002.

- - - . *Buzz Cut.* New York: Delacorte Press, 1996.

- - - .*Gone Wild.* New York: Dell Publishing., 1995.

- - - .*Tropical Freeze.* New York: W. W. Norton & Company, 1989.

- - - .*Red Sky at Night.* New York: Dell Publishing, 1997.

- - - .*Body Language.* New York: St. Martin's Press.1998.

Hiaasen, Carl. *Tourist Season.* New York: Warner Books, 1986.

- - - . *Strip Tease.* New York: Alfred A. Knopf, 1993.

- - - . *Sick Puppy.* New York: Warner Books, 1999.

- - - . *Basket Case.* New York: Alfred A. Knopf, 2002.

- - - . *Lucky You.* New York: Alfred A. Knopf, 1997.

- - - . *Stormy Weather.* New York: Alfred A. Knopf, 1995.

- - - . *Native Tongue.* New York: Fawcett Crest Books, 1991.

- - - . *Double Whammy.* New York: G. P. Putnam's Sons, 1989.

- - - . *Kick Ass.* New York: Berkley Books, 1999.

- - - . *Paradise Screwed.* New York: G. P. Putnam's Sons, 2001.

Hirshberg, Edgar W. John D. MacDonald. Boston: Twayne Publisher, 1985.

- - -. "John D. MacDonald and Travis McGee: Heroes for Our Time." *Florida Noir, Crime Fiction & Film in the Sunshine State.*(Bowling Green: Bowling Green State University Popular Press, 1997.

Jackson, John Brinckerhoff. "A Sense of Place, A Sense of Time," *A Sense of Place, A Sense of Time.* New Haven: Yale University Press, 1994.

Hundley, Norris Jr. The Great Thirst: Californians and Water: A History. Berkley, 2001.

MacDonald, John D. *The Green Ripper.* New York: Fawcett Publications, 1979.

- - - .The *Executioners.* New York: Simon and Schuster. 1957.

- - - .*A Dreadful Lemon Sky.* New York: J.B. Lippincott Company, 1974.

- - - .*Dead Low Tide.* Greenwich: Fawcett Publications, 1953.

- - - .*The Brass Cupcake.* Greenwich: Fawcett Publications, 1950.

- - -. *Condominium.* Philadelphia. J. B. Lippincott Company, 1977.

- - - .*A Flash of Green.* Greenwich: Fawcett Publications, 1962.

- - -. Judge *Me Not.* Greenwich: Fawcett Publications, 1951.

- - - . Introduction. *Great Tales of Mystery & Suspense.* Comp. by Bill Pronzine, Barry N. Malzberg & Martin H. Greenberg. New York: Galahad Books, 1985.

- - - . *Reading for Survival.* Washington, D.C.: Center for the Book in the Library of Congress, 1987.

- - -. Afterward. *Other Times, Other Worlds.* Edited by Martin Greenberg, New York: Fawcett Gold Medal, 1978. 279-82.

- - - . *The Deep Blue Good-by.* New York: Fawcett Books, 1964.

McArthur, Tom. Ed. The Oxford Companion to the English Language. Oxford: Oxford University Press, 1992.

Merrill, Hugh. *The Red Hot Typewriter: The Life and Times of John D. MacDonald.* New York: St. Martins Press, 2000.

Moore, Lewis D. *Meditations on America: John D. MacDonald's Travis McGee Series and Other Fiction.* Bowling Green: 1994.

Nelson, Michael P. "Lynn White, Jr." *Fifty Key Thinkers on the Environment.* Comp. And ed. Joy A. Palmer. London and New York: Rutledge, Taylor & Francis Group, 2001.

Nugent, Harold and Susan. "Noir: Keys' Style." *Florida Noir, Crime Fiction & Film in the Sunshine State.* (Bowling Green: Bowling Green State University Popular Press, 1997. 85-101.

O'Sullivan, Maurice. "Ecological Noir." *Florida Noir, Crime Fiction & Film in the Sunshine State.* (Bowling Green: Bowling Green State University Popular Press, 1997. 119-126.

Poole, Leslie Kemp. "Florida: Paradise Redefined." Unpublished Diss. Rollins College, 1991.

Rothchild, John. *Up for Grabs. A Trip through Time and Space in the Sunshine State.* New York: Viking Penguin Inc., 1985.

Siry, Joseph V "Politics and Preservation of Estuaries." *Marshes of the Ocean Shore, Development of an Ecological Ethic.* College Station: Texas A&M University Press, 1984.

Steingraber, Sandra. Prologue. *Living Downstream,* New York: Vintage Books,

1977.
Storer, John H. *The Web of Life*. New York: New American Library, 1952
White, Randy Wayne. *Everglades*. New York: G.P. Putnam's Sons, 2003.
- - - . *Sanibel Flats*. New York: St. Martin's Press, 1990.
- - - . *The Man Who Invented Florida*. New York: St. Martins Press, 1993
- - - . *The Heat Islands*. New York: St. Martins Press, 1992.
- - - . *The Mangrove Coast*. New York: Berkley Publishing Company, 1998.
- - - . *Everglades*. New York: G. P. Putnam's Sons, 2003.
- - - . *Twelve Mile Limit*. New York: G.P. Putnam's Sons, 2002.
- - - . *Captiva*. New York: Berkley Publishing Company, 1996.
- - - . *North of Havana*. New York: Berkley Publishing Company, 1997.
- - - . *Ten Thousand Islands*. New York: Berkley Publishing Company, 2002.
Williams, Terry Temple. *An Unspoken Hunger*. New York: Vintage Books, 1994.
Wright, Robert. *The Moral Animal, Why We Are the Way We Are: The New Science of Evolutionary Psychology*. New York: Vintage Books. 1994.

Articles

Brookman, Rob. "Excitable Boy: Carl Hiaasen Gets Fired Up with a Rant Against Lousy Journalism and Florida's Scumbags." *Book Magazine*. Jan. 1, 2002. No pag. Online. HighBeam Research. March 17, 2004.
Grant, Meg. "Tree Hugger from Hell (Carl Hiaasen's Campaign Against Over-development in Florida.) *People Weekly*. Sept. 21, 1991. n pag Online HighBeam Research. March 3, 2004.
Kenen, Joanne. "Call of the Wild." *American Journalism Review*. Oct. 1, 1993. No pag. Online. HighBeam Research. March 17, 2004.
MacDonald, John D. "John D. and the Critics." *JDM Bibliophile*. No. 24. July 1979. 4-12.
MacDonald, Jay Lee. "Carl Hiaasen Takes a Bite Out of Crimes Against the Environment." *First Person Book Page*. no date, no pag. Online. Netscape. March 17, 2004.
Quinn, Judy. "SMP Plans Big Push for James W. Hall." *Publishers Weekly*. Jan. 12, 1998. no pag. Online. HighBeam Research. Jan. 22, 2004.
Raban, Jonathan. "The Gaudy Green Eden," *St. Petersburg Times*, March 13, 1983. 3-D.
Robertson, Milton. "James W. Hall: Serious South Florida Thrillers." *Publishers Weekly*. July 8, 1996. no pag. Online. HighBeam Research. Jan. 22, 2004.
Robinson, David. "Hoot: Wisest Bird in Florida." *The Scotsman*. (Edinburgh, Scotland.) Feb. 1, 2002. no pag. Online. HighBeam Research. March 17, 2004.
Sutcliffe, Thomas. "Who Says That Crime Doesn't Pay?" *The Independent* (London, England.) March 7, 2002. no pag. Online. HighBeam Research. March 17, 2004.
Weeks, Linton. "Landshark." *Smithsonian Magazine*. June 2003. no pag. Smithsonian.com. Feb. 6, 2004.
White, Randy Wayne. "Out There: The Big Queasy." *Outside Magazine*. September 1996. no pag. Online. Outside Online. Feb. 5, 2004.

ABOUT THE AUTHOR

Harry Straight is an award-winning writer and journalist, now retired, who plays saxophone and harmonica in the occasional rock and blues band, collects model trains, dabbles in photography and woodworking, and teaches a class in Environmental Literature at Rollins College in Winter Park, Florida. He was born in Miami Beach, grew up on the Gulf Coast and now lives in Orlando with his wife of 25 years, Kay Wolf.

Made in the USA
Charleston, SC
19 February 2013